THE THEOLOGY OF THE BOOK OF LEVITICUS

Leviticus is often considered to be one of the most challenging books of the Bible because of its focus on blood sacrifice, infectious diseases, and complicated dietary restrictions. Moreover, scholarly approaches have focused primarily on divisions in the text without considering its overarching theological message. In this volume, Mark W. Scarlata analyzes Leviticus' theology, establishing the connection between God's divine presence and Israel's life. Exploring the symbols and rituals of ancient Israel, he traces how Leviticus develops a theology of holiness in space and time, one that weaves together the homes of the Israelites with the home of God. Seen through this theological lens, Leviticus' text demonstrates how to live in the fullness of God's holy presence and in harmony with one another and the land. Its theological vision also offers insights into how we might live today in a re-sacralized world that cherishes human dignity and cares for creation.

Mark W. Scarlata is Senior Lecturer in Old Testament at St. Mellitus College, London. He also serves as the vicar-chaplain at St. Edward, King and Martyr, Cambridge, and as the director of the St. Edward's Institute for Christian Thought.

OLD TESTAMENT THEOLOGY

GENERAL EDITORS

Brent A. Strawn
D. Moody Smith Distinguished Professor of Old Testament and
Professor of Law
Duke University

Stephen B. Chapman
Associate Professor of Old Testament
Duke University

Patrick D. Miller†
Charles T. Haley Professor of Old Testament Theology, Emeritus
Princeton Theological Seminary

This series aims to remedy the deficiency of available published material on the theological concerns of the Old Testament books. Here, specialists explore the theological richness of a given book at greater length than is usually possible in the introductions to commentaries or as part of other Old Testament theologies. They are also able to investigate the theological themes and issues of their chosen books without being tied to a commentary format or to a thematic structure provided from elsewhere. When complete, the series will cover all the Old Testament writings and will thus provide an attractive, and timely, range of short texts around which courses can be developed.

PUBLISHED VOLUMES

The Theology of the Books of Ezra and Nehemiah, Roger S. Nam
The Theology of the Book of Samuel, John Goldingay
The Theology of the Books of Nahum, Habakkuk, and Zephaniah,
Daniel C. Timmer

The Theology of the Book of Proverbs, Katharine J. Dell
The Theology of the Books of Haggai and Zechariah, Robert L. Foster
The Theology of the Book of Kings, Keith Bodner
The Theology of the Book of Amos, John Barton
The Theology of the Book of Genesis, R. W. L. Moberly
The Theology of the Book of Jeremiah, Walter Brueggemann

THE THEOLOGY OF THE BOOK OF LEVITICUS

MARK W. SCARLATA

St. Mellitus College

CAMBRIDGE
UNIVERSITY PRESS

Shaftesbury Road, Cambridge CB2 8EA, United Kingdom

One Liberty Plaza, 20th Floor, New York, NY 10006, USA

477 Williamstown Road, Port Melbourne, VIC 3207, Australia

314–321, 3rd Floor, Plot 3, Splendor Forum, Jasola District Centre, New Delhi – 110025, India

103 Penang Road, #05-06/07, Visioncrest Commercial, Singapore 238467

Cambridge University Press is part of Cambridge University Press & Assessment, a department of the University of Cambridge.

We share the University's mission to contribute to society through the pursuit of education, learning and research at the highest international levels of excellence.

www.cambridge.org
Information on this title: www.cambridge.org/9781108845649

DOI: 10.1017/9781108980319

© Cambridge University Press & Assessment 2025

This publication is in copyright. Subject to statutory exception and to the provisions of relevant collective licensing agreements, no reproduction of any part may take place without the written permission of Cambridge University Press & Assessment.

When citing this work, please include a reference to the DOI 10.1017/9781108980319

First published 2025

A catalogue record for this publication is available from the British Library

Library of Congress Cataloging-in-Publication Data
NAMES: Scarlata, Mark William author
TITLE: The theology of the book of Leviticus / Mark W. Scarlata, St. Mellitus College, London.
DESCRIPTION: 1. | Cambridge, United Kingdom ; New York, NY : Cambridge University Press, 2025. | Includes bibliographical references and index.
IDENTIFIERS: LCCN 2025007734 (print) | LCCN 2025007735 (ebook) | ISBN 9781108845649 hardback | ISBN 9781108970112 paperback | ISBN 9781108980319 epub
SUBJECTS: LCSH: Bible. Leviticus–Criticism, interpretation, etc. | Bible. Leviticus–Theology
CLASSIFICATION: LCC BS1255.52 .S23 2025 (print) | LCC BS1255.52 (ebook) | DDC 222/.1306–dc23/eng/20250416
LC record available at https://lccn.loc.gov/2025007734
LC ebook record available at https://lccn.loc.gov/2025007735

ISBN 978-1-108-84564-9 Hardback
ISBN 978-1-108-97011-2 Paperback

Cambridge University Press & Assessment has no responsibility for the persistence or accuracy of URLs for external or third-party internet websites referred to in this publication and does not guarantee that any content on such websites is, or will remain, accurate or appropriate.

For EU product safety concerns, contact us at Calle de José Abascal, 56, 1°, 28003 Madrid, Spain, or email eugpsr@cambridge.org

Contents

General Editors' Preface	*page* xi
Preface	xv
List of Abbreviations	xviii

1 THE SACRED WORLD 1

    The Setting of Leviticus Within the Pentateuch   1
    A Theology of Holiness   8
    Critical Scholarship and Leviticus   16
    Leviticus, Decentralization, and the Israelite Home   22
    Conclusion   29

2 SIN, SACRIFICE, AND ATONEMENT (LEVITICUS
   1–7, 16) 32

    The Nature of Sacrifice   32
    Who Can Sacrifice?   39
    Types of Sacrifice   43
    Performing the Divine Drama   49
    The Life Is in the Blood   55
    A Theology of Sin and Atonement   61

Yom Kippur   70
Anselm, Atonement, and Leviticus   75

3 PURITY AND IMPURITY (LEVITICUS 11–15)   83

Defining Boundaries   83
Eating Our Way to Holiness   87
Purification and Childbirth   102
Purification, Skin Disease, and Bodily Discharge   109

4 INHABITING SACRED SPACE (LEVITICUS 8–10, 24–27) 114

A Priestly Theology of Space: The Tabernacle   114
Inhabiting Sacred Space: The Ordination of Priests   121
The Consecration of the Altar   130
Defiling Sacred Space   133
Holiness and the Land   140
The Jubilee   149

5 LOVE YOUR NEIGHBOR (LEVITICUS 17–22)   157

The Holiness Code   157
A Bridge from God's Home to Israel's Home   160
Sexual Ethics and the Health of the Family   169
The *Imitatio Dei*   179
From Lay Household to Priestly Household   195

6 LIVING IN SACRED TIME (LEVITICUS 23)   203

Holy Times and Seasons   203
A Priestly Theology of Time   209
Sabbath   212
The Festivals   217

7	LEVITICUS IN THE OLD TESTAMENT AND BEYOND	234
	Leviticus and the Old Testament	234
	Leviticus in the Second Temple Period	242
	Leviticus in the New Testament and Beyond	247
	Conclusion	260

Further Reading   263

Index   270

General Editors' Preface

Some years ago, Cambridge University Press, under the editorship of James D. G. Dunn, initiated a series entitled New Testament Theology. The first volumes appeared in 1991 and the series was brought to completion in 2003. For whatever reason, a companion series that would focus on the Old Testament/Hebrew Bible was never planned or executed. The present series, Old Testament Theology, is intended to rectify this need.

The reasons for publishing *Old Testament Theology* are not, however, confined solely to a desire to match *New Testament Theology*. Instead, the reasons delineated by Dunn that justified the publication of *New Testament Theology* continue to hold true for *Old Testament Theology*. These include, among other things, the facts that (1) given faculty and curricular structures in many schools, the theological study of individual Old Testament writings is often spotty at best; (2) most exegetical approaches (and commentaries) proceed verse by verse such that theological interests are in competition with, if not completely eclipsed by, other important issues, whether historical, grammatical, or literary; and (3) commentaries often confine their discussion of a book's theology to just a few pages in the introduction. The dearth of materials focused exclusively on a particular book's theology may be seen as a result of factors like these; or, perhaps, it is the cause of such factors. Regardless, as Dunn concluded, without adequate theological resources, there is little incentive for teachers or students to engage the theology of specific books; they must be content with what are mostly general overviews. Perhaps the most serious problem resulting from all this is that students are at a disadvantage, even incapacitated, when it comes to the matter of integrating their study of the Bible with other courses in religion and theology. There is, therefore, an urgent need for a series to bridge the gap between the too-slim theological précis and the too-full commentary where theological concerns are lost among many others.

All of these factors commend the publication of *Old Testament Theology* now, just as they did for *New Testament Theology* more than two decades ago. Like its sister series, *Old Testament Theology* is a place where Old Testament scholars can write at greater length on the theology of individual biblical books and may do so without being tied to the linear, verse-by-verse format of the commentary genre or a thematic structure of some sort imposed on the text from outside. Each volume in the series seeks to describe the biblical book's theology as well as to engage the book theologically – that is, each volume intends to *do* theology through and with the biblical book under discussion, as well as delineate the theology contained within it. Among other things, theological engagement with the composition includes paying attention to its contribution to the canon and appraising its influence on and reception by later communities of faith. In these ways, *Old Testament Theology* seeks to emulate its New Testament counterpart.

In the intervening years since *New Testament Theology* was first conceived, however, developments have taken place in the field that provide still further reasons for the existence of *Old*

Testament Theology; these have impact on how the series is envisioned and implemented and also serve to distinguish it, however slightly, from its companion series. Three developments in particular are noteworthy:

1. *The present hermeneutical climate*, often identified (rightly or wrongly) as "postmodern," is rife with possibility and potential for new ways of theologizing about scripture and its constituent parts. Theologizing in this new climate will of necessity look (and be) different from how it has ever looked (or been) before.
2. *The ethos change in the study of religion, broadly, and in biblical studies in particular.* No longer are the leading scholars in the field only Christian clergy, whether Catholic priests or mainline Protestant ministers. Jewish scholars and scholars of other Christian traditions are every bit as prominent, as are scholars of non- or even anti-confessional stripe. In short, now is a time when "Old Testament Theology" must be conducted without the benefits of many of the old consensuses and certainties, even the most basic ones relating to epistemological framework and agreed-upon interpretative communities along with their respective traditions.
3. Finally, recent years have witnessed *a long-overdue rapprochement among biblical scholars, ethicists, and systematic theologians.* Interdisciplinary studies between these groups are now regularly published, thus furthering and facilitating the need for books that make the theology of scripture widely available for diverse publics.

In brief, the time is ripe for a series of books that will engage the theology of specific books of the Old Testament in a new climate for a new day. The result will not be programmatic, settled, or altogether certain. Despite that – or, in some ways, *because* of that – it is hoped that *Old Testament Theology* will contain highly useful volumes that are ideally poised to make significant contributions on a number of fronts including (a) the ongoing discussion of biblical theology in confessional and nonconfessional mode as well as in postmodern and canonical contexts, (b) the theological exchange between Old Testament scholars and those working in cognate and disparate disciplines, and (c) the always-pressing task of introducing students to the theology of the discrete canonical unit: the biblical books themselves.

Brent A. Strawn
D. Moody Smith Distinguished Professor of Old Testament and Professor of Law, Duke University

Stephen B. Chapman
Associate Professor of Old Testament
Duke University

Patrick D. Miller†
Charles T. Haley Professor of Old Testament Theology, Emeritus
Princeton Theological Seminary

Preface

Studying the Book of Leviticus can be a challenge for even the most patient of readers. How many chapters can one plow through on the finer details of how to slaughter an animal or how to detect if there is a fungal infection in a wall? Leviticus is unlike any other book of the Old Testament and yet it sits firmly in the center of the Pentateuch as one of the critical articulations of God's law and the calling of his people Israel. Nowhere else do we find such an emphasis on holiness, purity, and ethical obedience as it relates to God's covenant people and their relationship to his tabernacle.

The world of Leviticus is filled with the rituals and symbols of an ancient society that often feel impenetrable to today's reader. Yet with a little perseverance, one can begin to discover how things like the drama of ritual, the use of sound and smell, and the symbolism of blood help contribute to a theology of what it means to dwell in the presence a holy God.

Israel's call to holiness is also shaped by their ethical treatment of the land and their relationships with family members and the aliens among them. Leviticus is not only concerned with ritual purity, but it offers moral and ethical commands that are critical to the life of a holy people. Israel is to care for the poor and the vulnerable, to create a society based in justice and mercy, and to love their neighbor.

For all its peculiar commands around eating, sex, or farming, Leviticus has a very simple message – the calling of God's people to be holy as he is holy (Lev 19:2) (Following the text of Leviticus, this study will maintain the use of the masculine pronouns for God throughout). Holiness, however, does not cease with God's people but it is meant to lead to the consecration of all creation. The holiness of the tabernacle extends to the holiness of Israel's home and to the land, but the vision of Leviticus is for the consecration of all things.

Part of this book was composed during the COVID-19 pandemic and the lockdowns we experienced here in the UK. It was fascinating to study ancient laws on purity, contamination, and contagious disease while the world was trying to find scientific answers to the global spread of a virus. What became quickly apparent was that governments around the world were wrestling with issues of contagion that are similar to those found in Leviticus. I'm grateful for those scholars who were part of the St. Edward's scriptorium during that time. Although they were subjected to my constant ramblings on Leviticus, their presence and support was welcomed during such difficult periods of isolation. I'm also thankful for the study leave I was granted by St. Mellitus College to finish this work and for my students who always stimulate creative ideas for new interpretations. This book would not have been possible without the gracious support and feedback given by the editors, Brent Strawn and Stephen Chapman. I'm grateful for the opportunity to participate in this series on the theology of the Old Testament. These books offer a critical theological voice in Old Testament scholarship that can often be overlooked in favor of other approaches to the text. Finally,

I am always most thankful for the support of my family and their willingness to consider what it means to walk together in holiness.

Mark W. Scarlata
St. Edward, King and Martyr, Cambridge
Michaelmas 2025

Abbreviations

AB	Anchor Bible
ABD	*Anchor Bible Dictionary.* Edited by David Noel Freedman. 6 vols. New York: Doubleday, 1992
ABS	*Archaeology and Biblical Studies*
AGJU	Arbeiten zur Geschichte des antiken Judentums und des Urchristentums
AnBib	Analecta Biblica
AOTC	Apollos Old Testament Commentary
ANET	*Ancient Near Eastern Texts Relating to the Old Testament.* Edited by James B. Pritchard. 3rd ed. Princeton, NJ: Princeton University Press, 1969
ASOR	American Schools of Oriental Research
BA	*Biblical Archaeologist*
BAR	*Biblical Archaeology Review*
BBB	Bonner biblische Beiträge
BibInt	*Biblical Interpretation*
CBQ	*Catholic Biblical Quarterly*
ConBNT	Coniectanea Biblica: New Testament Series
COS	*The Context of Scripture.* Edited by William W. Hallo. 3 vols. Leiden: Brill, 1997–2002

DDD	*Dictionary of Deities and Demons in the Bible.* Edited by Karel van der Toorn, Bob Becking, and Pieter W. van der Horst. Leiden: Brill, 1995. 2nd rev. ed. Grand Rapids, MI: Eerdmans, 1999
DJD	Discoveries in the Judaean Desert
ESV	English Standard Version
EQ	*Evangelical Quarterly*
FAT	Forschungen zum Alten Testament
H	Holiness legislation
HCOT	Historical Commentary on the Old Testament
HSM	Harvard Semitic Monographs
HTR	*Harvard Theological Review*
HUCA	*Hebrew Union College Annual*
IBC	Interpretation: A Bible Commentary for Teaching and Preaching
IEJ	*Israel Exploration Journal*
IVP	Intervarsity Press
JAOS	*Journal of the American Oriental Society*
JBL	*Journal of Biblical Literature*
JPS	Jewish Publication Society
JQR	*Jewish Quarterly Review*
JR	*Journal of Religion*
JSJ	*Journal for the Study of Judaism*
JSOT	*Journal for the Study of the Old Testament*
JSOTSS	Journal for the Study of the Old Testament Supplement Series
LHBOTS	The Library of Hebrew Bible/Old Testament Studies
LXX	Septuagint

NICOT	New International Commentary on the Old Testament
NIV	New International Version
NRSV	New Revised Standard Version
OTL	Old Testament Library
OTT	*Old Testament Theology*, 2 vols. Gerhard von Rad, trans. D. M. G. Stalker. Old Edinburgh: Oliver and Boyd, 1967.
P	Priestly source
PAAJR	*Proceedings of the American Academy of Jewish Research*
PEQ	*Palestine Exploration Quarterly*
PTMS	Princeton Theological Monograph Series
RSV	Revised Standard Version
SBL	Society of Biblical Literature
SBLDS	Society of Biblical Literature Dissertation Series
SJLA	Studies in Judaism in Late Antiquity
StBoT	Studien Zu Den Boğazköy-Texten
VT	*Vetus Testamentum*
VTSup	Supplements to Vetus Testamentum
WBC	Word Biblical Commentary
ZAW	*Zeitschrift für die alttestamentliche Wissenschaft*

CHAPTER 1

The Sacred World

THE SETTING OF LEVITICUS WITHIN THE PENTATEUCH

Leviticus is likely one of the least understood and least studied books of the Bible. The foreignness of ritual sacrifice, purity laws, or ancient agrarian life presents such a chasm for the modern reader that there is often little incentive to discern its theological meaning and its relation to the rest of Scripture. This is no modern phenomena. Similar sentiments were expressed by the early church scholar Origen, who argued that a literal reading of the text by "wicked presbyters" would result in a misinterpretation of its figurative meaning for the Christian reader.[1] Even Maimonides, the great medieval Jewish rabbi, remained highly critical of the sacrificial system and sympathized with prophetic condemnation of cultic abuses. He argued that sacrifice was only given to Moses as a guide against ancient pagan religious practices but that it was never God's intent for Israel to participate in sacrificial worship forever.[2] Interpreters over the centuries have

---

[1] Origen, *Homilies on Leviticus 1–16*, trans. Gary Wayne Barkley, The Fathers of the Church series (Washington, DC: Catholic University of America Press, 1990), 30.
[2] Isadore Twersky ed., *A Maimonides Reader* (New York: Behrman House, 1972), 332–34.

struggled to find value or coherence in the priestly writings of Leviticus, which makes it one of the most challenging books in the biblical corpus.

One immediate difficulty that presents itself when considering the theology of Leviticus is discerning how the work sits in relation to the rest of the Pentateuch and whether or not we may describe it as a "book" in its own right. Part of the problem comes from the LXX translation of the title as *Levitikon* ("Levitical") and the Latin *Liber Leviticus*, which both point to the priestly tribe of Levi but obscure the distinction between priests and Levites that is a critical part of the book. The rabbinic Hebrew name *tôrat kôhănîm* ("teaching of priests") is just as limited in its focus. The Hebrew Bible identifies the scroll (as it does for each Pentateuchal book) by its first word *wayyiqrā'* ("And he called") in reference to God calling to Moses from the *'ōhel mô'ēd* ("tent of meeting"), the newly constructed tabernacle. This setting is critical because Leviticus sits in the middle of the larger Exodus/Sinai narrative and at the center of the Pentateuch.

Though the earliest extant texts of Leviticus attest to its independence as a scroll, its literary character reflects careful integration into the series of salvific events in the exodus that conclude at Mt. Sinai with the design and construction of the tabernacle. On the seventh day, Yhwh called Moses (*wayyiqrā'*) to ascend further up Sinai into the cloud of glory to receive the tablets of the commandments (Exod 24:16).[3] The same phrase (*wayyiqrā'*) introduces Leviticus when God reveals the laws concerning offerings within the tabernacle (Leviticus 1–7). This time Moses is

---

[3] The seven introductions can be found in Exod 25:1; 30:11, 17, 22, 34; 31:1, 12.

called to the tent, which had previously been impossible to enter because God's glory had descended upon it (Exod 40:34–35). The continuation of the theophany at Sinai centers around the newly constructed tabernacle where Yhwh now dwells. Yet God's calling to Moses from the tent in Lev 1:1 introduces a transition in the story of Israel's salvation from Egypt. With the divine decent made manifest at the end of Exodus, the theological imperative of Leviticus is to articulate how Israel might maintain their holiness in relation to the holy God who dwells in their midst. From this new reality emerges a theology of holiness that hinges on the critical relationship between Yhwh's home (the tabernacle) and every Israelite home. The two spaces are inextricably linked in Leviticus because Yhwh's requirement of holiness is one that extends to every aspect of Israelite life.

The construction of the tabernacle at the conclusion of Exodus points to a new creation, a new Eden, and the beginning of a new people, Israel, who will live and worship in God's presence. As God ordered the universe in the beginning of Genesis and created his cosmic temple, so too does Moses take on God-like qualities as he brings to completion God's tabernacle on earth. When God calls to Moses the seventh time (Exod 31:12), the reader is reminded of the seventh day of creation and God's sabbath command that will sanctify Israel and will be the sign of a perpetual covenant. Finally, on the first day of the first month in the second year of wandering in the wilderness, the tabernacle is completed (Exod 40:16–33). The fullness of Yhwh's glory descends (Exod 40:34) but there is no mention of offerings or sacrifice. Nothing is said about the consecration of the altar or how Aaron and his sons will serve within. This is where Leviticus begins and where Yhwh's first words are uttered as a continuation of the instructions already received at Sinai. Now, however, God's initial commands in Leviticus 1–7 focus on the life of the cult and sacrifice.[4]

After the high drama at the end of Exodus, Leviticus may seem somewhat anticlimactic as we read God's next command, "Speak to the people of Israel and say to them, when any one of you brings an offering to the LORD, you shall bring your offering of livestock from the herd or from the flock" (Lev 1:1). What may seem to be a boring turn of events in the narrative is, in fact, critical to maintaining the order and holiness of God's abode. Without ongoing sacrifices, rituals, and purifications, the tabernacle cannot function as a place where the divine intersects with the world and brings blessing to the people. The abiding presence of God with Israel is, to borrow Brueggemann's phrase, one of its core testimonies that expresses a belief in the visible, tangible experience of God's glory.[5] This is, in part, why Leviticus stands on its own as an individual book of the Pentateuch – it reveals an entire system of worship that encompasses cultic, ethical, and family matters that teach the Israelites how to live in relationship to God and to their neighbor.[6]

If the inauguration of the tabernacle is the decisive narrative and theological link between Exodus and Leviticus, we can begin to

---

[4] For a more in-depth treatment of the timings around the ordination of Aaron and his sons, the consecration of the altar, and God's glory descending in Exodus, see Gary A. Anderson, *That I May Dwell Among Them: Incarnation and Atonement in the Tabernacle Narrative* (Grand Rapids, MI: Eerdmans, 2023), 19–48.

[5] See Walter Brueggemann, *Theology of the Old Testament: Testimony, Dispute, Advocacy* (Minneapolis, MN: Fortress Press, 1997).

[6] Cf. Martin Noth, *Leviticus: A Commentary*, OTL (Philadelphia: Westminster Press, 1965), 9–17. Interestingly, Leviticus makes no mention of hymnic praise, which was a typical Levitical activity in the Second Temple period (1 Chr 23:30).

understand why there is so much emphasis on sacrifice and purity. We may, however, question why so much detail is necessary since different types of sacrifices and offerings had already been a part of Israelite worship since the time of the patriarchs. Burnt offerings were made by Noah after the flood (Gen 8:20) and by Abraham in the place of his son Isaac (Gen 22:13). Sacrifices to God were known by Moses as he had argued with Pharaoh about not being able to make offerings in Egypt lest they caused an outrage among the Egyptians who would consider it an abomination (Exod 8:25–26; cf. 10:25). The altar laws of Exod 20:24–26 also give instruction for general sacrifices whether on earth mounds or stone. At the base of Mt. Sinai, to ratify the covenant, Moses instructs the young men to help offer two types of sacrifice – the ʿōlâ ("whole burnt offering") and the šəlāmîm ("peace offering" or "well-being offering") (Exod 24:5; cf. 32:6), which are later explained in detail in Leviticus. Following a chronological narrative from Genesis to Exodus, we might question why Leviticus offers further commandments regarding sacrifices.

The rhetorical force of Leviticus is that, with the consecration of God's holy abode on earth, there is now a need for "specialists" (i.e., priests) within the community to be set apart to make offerings according to God's specific prescriptions.[7] Only men of certain lineage may be consecrated as priests to draw near to God's holiness. This is emphasized by the continual refrain in the opening chapters of Leviticus where cultic functions, like the sprinkling of blood, are to be performed only by "Aaron and his sons" (Lev 3:2, 8, 13; 6:16; 10:12; 13:2). Israel's relation to the

---

[7] James W. Watts, *Leviticus 1–10*, HCOT (Leuven: Peeters, 2013), 104–7; James W. Watts, *Ritual and Rhetoric in Leviticus: From Sacrifice to Scripture* (Cambridge: Cambridge University Press, 2007), 73.

tabernacle, and the divine presence within, requires distinct cultic instructions that must be performed by authorized persons alone. These new regulations reform the previous altar laws of the covenant code since they describe the particularity of sacrifice *within the tabernacle space* with a rhetorical emphasis on the priestly role. The average Israelite was still involved in the sacrifice, but the priest's role becomes prominent in Leviticus as one who orders and oversees cultic life in and around the tabernacle. The result is an elevated theology of priesthood that maintains a high regard for lay participation and knowledge of the cult.

Leviticus, it will be argued, does not restrict the priesthood to a single, central shrine but implicitly allows for sacrifices to take place at multiple sites. What remains critical for the theology of Leviticus is not *where* sacrifices take place but that they take place at an *authorized altar* by an *authorized priest* according to God's prescriptions.[8] Leviticus is not concerned with a centralized shrine but, rather, it emphasizes the sanctity and holiness of the priesthood that serves the community within the presence of God's holy altar.

Leviticus is not, however, simply a manual for priests that is shrouded in mystery like some gnostic, esoteric text reserved for the elite who lived behind temple walls. Its instructions are made known to the people of Israel who, in turn, can hold the priests accountable for their actions. Though strict divisions made between layperson and priest seem to promote a social hierarchy, these divisions serve, instead, to demystify the cult and level out social relationships so that the prevailing call to holiness is incumbent on all of God's people (cf. Lev 19:2). As Brueggemann argues,

---

[8] This is one of the chief criticisms of Jeroboam in 1 Kgs 12:31–32 when he appoints priests for the sanctuaries at Bethel and Dan who are not Levites.

"This may suggest that the extended inventory of sacrifices and related materials in the book of Leviticus is to be understood not as a manual for practice, but as a liturgical, aesthetic act of imagination of what the world of Israel is like when it is known to be focused upon glad responses in obedience and sacrifice to YHWH."[9] Leviticus, therefore, seeks to order the cult as it consolidates, secures, and standardizes sacred traditions around ritual and sacrifice, but it does so by presenting (and sometimes explaining) how it functions so that religious power is not held by a select few.

The narrative connection between Exodus and Leviticus is critical in understanding the shift in focus from God's power revealed in the deliverance from Egypt to the power of his holiness revealed at Sinai, which is then made manifest in the tabernacle. Yhwh's home on earth is a sign of salvation, new creation, and the promise of his abiding presence with his people. His glory fills the tent at the end of Exodus, but its function is not complete until the altar is consecrated and atonement becomes possible through the priests. Though the narrative links to Exodus are clear, the book of Leviticus stands on its own as a priestly and prophetic book. Sacrifice, atonement, and how Israel can live as a holy people are at the heart of its *kerygma*, which offers a holistic theology through both ritual and ethical practice.

The emergence of such a "book" in Israel stems from ancient cultic traditions and liturgical rites that were collated, refined, edited, and passed on from generation to generation. Layers of tradition will be discernible in the text that may reflect different

---

[9] Walter Brueggemann and Tod Linafelt, *An Introduction to the Old Testament: The Canon and Christian Imagination*, 2nd ed. (Louisville, KY: Westminster John Knox Press, 2012), 98.

time periods or the theological interests and concerns of the authors, but the goal of the present study is to determine how these different theological strands come together to form the theology of the Book of Leviticus in its final form. Leviticus puts forward its own vision for Israel's calling as a priestly kingdom that reflects an overarching concern for the holiness of God and how that is reflected in the holiness of God's people.

A THEOLOGY OF HOLINESS

At the heart of the theology of the Book of Leviticus is holiness. Holiness resonates throughout each chapter and culminates in the all-encompassing command, "You shall be holy, for I the LORD your God am holy" (Lev 19:2). Holiness is to permeate every aspect of Israelite life whether it is offering a sacrifice, eating a meal, tending to the land or animals, having sex, or loving one's neighbor. The priestly world is defined by the sacred and the glory of God's permanent presence abiding with his people. William Blake once wrote, "everything that lives is holy,"[10] which expresses well the sentiment of Leviticus. Every aspect of life is holy because all things live in relation to the holy God of Israel who now dwells on earth. The emphasis on holiness is not, as P. R. Davies suggests, a type of "neurosis" to which all life is reduced as if it is merely the result of social, political, or economic forces.[11] Instead, holiness offers a vision for a world in which the

---

[10] William Blake, *Complete Writings*, ed. Geoffrey Keynes (London: Oxford University Press, 1966), 160.

[11] Philip R. Davies, "Leviticus as a Cultic System in the Second Temple Period: Remarks on the Paper by Hannah K. Harrington," in *Reading Leviticus: A Conversation with Mary Douglas*, ed. John F. A. Sawyer, JSOTSS 227 (Sheffield: Sheffield Academic Press, 1996), 230–37 (236–37).

divine presence is fully manifest in the tabernacle that sanctifies Israel and the land.

The biblical idea of holiness is difficult to grasp because it relates to the numinous, wholly otherness of God.[12] Only God is holy and people or objects become holy by being set apart to him. The Hebrew root *q-d-š* generally means to set apart for holy purposes. When used in the *piēl* verbal stem, it means "sanctify, make holy," which refers to something that is transferred from the profane into God's presence. This can relate to time (sabbath, festivals), to people (priests), or to offerings on the altar. For something to be set apart as holy means that it has been dedicated to God and thereby acquires a degree of God's holiness.

To become holy something must first be taken from the ordinary or profane. In English, the word "profane" often takes on negative moral connotations today, but it derives from the Latin *pro* ("before, outside") *fanum* ("temple"). The term originally referred to anything that dealt with matters of life and work outside the temple.[13] In biblical Hebrew, the verbal root for "profane" (*ḥ-l-l*) describes something that is no longer suitable to come into God's presence or that has been defiled. This more negative nuance, however, should not be confused with a permanent state of contamination. Instead, Leviticus understands that the consecration of life is an ongoing process. People and things can move toward Yhwh's holiness or they can become defiled and move away from his holiness. For most things, the state of uncleanness in the profane world is temporary and can be

---

[12] See Rudolf Otto, *The Idea of Holiness*, trans. John W. Harvey, 2nd ed. (Oxford: Oxford University Press, 1950), 5–11.
[13] Cf. Émile Durkheim, *The Elementary Forms of the Religious Life* (repr. London: George Allen & Unwin, 1976), 37.

remedied. As Baruch Levine argues, "The gulf between the sacred and the profane was not meant to be permanent. The command to achieve holiness, to become holy, envisions a time when life would be consecrated in its fullness and when all nations would worship God in holiness."[14] Though Leviticus is concerned with separation and division between the sacred and the profane, the end goal is for God's holiness to flow from his dwelling place to his people and to the world.

The theology of holiness in Leviticus is multilayered and is concerned with both ethical obedience to God's commands as well as cultic obedience expressed through ritual. Holiness in Leviticus is not presented as a set of propositional truths about God, but it is conveyed through signs, symbols, rituals, and actions that convey the drama of participating in God's salvation. To understand this drama, one must look to the culture and worldview that undergirds each ritual act in order to determine its meaning.[15] Clifford Geertz argues that "any religious ritual, no matter how apparently automatic or conventional ... involves this symbolic fusion of ethos and world view."[16] The dialectic nature between thought and action is critical in the study of Leviticus because its theology is expressed through word, symbol, and ritual performance. This can be a challenge for modern readers due to the fact that the rituals of Leviticus stem from an ancient agrarian culture where life consisted largely of subsistence farming and religious beliefs that centered around blood sacrifice.

---

[14] Baruch A. Levine, *Leviticus*, JPS Torah Commentary (New York: Jewish Publication Society, 1989), 257.

[15] Frank H. Gorman Jr., *The Ideology of Ritual: Space, Time and Status in the Priestly Theology*, JSOTSS 91 (Sheffield: Sheffield Academic Press, 1990), 15.

[16] Clifford Geertz, *The Interpretation of Cultures: Selected Essays* (New York: Basic Books, 1973), 113; cf. 126–41.

This is a far cry from religious practice in the contemporary world. Yet to understand the depth and breadth of Leviticus' theology, the reader is required to move beyond purely rational approaches to the Bible and to open their imaginations to the signs and symbols of an ancient world to determine how these might convey theological belief.[17]

To interpret ritual is to understand how the body is actively engaged in worship as an act of world shaping and world creating. Catherine Bell argues that "acting ritually emerges as a particular cultural strategy of differentiation linked to particular social effects and rooted in a distinctive interplay of a socialized body and the environment it structures."[18] Rituals are not merely static, repetitive acts but, rather, they help construct social and religious relationships of power. In Leviticus, this encompasses both the human authority of Moses and the priests within the Israelite camp but also the divine authority of Yhwh. Leviticus centralizes the locus of divine power in the tabernacle, which is the physical representation and sign of the reordering of the world. The hierarchy of priests and laypeople establishes a social structure that allows Israel to move from the threat of chaos produced by sin to the order and stability of God's creation. The social and religious power dynamics advocated in Leviticus are ultimately for the sake of preserving the holiness of God's people and thus preserving the holiness and life of the world.

Rituals also link communities to the rhythms of the environment. Harvest, summer rains, sowing seed, and care for the land

---

[17] See Mary Douglas, *Leviticus as Literature* (Oxford: Oxford University Press, 1999), 13–40.

[18] Catherine Bell, *Ritual Theory, Ritual Practice* (Oxford: Oxford University Press, 1992), 8.

are tied to festivals and life around the altar. Samuel Balentine contends that the "priestly conviction is that God's *creational order* is generative of and sustained by human observance of an imaging *ritual order*."[19] To be attuned to the natural rhythms of the world is one way that Leviticus expresses a theology of holiness. The seasons draw the community back to the story of salvation year after year, which leads to the right ordering of God's people and protects them from the forces of chaos and death.

A theology of holiness in Leviticus, however, is not limited to ritual acts. The priestly text that guides the reader through blood, atonement, and purification also contains moral and ethical commands for social justice and the preservation of the family and the land. Leviticus is as much a prophetic text that condemns the mistreatment of the poor and vulnerable in society as it is a cultic text.[20] For Israel to be a holy people they must strive for ritual *and* ethical purity. At the core of such belief is the idea that holiness is a corporate undertaking that can never be achieved by the individual alone. To be holy necessarily means to be in community and in loving relationships characterized by God's justice, righteousness, and goodness. Israel's call to holiness can only be achieved through its communal response to God's command.[21]

---

[19] Samuel E. Balentine, *Leviticus*, IBC (Louisville, KY: Westminster John Knox, 2002), 4.

[20] S. R. Driver, *Introduction to the Literature of the Old Testament*, 9th ed. (Magnolia, MA: Peter Smith, 1972), 151.

[21] For a summary of John Wesley's views on social holiness, see Brent A. Strawn, "Leviticus," in *Wesley One Volume Commentary*, ed. Kenneth J. Collins and Robert W. Wall (Nashville, TN: Abingdon Press, 2020), 66–89 (79–81).

Leviticus also highlights the critical connection between the holiness of Yhwh's home and the holiness of the Israelite home. The two are inextricably tethered because the tabernacle's purity is linked to the purity of Israel's most intimate family relationships. With the advent of the divine descent, God tells Israel, "I will place my dwelling in your midst, and I shall not abhor you. And I will walk among you, and will be your God, and you shall be my people" (Lev 26:11–12). The language of walking among the Israelites recalls Eden (Gen 3:8) and foresees a time of re-creation, re-birth, and the reclaiming of God's rightful place as king over all the earth. The humble dwelling of a tent in the wilderness has cosmic implications and represents the order of the divine kingdom being re-established on earth through God's holy presence, which is to be mirrored in every Israelite home.

The most basic social structure in ancient Israel begins in the home and extends to the clan and tribe. Leviticus makes no mention of a king, a royal court, or those of privileged position apart from the "elders" or "chieftains" (Lev 4:15, 22; 9:1; 19:32). Instead, we find what is often referred to as a "democratization of holiness."[22] Though there are distinctions between the priests and laypeople, all of God's covenant community is called to the *imitatio Dei* without exception (Lev 11:44–45; 19:2; 20:26). Thus, every Israelite family is meant to reflect the purity and holiness of the tabernacle, which means that everyday things like

---

[22] See Robert A. Kugler, "Holiness, Purity, The Body, and Society: The Evidence for Theological Conflict in Leviticus," *JSOT* (1997): 3–27; Jacob Milgrom, "The Changing Concept of Holiness in the Pentateuchal Codes with Emphasis on Leviticus 19," in *Reading Leviticus: A Conversation with Mary Douglas*, ed. John F. A. Sawyer, JSOTSS 227 (Sheffield: Sheffield Academic Press, 1996), 65–75.

eating, drinking, farming, sexual relations, and familial relationships are all tied to God's home. If God's home represents a microcosm of the cosmic temple where his purity and holiness dwell, then every Israelite home must imitate this same purity and holiness.

One of the significant and unique contributions of Leviticus' theology in the scriptures is its understanding of holy space and time. We shall discuss holiness in more detail later, but it is important to grasp the critical links that are made throughout the book between purity in the space of Israel's tent and how that is directly connected to Yhwh's tent. Holiness in Leviticus is not simply about the divine presence in the shrine where the deity resides, as it was for many other ancient religions. Instead, holiness in Leviticus is something so pervasive that it extends to the home and to the land to the extent that if any of those places are defiled it affects God's dwelling. Such an emphasis on purity and holiness presents a theological vision of a sacralized world where Yhwh is actively consecrating his people and the land through his glory and abiding presence. To read Leviticus through this theological lens is to see how and why its arrangement moves from purity in the tabernacle (chapters 1–16) to purity in the covenant community (chapters 17–27). What has traditionally been seen as a division in authorship of the book is the natural theological flow for instructions on how to live in Yhwh's presence and in his consecrated land. The unity of holiness between tabernacle, home, and land is key to understanding how Leviticus represents its vision for a world where God is reconsecrating his people and his kingdom on earth.

A theology of holiness in the home in Leviticus also expresses a theology of power. God's divine power in the tabernacle can provide blessing or it can be a force that brings death.

Oftentimes, the instructions given to Moses or the priests are made with the proviso that the priests act accordingly or else they will die (Lev 10:7, 9; 16:2, 13). What is true in the tabernacle is also true of the Israelite home. Most of the commands concerning the household have as their assumed audience the male head of household (*paterfamilias*) with the understanding that his actions can bring about the life or potential destruction of the family. The ritual sacrifices found in Leviticus 1–16 often have the *paterfamilias* as the presumed offerer. The more ethical focus of Leviticus 17–27 is also directed at the male head of household especially in the chapters on sexual purity (Leviticus 18 and 20). Issues concerning land management, ethical treatment of slaves or sojourners, enforcement of sabbath rest for family and livestock, and treatment of one's neighbor are almost all aimed first at the male head of the household. This is not to diminish the critical role of the matriarch or women in the family, but the commands of Leviticus presume a theology of home under the primary authority of the patriarch who, like the priests, must be obedient to God's commands for holiness to prevail in the household.

When considering a theology of holiness in Leviticus, the contemporary reader must be willing to suspend prejudices and attempt to enter into the sacred world of its authors. In Leviticus, all of life is wrapped in a beautiful web of holiness and all of life must be consecrated as holy if it is to remain in unity with the God who is wholly other. The epicenter of holiness lies in the heart of God's home, the tabernacle, but it does not end there. Reflections of his glory are meant to be found in the homes of his covenant people as they set themselves apart from the world so that God's holiness might be made manifest to all nations. Though Leviticus may seem preoccupied with the minutiae of sacrifice or the appropriate divisions between the pure and impure, it is only because it sees the possibility of a world that is fully healed, restored, and consecrated to the God whose holiness will fill all the earth.

CRITICAL SCHOLARSHIP AND LEVITICUS

Since the nineteenth century, Pentateuchal scholarship has focused mainly on the sources behind the Torah and how it was brought together in its final form. Julius Wellhausen's Documentary Hypothesis (DH) argued for four distinct sources (J, E, P, and D) that made up the Mosaic Pentateuch. The latest of these, dated to the fifth century BCE, was the priestly source (*Priesterschrift* or P), which includes the law code of Leviticus 17–26 (Holiness Code or H) that emphasized the centrality of the Jerusalem temple.[23] Wellhausen traced the development of Israelite religion and argued that it moved from a simple, free form of worship to an increasingly legalistic and ritually focused practice established by the priestly classes. Unfortunately, Wellhausen's negative characterization of priestly influence reflected sentiments of his own Protestant cultural milieu. Since Wellhausen, some scholars such as Yehezkel Kaufmann have argued for the antiquity of P and its pre-dating of Deuteronomy (D),[24] but many have held to the position that P is the latest document of the Pentateuch and is responsible for its final formation.[25]

---

[23] Julius Wellhausen, *Prolegomena to the History of Ancient Israel* (1878; repr., Cleveland: World, 1965) 34–38.

[24] Yehezkel Kaufmann, *The Religion of Israel from Its Beginnings to the Babylonian Exile*, trans. and ed. Moshe Greenberg (Chicago: University of Chicago Press, 1960).

[25] See, e.g., Konrad Schmid, *The Scribes of the Torah: The Formation of the Pentteuch in Its Literary and Historical Contexts*. Ancient Israel and Its

More recent approaches have called into question the DH and the idea of a specific priestly source. Some have argued that the growth of Leviticus and the Pentateuch can be understood as a more organic transmission over time whereby narratives, laws, poems, and other forms of literature were gradually brought together in different generations that reflected their own use and understanding of the Mosaic tradition.[26] If this was the case, then we may speak more generally about "priestly writings" in the Pentateuch rather than a "Priestly Source" or even a "Holiness Code."[27]

Despite the preference of scholarship to dissect the Pentateuch into its constituent parts, the literary unity of Leviticus has been defended by anthropologist Mary Douglas in her work *Leviticus as Literature*. She argues for a tripartite ring structure in the book, which reflects the tripartite structure of the tabernacle. Douglas sees the division between P and H as an artificial scholarly construction that does not take into account the thematic unity and structure of the priestly writers. She contends that the alleged split between P and H more likely reflects Christian theological preferences imposed on the text. P is characterized as the pedantic priest incessantly worried about the precision of ritual while H is the good liberal concerned with social issues and the treatment of the poor. She argues, however, that "according to the anthropological

---

Literature, 45 (Atlanta: SBL Press, 2023); Joel S. Baden, *The Composition of the Pentateuch: Renewing the Documentary Hypothesis* (New Haven: Yale University Press, 2012).

[26] Rolf Rendtorff, *The Problem of the Process of Transmission in the Pentateuch*, JSOTSS 89 (Sheffield: Sheffield Academic Press, 1990); Gordon J. Wenham, *The Book of Leviticus*, NICOT (Grand Rapids, MI: Eerdmans, 1979), 6–12.

[27] See Konrad Schmid and Friedhelm Hartenstein, *Farewell to the Priestly Writing? The Current State of the Debate* (Atlanta: SBL Press, 2022).

analysis, the differences between the two halves of Leviticus do not quite follow these lines. Both halves of the book use analogies in the same way, and neither demonstrates 'causal', 'logical', 'discursive', or 'dialogic' reasoning."[28] Her analysis leads to the conclusion that Leviticus was likely authored by someone bringing together a variety of sources from different periods in a distinctly mythopoetic style that varies throughout the composition but remains unified in its structure.[29]

Though some have agreed with Douglas' work, ever since August Klostermann's use of the phrase "Holiness Code," most scholars have continued to divide the book into two main sections to differentiate between the P legislation found in Leviticus 1–16 and the H writings in 17–26 (27).[30] The holiness writings are thought to be a later (priestly) development, possibly composed as early as the eighth century BCE or as late as fifth century BCE. They demonstrate a thematic unity summed up in the command, "You shall be holy, for I the LORD your God am holy" (Lev 19:2). The call to be holy is often repeated throughout H (cf. 20:7–8; 21:8, 15, 23; 22:9, 16, 32) but can also be found in other redactions such as within the dietary restrictions of Lev 11:44–45.

There is extensive debate about the nature and scope of H in Leviticus and the rest of the Pentateuch.[31] Scholars such as

---

[28] Douglas, *Leviticus as Literature*, 34.
[29] Douglas, *Leviticus as Literature*, 34, 40, 150.
[30] August Klostermann, *Der Pentateuch* (Leipzig: A. Deichert, 1893), 1:368, 418. For a full summary of scholarship on H, see John E. Hartley, *Leviticus*, WBC (Dallas, TX: Word Books, 1992), 251–60.
[31] E.g., see Israel Knohl, *Sanctuary of Silence: The Priestly Torah and the Holiness School* (Winona Lake, IN: Eisenbrauns, 2007), 199–224; Jacob Milgrom, *Leviticus 17–22: A New Translation with Introduction and Commentary*, AB 3A (Garden City, NY: Doubleday, 2000), 1337–44; Jacob Milgrom, "HR in Leviticus and Elsewhere in the Torah," in *The Book of*

Jacob Milgrom and Israel Knohl have argued that H is a redactional layer that is distinct from P. Knohl contends that a "Holiness School" was responsible for the final editing of the Pentateuch, while Milgrom prefers the term "Holiness Source." Both argue that H was influenced by Isaiah's call to social justice and ethical holiness. Though Knohl highlights linguistic differences between what he calls the "Priestly Torah" and the "Holiness School," his interpretation of these differences is often reductionistic.[32] He tends to depict the priests as an elite circle isolated within the walls of the Jerusalem temple concerned only with esoteric cultic matters. He sees them as a religious class who care little for ethical behavior and are obsessed with maintaining the purity of the temple.[33] While those from the "Holiness School" appeal to ethical holiness and the popular religion of the people. Such a bifurcation of Leviticus is unnecessary, and we shall see that the connections made between Yhwh's home and Israel's home provide a natural link between chapters 1–16 and 17–27 and for the overarching vision of holiness offered by the authors.

It is clear that Leviticus contains various layers of tradition that express different themes and motifs, but this does not mean that we cannot speak about a theology that emerges from the book as a whole.[34] Knohl rightly argues that one should not speak casually

---

Leviticus: Composition and Reception, ed. Rolf Rendtorff and Robert A. Kugler, VTSup 93 (Leiden: Brill, 2003), 24–40. See also Christophe Nihan, *From Priestly Torah to Pentateuch: A Study in the Composition of the Book of Leviticus*, FAT 252 (Tübingen: Mohr Siebeck, 2007), 559–75.

[32] Cf. Jacob Milgrom's critique in "HR in Leviticus and Elsewhere in the Torah," 26–40.

[33] Knohl, *Sanctuary of Silence*, 214–16, 220–22, 226.

[34] Cf. Baruch J. Schwartz, *The Holiness Legislation: Studies in the Priestly Code* (Jerusalem: Magnes, 1999) (Hebrew), 17–24.

of "the priestly theology" in view of the different traditions that have been collected in the Pentateuch. We can, however, examine Leviticus in its final form as an expression of priestly theology that is multivalent since it speaks with resonances of Israelite religion that have grown throughout centuries of worship and obedience to the Mosaic laws. Rather than separating P and H, they will be analyzed synchronically since both earlier and later priestly traditions have been joined together in Leviticus to form a distinct theological voice.[35]

Another issue that critical scholarship has addressed is the dating of Leviticus' final form. Since Wellhausen, P has been viewed as the product of postexilic authors writing during the Persian period. This would account for similarities between P and the more elaborate cultic descriptions found in Chronicles as well as the lack of any reference to a king. However, more recent proposals from Knohl and Milgrom have argued for an eighth-century BCE provenance sometime during the reigns of Ahaz and Hezekiah following the Assyrian destruction of the northern tribes.[36] Allowing for various layers of redaction, this view generally argues for the antiquity of P and its cultic traditions, which have been modified and updated by H to form the Book of Leviticus.

Historical background is important in understanding why certain beliefs emerged in Israelite religion at particular times and these will be addressed in the following chapters. Theology in the Old Testament is not a matter of timeless truths created in a religious vacuum. The beliefs of ancient Israel stem from

---

[35] See Nihan, *Priestly Torah*, 546–47; Erhard S. Gersternberger, *Leviticus*, OTL (Louisville, KY: Westminster John Knox, 1996), 18.
[36] Knohl, *The Sanctuary of Silence*, 199–224.

traditions that were passed down in both oral and written form. These were ultimately integrated, composed, and redacted into the Book of Leviticus. The focus of the present volume, however, demands one avoid being overly dependent on compositional debates. Attempts to date different layers of priestly tradition are fraught with difficulties. One often finds the scholarly assumption that any variation within the text points to different authorship or distinct documents that once circulated independently of one another. These presuppositions, at times, make for circular arguments that cannot be sustained. This makes it almost impossible to come to any firm conclusions regarding the date and final composition of Leviticus.[37] Though arguments for preexilic or postexilic authorship have their merits, this work will assume, with Milgrom and Knohl, that the antiquity of Israel's cultic traditions were standardized by later priestly authors around the eighth or seventh century BCE but thereafter went through later redactions.[38] This periodization will be defended as different theological points are discussed. In the present volume, however, the concern will be to examine Leviticus through a synchronic approach that seeks to discover how the final form of the text articulates its theological vision.

---

[37] For a history of proposals on dating and the Holiness Code, see Paavo N. Tucker, *The Holiness Composition in the Book of Exodus*, FAT 2/98 (Tübingen: Mohr Siebeck, 2017), 18–28. See also Rolf Rendtorff, "Is It Possible to Read Leviticus as a Separate Book?," in *Reading Leviticus: A Conversation with Mary Douglas*, ed. John F. A. Sawyer, JSOTSS 227 (Sheffield: Sheffield Academic Press, 1996), 22–35; Rolf Rendtorff, *The Old Testament: An Introduction* (London: SCM Press, 1985; Philadelphia: Fortress Press, 1986), 145.

[38] This also assumes that Leviticus is shaped prior to the book of Deuteronomy and Ezekiel. See Moshe Weinfeld, *Deuteronomy and the Deuteronomic School* (Oxford: Clarendon, 1972), 179–89.

LEVITICUS, DECENTRALIZATION, AND THE ISRAELITE HOME

One of the key theological themes that emerges from Leviticus is the significance of sacrifice at an authorized shrine by the hands of authorized priests. This has often been interpreted as Leviticus' support for a centralized sanctuary, but we shall see that this is not necessarily the case. The theology of Leviticus actually promotes a *decentralized* form of worship where the standardization of priestly practice allows for regional, authorized shrines to be active in the everyday life and worship of Israelite communities. Just as cultic restrictions around the altar are standardized, so too does Leviticus advocate a standardization that shapes the life of the laity through purity laws, festivals, ethical behavior in the home, and work on the land. Leviticus offers a holistic pattern for life and worship both in the home and in the tabernacle.

Wellhausen argued that cult centralization was originally the result of Deuteronomic reforms under Josiah. According to his dating of P (and H) as postexilic, he contended that cultic texts in Leviticus represented continued support for a single, centralized sanctuary that was initiated under D.[39] Scholarship since then has continued to support and build on this theory, but there have been dissenting voices. Kaufmann argued that the priestly material predates Deuteronomy and that centralization was not a concern of Leviticus since multiple sanctuaries had existed in Israel throughout its history in the land and well into the postexilic period.[40] He saw no literary connection between P and D concerning the centralization of a worship site and argued,

---

[39] Wellhausen, *Prolegomena*, 376–85.
[40] Kaufmann, *The Religion of* Israel, 175–205.

instead, that the portability of the shrine points to a time of worship that best reflects the earliest phases of ancient Israel's history in the land.[41] Kaufmann also argued that the language and laws of Leviticus better reflect a preexilic rather than postexilic period and that Leviticus shared more similarities with second millennium BCE Mesopotamian traditions than it did with postexilic Persian documents. In support of this, E. A. Speiser also argued that the priestly laws came together over a lengthy period of time and contain both earlier and later material but were not reliant on D and did not push for centralization.[42]

Milgrom departs slightly from Kaufmann by arguing that P probably intended the tabernacle to support limited centralization at a regional sanctuary (possibly Shiloh) but that the priestly authors accepted the existence and legitimacy of other regional sanctuaries.[43] Milgrom highlights early Israelite histories that focus on different offerings being made at Shiloh in premonarchic times and the fact that this is the first site where the tabernacle resides when entering the land (Josh 18:1). This tradition finds confirmation in the independent text of 2 Sam 7:6-7 (1 Chr 17:5-6).

Early narratives of life in the land depict both the use of local altars and common slaughter as well as a regional shrine where households would visit for annual pilgrimages (1 Sam 1:3; 2:19) or festivals (Judg 21:19). Shiloh seems to have been the regional center primarily for the northern tribes of Ephraim and Manasseh, but other sites of worship are mentioned such as

---

[41] Kaufmann, *The Religion of Israel*, 183-84.
[42] E. A. Speiser, "Leviticus and the Critics," in *Yehezkel Kaufmann Jubilee Volume*, ed. M. Haran (Jerusalem: Magnes Press, 1960), 29-45.
[43] Jacob Milgrom, *Leviticus 1-16: A New Translation with Introduction and Commentary*, AB 3 (New Haven: Yale University Press, 1991), 29-35.

Mizpah (Judg 11:11; 20:1; 21:5, 8; 1 Sam 7:5–6) and Bethel (Judg 20:18, 23, 26, 27). Milgrom concludes that neither P nor H advocates the centralization of worship but that H innovates cultic tradition by banning all common slaughter that originates prior to the centralization of Josiah.[44] Pitkänen comes to a similar conclusion in his analysis of the Priestly source and writes, "in many ways the Priestly material argues for a central sanctuary as an ideal in the strongest possible way, but more or less tacitly allows other options as well."[45]

Further examination of the evidence in Leviticus is in order, but Lev 26:31 stands out as one text that acknowledges multiple sites of worship. Yhwh warns the Israelites that he will lay waste to their cities and their "sanctuaries." The use of the plural here, and in v. 31b referring to "pleasing odors," indicates that multiple sites of worship were employed throughout the land.[46] Gerstenberger, however, rightly points out the polemical context of Lev 26:30–31 and argues that the parallel reference to the destruction of "your high places" in v. 30 strongly suggests that this condemns the use of local sanctuaries.[47] Yet Gerstenberger also acknowledges that the plural "sanctuaries" is used in Lev 21:23 (in a non-polemical context) and concedes that there may have been a multiplicity of sanctuaries in use (cf. Jer 51:51; Ezek 7:24; 21:2; Amos 7:9).

Other scholars have supported a theology of decentralization in Leviticus. Benjamin Sommer argues that the priestly concept of

---

[44] Milgrom, *Leviticus 1–16*, 29, 34.
[45] Pekka Pitkänen, *Central Sanctuary and Centralization of Worship in Ancient Israel: From the Settlement to the Building of Solomon's Temple* (Piscataway, NJ: Gorgias, 2003), 94; 69–74.
[46] Jacob Milgrom, "Does H Advocate the Centralization of Worship?" *JSOT* 88 (2000): 59–76 (59–60).
[47] Gerstenberger, *Leviticus*, 421–22.

divine presence favors an alternative to that of a centralized sanctuary. Sommer contends that the "locomotive" notion of God's abode is critical to understanding how the divine presence can move with the covenant community.[48] Sacred space can exist anywhere God chooses to abide and thus the divine presence is not limited to a central temple. With the mobility of the tabernacle, Israel is instead taught that a single cultic site could be established at multiple places within tribal territory where the peripheries are only determined by the boundaries of the allotted land.[49]

In a similar manner, Douglas argues that the tabernacle is concerned with "virtual space" and "virtual time" where the primary importance is not on how often the shrine is re-created but that its construction is done according to the one standard revealed in the wilderness.[50] The tabernacle is the physical sign that becomes representative of the theophany at Sinai. The proportions of the tabernacle given in Exodus mirror the divisions of God's cosmic tabernacle and the gradations of holiness revealed at Sinai. "In this sense, the tabernacle is spiritualized, like the celestial Jerusalem and the celestial Israel. Leviticus does not need to legislate for secular slaughter because it expects multiple sanctuaries throughout the land, [based] on the one sanctified design of the desert tabernacle, Mount Sinai, and the body."[51]

Indeed, the "spiritualization" of the tabernacle is also witnessed through the idealized setting in which its construction takes place.

---

[48] Benjamin D. Sommer, "Conflicting Constructions of Divine Presence in the Priestly Tabernacle," *BibInt* 9 (2001): 41–63.
[49] Benjamin D. Sommer, *The Bodies of God and the World of Ancient Israel* (New York: Cambridge University Press, 2009), 80–108.
[50] Douglas, *Leviticus as Literature*, 96–97.
[51] Douglas, *Leviticus as Literature*, 97.

Exodus 35 presents the extreme generosity of the Israelites in their giving toward the materials for God's home. The ideal tabernacle is one that comes into existence through communal participation out of gratitude for Yhwh's salvation, which brings forth creativity and unity among the people. The construction of the shrine becomes a metaphor for Israel's grateful worship as a whole community where each one contributes to the site where Yhwh will be worshipped. It is possible that this model was repeated in tribal settlements with the construction of shrines at Shiloh, Bethel, or Ramah where Samuel constructed an altar to Yhwh (1 Sam 7:17).

More recent approaches to Leviticus have offered a more nuanced approach to the notion of centralization. Julia Rhyder argues that centralization should be understood through the various means of social organization that structure power and authority in a concentrated manner. Centralization is, therefore, dependent not only on physical place but also on how social or religious structures are set up within certain spaces to create hierarchies and institutions. The standardization of the cult is a way for Leviticus to centralize the social and religious authority of the priesthood.[52] Thus Leviticus 17–26, and the stipulations for holiness, become a means for the temple/priests to control Israelite behavior both in cultic matters and in all aspects of life including family, festivals, agriculture, and other socioeconomic relationships. Rhyder goes on to argue that "the nexus between centralization and standardization that is strongly developed in H, as well as in the earlier P materials, serves as a device for developing norms and

---

[52] Julia Rhyder, *Centralizing the Cult: The Holiness Legislation in Leviticus 17–26* (Tübingen: Mohr Siebeck, 2019), 112–89.

scripts that regulate behavior in order to silence local discretion in favor of conformity with centralized authority."⁵³

One difficulty with Rhyder's argument is that she closely associates the concept of "centralization" with "standardization," which seems to confuse the force behind the priestly legislation of Leviticus. It is apparent that the standardization of cultic traditions can connote the power of a central authority, but this does not necessitate the silencing of local discretion. As detailed as Leviticus is about cultic and ethical matters, it is not exhaustive and leaves many issues around life and worship unaddressed. Questions such as where animals were slaughtered, what type of wood could be used for the altar, or what type wine could be offered were all debated later by the rabbis because Leviticus did not provide such details. What is important for Leviticus is not merely the regulating of practice but a standardization that produces or elicits a theological orthodoxy among tribes and clans.

Restricting sacrifices to an authorized altar was not for the sake of institutional power but, rather, it was to prohibit the Israelites from participating in pagan or chthonic worship (Lev 17:7).⁵⁴ The theological imperative found in Leviticus is not one interested in creating social power structures; instead, it is a call to cultic and moral holiness for all Israelites that eschews the religious practices of the Canaanites. Rather than an authoritarian class of priests seeking to establish centralized power through standardization, Leviticus depicts Aaron and his sons as being called to the dangerous role of serving in the tabernacle that is instituted to maintain Israel's ongoing relationship with a holy God. Leviticus presents the cultic commands not as a means of power to silence

---

[53] Rhyder, *Centralizing the Cult*, 389.
[54] Milgrom, "Does H Advocate the Centralization of Worship?" 71–72.

and control the laity but, rather, they are given so that Israel might have a perpetual mediator through the lineage of Aaron that will offer a continuity in the covenant for future generations.

What we might consider innovative in Leviticus are the links created between the sanctity of God's home which is to be mirrored in the purity of the Israelite home. Leviticus does not advocate for a socioreligious system based on institutional power, but it demonstrates a desire for orthodoxy and orthopraxy within the tabernacle and within Israelite homes and communities. The imperative for holiness in Leviticus is one that emerges from a *theological motivation* that creatively tethers the tents of Israel to the tent of Yhwh.

What is of primary concern in Leviticus is not the centrality of a single sanctuary but *the decentralizing of worship through the authorization of particular spaces and of a particular people to operate within and around those spaces*. The altar and the surrounding shrine must be maintained according to the priests, while the Israelite home is maintained by the head of the household. In this way, Leviticus upholds some of the earliest traditions in the land where several authorized shrines existed throughout the Israelite territories, but it also reiterates and intensifies the call to holiness among the laity. James Watts is correct to argue that the rhetoric of Leviticus is about establishing the authority of the Aaronide priesthood and the sanctuary, but this need not be portrayed as a mere power grab or a desire for a single sanctuary.[55] Instead, cultic authorization stems from the desire to ban ancestral worship or other rites associated with the "high places" (*bāmôt*) or open-air altars where Israelites often offered their sacrifices. In an effort to curtail such practices, Leviticus presents a theology of

---

[55] Watts, *Ritual and Rhetoric*, 142–51.

holiness that mandates the purity of *every Israelite home as it relates to the only authorized place of sacrifice, Yhwh's home.*

CONCLUSION

The final form of Leviticus within the canon represents fragments of cultic and ethical traditions that stretch back to the earliest history of Israel. These traditions were brought together by the priestly authors and shaped into a standardized model for Israel's cultic practice even in cases where those practices may appear contradictory. The authors of Leviticus appear to be concerned with maintaining the Mosaic cultic tradition to preserve the right practice of worship in Israel. Yet with cultic legislation found in both Exodus, Numbers, and Deuteronomy, we might ask why a biblical book on ritual, ethical obedience, and a call to holiness was written in the first place? Standardization of practice in religion is a powerful tool to bring about a catholicity in worship and doctrine. Whether this occurred after the fall of the northern tribes to the Assyrians or the Babylonian destruction of Jerusalem, Leviticus provides a comprehensive overview both of Israel's cultic practice and their moral calling as God's holy people. The original audience may have been eighth-century Israelite refugees or fifth-century Judeans. Whoever it was, Leviticus presents a way for faithful communities in Jerusalem and beyond to live in devotion and obedience to Yhwh through authorized sacrifice, moral and ethical living, yearly festivals, and care for the land.

The theology of the Book of Leviticus is concerned with the whole covenant community. Though the priests are set apart for specific duties in the tabernacle, they remain intimately bound to all the tribes of Israel. They are not a magical, arcane class of professionals. Their duties are composed in written form which is read to the whole of Israel (Neh 8:1–3) for their understanding. By preserving and conveying the Mosaic traditions this way, Leviticus establishes a priestly authority that can be held to account by the whole community. The divisions between priest and lay person in Leviticus is less about hierarchy and more about idealized service within the covenant community that results in God's blessing upon his whole people.

Though Leviticus is often referred to as "law," it may be better to think of it in terms of Mosaic *tôrāh*, or "teaching." The term "law" in contemporary settings can often be associated only with legal restrictions that are instituted for the good of society. Though Leviticus does contain such laws, many of its instructions, both cultic and ethical, seek to offer a way for how Israel can live in purity and holiness in the presence of a holy God. Moses' teachings present a vision for a people of faith who live in social and economic harmony, who care for the land, and who maintain the purity of God's home through the mediation of the priests. Leviticus presents a people whose homes reflect the holiness of God's home and whose lives reflect Yhwh's justice, compassion, and mercy.

There are compelling reasons to study Leviticus and its theology in a post-Enlightenment culture that often substitutes rationality for religious experience. David Brown argues that we have lost the "enchantment of place" in our modern context and that current thinking suggests that once we can explain religious phenomena there is no further need to address related religious questions.[56] When life is reduced to a series of propositional truths and empirical evidence, we are in danger of stripping away

---

[56] David Brown, *God and Enchantment of Space: Reclaiming Human Experience* (Oxford: Oxford University Press, 2004), 22.

mystery and how we perceive the divine presence in the world. Leviticus reminds us that a holy God has come to dwell on earth and that he has called his people to live as the expression of his holiness. This holiness is one that is conveyed through symbol, ritual, seasonal festivals, and ethical behavior. It is a holiness that reminds Israel of the sacredness of all life. As Walter Brueggemann writes, "The holiness of God is urgent in the face of profanation, which empties life of larger passion and dignity. The holiness of God is urgent in the face of pervasive brutality, which trivializes God's purpose and abuses God's world. The holiness of God is urgent in the face of growing authority of technique, which diminishes mystery that keeps life open."[57] Leviticus invites its readers into a sacred world where the God of Israel is present, where his glory emanates from his tabernacle, and where his people might draw near to him as they tread on holy ground.

---

[57] Walter Brueggemann's foreword in John G. Gammie, *Holiness in Israel*, OBT (Minneapolis, MN: Fortress Press, 1989), xii.

CHAPTER 2

Sin, Sacrifice, and Atonement (Leviticus 1–7, 16)

THE NATURE OF SACRIFICE

Leviticus 1–7 begins with detailed instruction on how to offer different types of sacrifices. This raises the question as to whether these chapters were intended to serve as a manual for priests on how to perform their cultic duties. The difficulty with limiting Leviticus 1–7 to instructions for priests is that it fails to consider the narrative within its broader context of the exodus events. The laws concerning sacrifices and offerings were written not only for the benefit of the priests but for the benefit of all those who hear the laws.[1] Though the majority of instructions are specifically for the priests, the regulations concerning ritual sacrifice also include prescriptions for the laity so that they too might understand the significance of God's holiness and how to approach him with their offerings. The sacrifices described in these chapters provide typological priestly ideals for cultic traditions that had been passed down throughout Israel's history. Though likely formed and redacted by later priestly authors, the "canonization" of centuries of cultic

---

[1] Cf. Liane M. Feldman, *The Story of Sacrifice: Ritual and Narrative in the Priestly Source*, FAT 141 (Tübingen: Mohr Siebeck, 2020), 45–49.

practice is brought together in the narrative context of the wilderness wanderings at Sinai.

A common stereotype of Leviticus is that it is a barbaric text because it promotes the cruel slaughter of animals. In an industrialized world where so many are detached from food production, there is a vast gulf between what we find neatly packaged in our grocery stores and the mass killing of animals happening in factories around the world.[2] The often inhumane conditions that animals face before slaughter are hidden from view and so the detailed sacrifice of a single animal somehow seems brutal in comparison. Modern readers often associate the practice of animal sacrifice with primitive superstitious cultures and though these types of offerings are remnants of the past, the significance of blood and sacrifice remains central to understanding the theology of Leviticus and the meaning of Israel's cult.

In approaching sacrificial texts, it is important to consider that, in spite of what may seem like endless detail and repetition, Leviticus does not provide a full description of what happens nor does it frequently offer explanation for why something is done in a certain way. This was the cause for so many significant debates around sacrifice in the Mishnah, which is a collection of rabbinic writings from the Second Temple period and beyond. The gaps in the biblical text are vast and assume a degree of knowledge about offerings and their meaning. Yet, as Robert Alter argues, "an essential aim of the innovative technique of fiction worked out by the ancient Hebrew writers was to produce a certain indeterminacy of meaning, especially in regard to

---

[2] See Norman Wirzba, *Food and Faith: A Theology of Eating* (Cambridge: Cambridge University Press, 2011), 71–109.

motive, moral character, and psychology."[3] These deliberate gaps in the narrative open up the process of revision and discernment of multiple possible interpretations. The consolidation of sacrificial traditions in Leviticus does not shut down interpretive possibilities but, rather, it leaves room for various layers of meaning and understanding.

What we seem to have in Leviticus is something like a set of notes from centuries of Israelite sacrificial tradition that have been synthesized in textual and narrative form. They present a single, idealized method for each type of offering yet remain general in scope. If this was intended as a manual for priests, we might expect more detail and explanation devoted to each type of offering. Instead, we have simplified instructions that could be practiced, in most cases, at any authorized shrine.[4] The priestly authors have gathered centuries of northern and southern religious traditions to produce the "scripturalization of the cult"[5] where ritual practice is transmitted through the written word. This process of narrating rituals creates a standardized model in textual form that could be upheld up by communities and priests worshipping in, or outside of, Jerusalem. By committing rituals to text, the priestly authors preserve sacrificial traditions and establish liturgical norms for Israelite worship.

---

[3] Robert Alter, *The Art of Biblical Narrative*, rev. ed. (New York: Basic Books, 2011), 12.
[4] An example of this lack of specificity is the command for the priests to arrange the wood on the altar for the fire (Lev 1:7) without explaining what type of wood to use. Other writings address the need for wood from the priests (Neh 10:34, 13:31; cf. *Ta'an.* 4:5), but *Jubilees* 21:12–14 specifies which wood may be used.
[5] Gary Anderson, "Sacrifice and Sacrificial Offerings (OT)," in *ABD*, 5: 870–86 (874).

In Leviticus, the offering of an animal's blood is a sacred event and is never taken lightly. In fact, the slaughtering of an animal as an act of worship demonstrates the highest regard and respect for the animal because it is by the gift of its blood that humanity may be reconciled with God in the priestly theology (Lev 17:10). The blood itself did not have expiatory power but it contained the life of the animal, given by Yhwh, to be the agent of atonement. Blood carries the life-giving breath of the divine and it is only under strict regulations that it might be used for cleansing and atoning. The Levitical prescriptions for sacrifices, and the theology that undergirds them, represent the utmost respect for life and its capacity to bring about purgation and reconciliation with the divine.

Unlike other ancient cultures, Leviticus firmly rejects the notion that sacrifices are to appease the gods and change their actions. One such example comes from Homer's *Illiad* where Chryses, the priest of Apollo, appeals to the god to help him get his daughter back from her Greek kidnappers. Chryses reminds Apollo that he has made generous burnt offerings to which the god should respond. Following his prayer, Apollo "rained down death upon the troops" of the Greeks mainly because the god was overly concerned with his honor.[6] The theological implication is that if the priest makes enough offerings, and appeals to the pride of the god, he will get his way. Nothing is said about the justice of Apollo's actions nor the innocent who were killed. There is no sense of the god's morality, but everything points to his capriciousness and capacity to be manipulated by the blood and flesh

---

[6] Homer, *Iliad*, trans. Ian Johnston (Arlington, VA: Richer Resources, 2006), Bk. I, ll.40–42.

of bulls. This type of offering, initiated by humans to manipulate the divine, is absent from the priestly authors of Leviticus.

Cultural anthropologists have proposed different models for approaching ritual sacrifice in the ancient world. Some argue that its purpose was to provide food for the gods, to appease the gods, to entreat the deity for help through their gifts, or to curb human violence.[7] With these possible motivations, the animal (or other offering) becomes the device for mediation as its physical state is turned into a spiritual offering through fire on an altar. The offering is transferred from the profane world into the realms of the divine as it ascends in the rising smoke. A similar sense may be found in the Hebrew where offerings can be "burned" (*śārap*) on the altar, or they are described as being "turned into smoke" (*hiqṭîr*). Sacrifice in Leviticus is not just killing an animal but, rather, it is transforming it from one existence into another.[8]

It was also a common belief in the ancient Near East that sacrifices fed the gods in return for blessings of fertility and life.[9] This anthropomorphism of the divine is also reflected in Leviticus where Yhwh smells the "pleasing odor" of the sacrifice (Lev 1:9, 13, 17, et al.), but other biblical texts decry the notion that God is in need of food or drink like the other gods (cf. Ps 50:12–14). Anderson argues that it is preferable to "see sacrifice as a *multivalent entity*" where the scriptures offer various perspectives on

---

[7] See René Girard, *Violence and the Sacred*, trans. Patrick Gregory (Baltimore, MD: Johns Hopkins University Press, 1979; rev. ed. New York: Bloomsbury, 2013); Bell, *Ritual Theory*, 173–75.
[8] Douglas, *Leviticus as Literature*, 68–69.
[9] In the Gilgamesh epic, Utnapishtim makes an offering after the flood resides and, "The gods smelled the savor,/ The gods smelled the sweet savor,/ The gods crowded around the sacrificer like flies" (*COS* 1:460). Cf. Gen 8:20–22.

Sin, Sacrifice, and Atonement (Leviticus 1–7, 16) 37

how sacrifice is connected to the worship of Yhwh.[10] Rather than being reduced to a single definition, sacrifice must be understood within its particular context to determine its potential layers of theological meaning.

Regulations around sacrifice in terms of what can and cannot be eaten follow patterns in Leviticus that mirror dimensions of their social world. The classifying of animal parts according to totemic principles likely had historical roots that remain unknown to the modern reader and were possibly also unknown to Second Temple readers of Leviticus. The origins of these principles, however, are of less significance since in their written form they offer a system of categories for sacrifice that had religious and social meaning. Douglas argues, "Extending totemism to the partitions within an animal postulates a logical equivalence projected upon the parts of the organism and the parts of the social world. This is just what a microcosm is. Microcosmic thinking uses analogies as a logical basis for a total metaphysical framework. A distinctive way of thinking, it is the essentially other thought style, foreign to our own."[11] Though foreign to the modern reader, Leviticus' theology of sacrifice reflects a cultic system that corresponds to the larger macrocosm of creation where all things have been ordered and arranged according to Yhwh's wisdom.

Though animals are sacrificed to the divine, it is important to recall that all creatures are part of God's "good" creation (Genesis 1) in the priestly cosmology. God does not despise his creatures or want Israel to kill them needlessly to satisfy his appetite for atoning blood (cf. Ps 51:16–17). Animals play a significant role in the mystery of creation, sin, and atonement. They are sacred in

---

[10] Anderson, "Sacrifice", 873.
[11] Douglas, *Leviticus as Literature*, 25.

God's eyes and play a critical part within the breadth of his cosmic order.[12] Thus the blood of animals is to be treated with the utmost respect by the Israelites because part of the goodness and life of God's creation is sacrificed for the sake of Israel's ongoing life and fellowship with God.

In Leviticus, the life of the animal is also tied to the purification of Israel and the tabernacle. Transgression can take place on the individual or corporate level and can be committed intentionally or unintentionally. Whether sin is done in public or in secret, Leviticus understands the result to be like a metaphysical residue or stain left on the tabernacle that must be purged and cleansed. Sin has a type of materiality, or what might be called the *materia peccans* ("substance of sin"), which remains on the physical space of the tabernacle until it is cleansed by blood.[13]

Sacrifice is not depicted in Leviticus as a form of magic nor is it efficacious by itself. Leviticus presents the cultic system as a gift from Yhwh, enacted on the altar, that allows Israel to worship, give thanks, and offer atoning sacrifices. Ritual sacrifice also acts as a pedagogical tool that teaches Israel about the holiness of Yhwh and the need for worship, atonement, and purification of sin.

It is important, however, to remember that the most frequent sacrifices presented on the altar were not for atonement. The daily burnt offering, or the *tamid* (Exod 29:38–41; Num 28:3–4; cf. Lev 1:10–13), was sacrificed every morning and evening as part of the

---

[12] Douglas, *Leviticus as Literature*, 137.
[13] Bernd Janowski, "Das Geschenk der Versöhnung. Leviticus 16 als Schlussstein der priesterlichen Kulttheologie," in *The Day of Atonement: Its Interpretations in Early Jewish and Christian Traditions*, ed. Thomas Hieke and Tobias Niklas (Leiden: Brill, 2012), 3–31 (11–12).

temple's liturgical life.[14] Every day the Israelite priests offered gifts at the altar to give thanks and to entreat the divine for ongoing blessing. Though atonement for sin was an important part of cultic life, the daily practice of worshipping through blood, grain, wine, and oil was critical in praising the creator God who came down to dwell in their presence. Jonathan Klawans argues that for many biblical scholars sacrifice is primarily seen as a response to transgression that corrects or restores a wrong that has been committed, but he believes the opposite to be true. "It is not that the daily sacrifice undoes the damage done by grave transgression. Quite the contrary: grave transgression undoes what the daily sacrifice produces."[15] His argument offers an important corrective to the idea that expiation is the primary significance of sacrifice. Instead, Leviticus presents sacrifice as a positive and productive act of worship in response to the continued grace and benevolence of God.

WHO CAN SACRIFICE?

Leviticus contends that the priestly role comes only through the Aaronide line of the Levites. During the early tribal period in the land, the priest seems to have taken on some sort of paternal role as they were sometimes referred to as "father" (Judg 17:10; 18:19). The ancient term *kôhēn* ("priest") is the same terminology used by the Canaanites and the role was likely adapted from their cultic rituals and practices.[16] Pagan priests served to protect the king and the people from malevolent powers and demons that could

---

[14] See Anderson, *That I May Dwell among Them*, 84–99.
[15] Jonathan Klawans, *Purity, Sacrifice and the Temple: Symbolism and Supersessionism in the Study of Ancient Judaism* (Oxford: Oxford University Press, 2006), 71.
[16] Cf. *ANET*, 656–67; *COS*, 1:299–301.

bring about calamity. Milgrom contends that Israelite priestly theology replaces demons with human sin and shifts the focus from external evil powers to the human will that can desecrate the holy sanctuary.[17] Rather than protection from malevolent spirits, Israelite priests function as mediators by making offerings for transgressions that defile the tabernacle and have the potential to drive the deity from his dwelling.

Narratives from Judges offer a distinctly different picture of priesthood compared to Leviticus. In pre-monarchic Israel, the head of a household could ordain a son as priest over the family shrine as is seen in the story of Micah (Judg 17:5). It appears, however, that to have a Levite serving at the altar was even better (Judg 17:13). We do not know the specific duties of the Levite, but the story describes sacred items such as the ephod, teraphim, and metal idols. The story tells of the success of the Danites and their ordering of "the house of God" (*bêt-hā 'ĕlōhîm*) established in Shiloh (Judg 18:31; cf. Josh 18:1).[18] The priest ordained for service there, however, was not the Levite but, rather, it was "Jonathan son of Gershom, son of Moses" who were "priests to the tribe of the Danites" (Judg 18:30). The northern tradition traces priestly lineage to Moses and not Aaron, which stands in sharp contrast to the authorized priests of Leviticus.

Another figure from pre-monarchic times also stands in contrast to Levitical regulations around ordination. Samuel is the

---

[17] Milgrom, *Leviticus 1–16*, 43.
[18] The rabbis argued that this was the first place that a permanent structure for the tabernacle was built. "After they came to Shiloh, the high places were forbidden. There was no roof-beam there, but below was a house of stone and above were hangings and this was the 'resting place'" (*m. Zebaḥ.* 14:6). The building was likely a Canaanite temple that had been reconstructed into an Israelite place of worship.

prophet that bridges tribal Israel and the monarchy. Though he is from the tribe of Ephraim, he intercedes on behalf of all Israel, offers sacrifices to Yhwh (1 Sam 7:9), and blesses the people's sacrifices (1 Sam 9:12-13). His annual circuit consisted of trips to Bethel, Gilgal, and Mizpah where he judged on behalf of Israel and where he likely made offerings at the local shrines. We are told he did the same in his hometown of Ramah where he set up an altar to the Lord (1 Sam 7:15-17). In an effort to harmonize this incongruity with Leviticus and the priestly regulations the Chronicler provides Samuel with a Levitical genealogy (1 Chr 6:28).

For the authors of Leviticus, however, the priestly role was reserved for men of a particular lineage. The only authorized personnel who could approach Yhwh's holy tabernacle were those from the line of Aaron and the tribe of Levi. Challenges to this understanding are seen in the wilderness wanderings (cf. Numbers 16), but the sole lineage of Aaron is affirmed. Genealogy, however, was not the only requirement for working in the tabernacle. Strict obedience to Yhwh's command was also imperative for the priest to survive their encounters with holiness. The story of Nadab and Abihu (Lev 10:1-2) illustrates this point and Leviticus reminds Israel that one's priestly pedigree means nothing in the presence God's holiness if one does not abide by his command.

The priests also needed to maintain their own state of purity and holiness. Improper contact with unclean things could lead to their defilement and need for purification. Aaron, as the high priest, was not allowed to bury his sons for fear of coming in contact with the dead (Lev 10:6-7). In the later rabbinic writings of the Mishnah, there are stories of keeping the high priest awake the night before the Day of Atonement (*Yom Kippur*) for fear that he might have a nocturnal emission and therefore be unable to perform his duties on behalf of Israel (*m. Yoma* 1:17). Priestly purity was essential to the proper maintenance of the tabernacle to ensure the ongoing presence of the divine.

Along with the work of sacrifice came the work of administration. In the ancient world, temples often functioned as types of banks. Sacrifices could be monetized and the priests could exact taxes from the people as part of their role in making offerings to the gods (cf. Lev 5:15). In Leviticus, we find a similar picture of priests who were to assess the worth of animals or land sacrificed to God (Lev 27:12-20). The monetary value of human beings was determined by the priests when people would make specific vows (Lev 27:3-8). The priests were also in charge of booty from war (Josh 6:19, 24) and any other gifts that were given in service to Yhwh. In the Second Temple period, deposits were also held in the temple to help the poor. These funds were distributed by the priests who acted as accountants entrusted with much of the community's wealth (2 Macc 3:9-14).

Though the priesthood was limited to certain stock, the language of Leviticus is more open regarding who can bring sacrifices to the altar. In many instances, the altar was open to any "person" (*nepeš*) who approached the tabernacle with an offering (Lev 2:1; 4:2, 27; 5:1, 17; 6:2), or any "human being" (*'ādām*) (Lev 1:2; 13:2, 9), or a "man or woman" (Lev 13:29, 38). The inclusivity of the language is important as it highlights the participation of the whole covenant community in the act of sacrifice. Among the Israelites were also Canaanites from the land or sojourners who were not barred from making offerings to Yhwh. The openness of the altar to the whole community expresses an important theology that emphasizes the desire and ability for both circumcised and uncircumcised to participate in worship.

TYPES OF SACRIFICE

In the Old Testament, there are two main categories for sacrifices. The more general term *minḥâ* ("offering") is common in the Pentateuch and can describe any generic sacrifice. If the offering is an animal, then the root *z-b-ḥ* ("slaughter") is used to describe how it is killed. The altar is the "place of slaughter" (*mizbēaḥ*) where sacrifices occur and where other things like "libations" (*nesek*) are poured out. In the priestly texts, the term *qôrbān* ("gift") is often used and derives from the root *q-r-b*, which means to "draw near." This implies that something is brought near to the presence of God at the altar.

Before we examine each type of offering individually, it is important to recall that some of the language of Leviticus is distinct from the rest of the Old Testament. The vocabulary employed is often technical and used within cultic instruction.[19] Many of these terms are absent from the rest of the Old Testament or, if they are used, offer different meanings.[20] The uniqueness of the priestly language around sacrifice poses difficulties in identifying its exact meaning since it is often unfruitful to try to compare them to non-priestly texts. In Leviticus, there is also theological meaning behind the language used concerning

---

[19] Innocent Himbaza, "Textual Witnesses and Sacrificial Terminology in Leviticus 1–7," in *Sôfer Mahîr: Essays in Honour of Adrian Schenker Offered by the Editors of Biblia Hebraica Quinta*, ed. Yohanan A. P. Goldman, Arie van der Kooij, and Richard D. Weis, VTSup 110 (Leiden: Brill, 2006), 95–111.

[20] E.g., Lev 2:1 designates a cereal offering as a *minḥâ*, whereas the same word is used in Gen 4:3–4 to describe Cain's grain offering and Abel's animal sacrifice. See Gary A. Anderson, *Sacrifices and Offerings in Ancient Israel: Studies in Their Social and Political Importance*, HSM 41 (Atlanta: Scholars Press, 1987), 27–34.

cultic issues like purification and atonement. The necessity of technical terms was likely the result of later theological reflection on the cult and the development of particular rituals associated with approaching Yhwh's holiness. In earlier Israelite history, such meticulous detail and vocabulary is largely absent as more general sacrifices could be offered in a variety of ways and in various places.

In Leviticus, however, all offerings take place at the sanctuary on the altar. The only occasion where profane slaughter was permitted away from the altar in Leviticus was for ritually clean wild animals, such as deer or some species of birds, as long as their blood was drained and covered with earth (Lev 17:13). This permission reflects the realities of hunting that may have taken place away from the shrine. The meat might have spoiled by the time it was brought to the altar and so permission was given to pour the blood back into the earth.

The burnt offering (*ʿōlâ*): One of the most common sacrifices was the burnt offering, which might be translated literally as "the offering that ascends" (Latin = *holocaustum*). The whole of the animal was consumed in fire and the smoke ascended to Yhwh as a pleasing aroma. The antiquity of the offering is demonstrated by its prevalence in older biblical texts (Gen 8:20; 22:2, 7, 8, 13; Exod 10:25; 18:12; Judg 6:26; 13:16; 1 Sam 7:9; 13:9). The practice of consuming the entire animal on the altar represented the most complete sacrifice to God since no part of it was left for consumption either by the priest or the offerer. This was the most costly sacrifice an Israelite could make.

The burnt offering was also thought to have an expiatory function according to Lev 1:4. Levine, however, contends that the phrase "for atonement" (*ləkappēr*) in this instance does not refer to a normal expiatory rite since this practice was not usually associated with the burnt offering. Instead, he argues that it refers to a sign of favorable acceptance before God to avert his divine wrath.[21] Though the notion of appeasement may partially be the sense of the passage, in a wide range of ancient cultures the burnt offering did have expiatory value. This is also alluded to in other biblical texts such as Saul's hasty burnt offering made in Samuel's stead (1 Sam 13:12) or David's burnt offering to stop the plague (2 Sam 24:21-25). The rabbis argued that the burnt offering atoned for sinful thoughts, neglected obedience to the commandments, or for sins otherwise unmentioned in other sacrifices of atonement.[22] Though the primary sense of the burnt offering was a gift given wholly to God out of joy and thanksgiving (or possibly appeasement), the goal of cleansing or purifying could also be part of its function.

Different types of animals could be brought for the burnt offering depending on the economic circumstances of the offerer. Milgrom notes the inclusivity of the sanctuary for sacrifice and the desire to make offerings possible for the poor.[23] Leviticus demonstrates its concern for sacrifices to be open to people from every social and economic background so that all might have the opportunity to worship.

The well-being offering (*šəlāmîm*): In the earliest altar laws from the covenant code (Exod 20:24), the *šəlāmîm* is included with the burnt offering. Both are given as signs of worship to Yhwh, but there is no theological significance attached to them beyond a gift that is presented before God.[24] Other translations

---

[21] Levine, *Leviticus*, 7.
[22] See Milgrom, *Leviticus 1-16*, 174-76.
[23] Milgrom, *Leviticus 1-16*, 54.
[24] Ronald S. Hendel, "Sacrifice as a Cultural System: The Ritual Symbolism of Exodus 24, 3-8," *ZAW* 101 (1989): 366-90 (371-72).

might include a "peace offering" or "wholeness offering," which express part of the sense of the Hebrew šālôm. The term may have come from the idea of completeness or wholeness in relationship to Yhwh and in relationship to one's neighbor. It constituted a sacred meal that was shared by both priest and offerer as they ate celebrating the šālôm of God's blessing.

In Leviticus, however, the well-being offering is described with particular detail in terms of how the sacrifice was to be conducted. Specific regulations are given concerning blood and fat and what was to be burned. The "fat" (*ḥēleb*) was forbidden for human consumption and was always offered to God alone (cf. Lev 3:16–17). Details regarding other body parts (liver, kidneys, entrails, etc.) are explained as to what can and cannot be consumed.

The main difference between the well-being offering and the burnt offering is that the priests receive a portion of the animal offered in the *šəlāmîm*. In Lev 7:28–36, and numerous references elsewhere (e.g., Lev 8:25–26, 9:20–21, 10:14–15), the priests are given the "hindlimb" from the right side along with the "breast."[25] The offerer would also receive a portion of the boiled meat. Reflecting on what kind of social and economic setting this type of system would function best in, it is more logical to envisage the well-being offering being presented at a regional shrine rather than traveling great distances to a central sanctuary (cf. 1 Sam 2:12–16). The local priests needed provision and the Levitical regulations provided support for the officiating priest whether in

---

[25] For the different biblical practices regarding the priestly portion, see Jonathan S. Greer, "The 'Priestly Portion' in the Hebrew Bible: Its Ancient Near Eastern Context and Its Implications for the Composition of P," *JBL* 138 (2019): 263–84; Jan Joosten, "Divergent Cultic Practices in the Septuagint: The 'Shoulder' (Βραχίων) of the Priest," *Journal of Septuagint and Cognate Studies* 48 (2015): 27–38.

Jerusalem or beyond. This type of mutually beneficial relationship would be difficult to conceive of for those living greater distances from a regional temple. Instead, Leviticus recognizes the viability and importance of shrines that sustain the priesthood and provide a means for slaughter on a local level.[26] Milgrom contends that this likely represents an older strata of P (along with Lev 9:21 and 10:15) that reflects a Shilohnite tradition where multiple shrines were in existence.[27]

The grain offering (*minḥâ*): Also called the "cereal offering," the *minḥâ* was shared with the priests. Details of preparation are given and specifics regarding what should be offered (flour, oil, frankincense, salt) and what should not (leaven, honey). The offering was appropriate for a variety of circumstances and provided a less costly form of worship for those who might not be able to afford animals. There is little in the description of the grain offering that points to its theological meaning or how it affected the relationship between the offerer and God or the tabernacle. Since grain and bread were the primary food source in ancient Israel, an offering of fine flour or baked cakes at the altar might have expressed a gift to feed God, but there was also the practical side of feeding the priests. A "token portion" (*'azkārātāh*) of the *minḥâ* was taken from the offering and given to Yhwh while the rest was consecrated as "the most sacred" portion for the priests to consume (Lev 2:2–3).

In other Old Testament texts, the *minḥâ* takes on different characteristics, which may include animal or grain sacrifices

---

[26] Greer, "The 'Priestly Portion,'" 283–84, contends the blended hindlimb and forelimb traditions represent the priestly authors' attempt to retain both early northern and southern cultic traditions.

[27] Milgrom, *Leviticus 1–16*, 435.

(Gen 4:2–4; 1 Sam 2:17, 29; 26:19). The general sense is that the offering represents a gift or tribute, possibly entreating another person or God for their favor or blessing (cf. Gen 32:21; Gen 43:11–15). In Leviticus, the grain offering takes a particular form, but the notion of a tribute or gift remains as the people bring offerings of thanksgiving to Yhwh as a pleasing aroma (Lev 2:2, 9, 16).

The purification offering (*ḥaṭṭā't*): Often translated as "sin offering," the *ḥaṭṭā't* was presented in the case of individual/corporate moral transgressions as well as for physical impurities (Lev 5:2–3). Milgrom makes a compelling argument that it is misleading to translate *ḥaṭṭā't* as "sin offering" because the primary purpose of the offering had to do with purification. He proposes that *ḥaṭṭā't* be rendered "purification offering" because it represents the purgation of the tabernacle and the movement of the unclean person to a purified state so that they might be brought back into fellowship with God and the covenant community (cf. Lev 12:6–8; 14:18–20).[28] Though the *ḥaṭṭā't* was offered to release an individual from their guilty status, its primary intent was to purify the altar because of the effects of sin on the tabernacle. This will be discussed further in the section below on sin and atonement.

The reparation offering (*'āšām*): This was the penalty paid when a specific offense was committed against God. The sacrifice represented a "guilt offering" for one who had sinned unintentionally whether in relation to property of the sanctuary, swearing falsely, making rash oaths, or concerning responsibility toward a neighbor's property (Lev 5:14–6:7). The sacrifice did not absolve

---

[28] Milgrom, *Leviticus 1–16*, 232, 253–58; Jacob Milgrom, *Studies in Cultic Theology and Terminology*, SJLA 36 (Leiden: Brill, 1983).

the offender of all guilt since they were also required to make restitution often with the provision of an extra 20 percent to make amends.

Other Types: Other types of sacrifices are also mentioned in Leviticus including the "daily offering" (*tāmîd*), "tithe" (*ma'ăśēr*), "firstfruits" (*bikkûrîm*), "wave-offering" (*tĕnûpâ*), and the "heave-offering" (*tĕrûmâ*). These may fall under the general category of "gift, tribute" for different times and seasons. What they express is the ongoing need for Israel to acknowledge God in the form of ritual offerings as a central part of their daily lives. Israel is to remain in communion with their God through the altar and the priests who minister there. Yhwh's holy dwelling is the place where they can most fully express their allegiance to him and, in turn, receive his blessing of salvation, forgiveness, and the promise of his continued presence.

PERFORMING THE DIVINE DRAMA

The drama of sacrifice is also something that must be considered when discerning how Leviticus conveys its theology through ritual acts.[29] The slaughter of an animal is a powerful image of death and lifeblood spilled as a sign of purification and the reordering the cosmos. Whether making atonement for sin or giving thanks to God, the ritual actors of the offerer, the victim/offering, the priest, and the audience all give witness to symbolic actions that sum up a subplot in the wider story of salvation. Placing hands on the head of an animal, lifting up and waving sheaths of grain,

---

[29] See Bell, *Ritual Theory*, 39–46, on performance theory. See also Dru Johnson, *Knowledge by Ritual: A Biblical Prolegomenon to Sacramental Theology* (Winona Lake, IN: Eisenbrauns, 2016), 71–119.

sprinkling blood around the altar, pouring out wine, all performed in the presence of fire and smoke, are performative acts that teach the community about thanksgiving, sin, holiness, and their relationship with the divine. As Milgrom argues, "every act, whether movement, manipulation, or gesticulation, is pregnant with meaning."[30]

The power of ritual is that it brings together physical actions with theological beliefs that express the ongoing drama of salvation where past, present, and future are celebrated. Douglas argues that "ritual focuses attention by framing; it enlivens the memory and links the present with the relevant past. In all this it aids perception. Or rather, it changes perception because it changes the selective principles."[31] The intentional framing of God's salvation around the rituals in the tabernacle help Israel to remember their relationship with Yhwh and the provision he has made for worship and atonement. Balentine contends that "Ritual invites something different: the active participation in 'embodied' theological reflection. Both the knowledge and the learning of theology come from performing the ritual act itself."[32] Ritual is an enacted worldview where the drama of the cosmic order is expressed through ongoing acts of worship.

The priestly creation narrative of Genesis 1 presents a God who delights in separating, forming, and shaping the universe to create a rhythm and order in the cosmos. The division of day and night and the creation of the sun, moon, and stars allow times and seasons that help the worshipper enter into the rhythm that God has created. Gorman argues that rituals are concerned with the way they relate to the maintenance and ongoing renewal and

---

[30] Milgrom, *Leviticus 1–16*, 42.
[31] Douglas, *Purity and Danger*, 65.
[32] Balentine, *Leviticus*, 5.

restoration of the created order, which become a means for Israel to construct the world around them.[33] Sacred rituals and symbols, as Geertz argues, are ways that cultures create a blueprint or template of reality.[34] For Israel, that blueprint is determined by the tabernacle, which represents both a physical structure and a metaphysical structure as a microcosm of God's cosmic temple. Their ritual practice in God's tent in an outworking of their broader connection to his entire creation.

To preserve the community's closeness to the deity, Israelites participated with the priests in the divine drama. Many of the sacrifices occurred at "the entrance of the tent of meeting" (Lev 1:3, 5; 3:2; 4:4, 7, 18; 8:3-4). The layperson helped the priest with the slaughtering of the animal at the tent, along with others, to witness the transferal of the offering to God. The social nature of sacrifice is significant in understanding the place of drama within the community. Though the priests played the leading role, they were not the only participants.[35] Instead, they are seen in their capacity as the bridge between the people and Yhwh's holiness.[36] In Leviticus, ritual laws are made known to the whole congregation, both lay and ordained (Lev 21:1, 24), as a way of decentralizing the power of the priests and empowering laypeople to resist and protest potential abuses of authority.[37] Though the text may

---

[33] Gorman, *The Ideology of Ritual*, 14-16, 59.
[34] Geertz, *The Interpretation of Cultures*, 90-94.
[35] Cf. Feldman, *The Story of Sacrifice*, 48-49.
[36] See Michael B. Hundley, "Before YHWH at the Entrance of the Tent of Meeting: A Study of Spatial and Conceptual Geography in the Priestly Texts," *ZAW* 123 (2011): 15-26, for the connection between architecture and the spatial significance of the entrance to Yhwh's tent for the average Israelite.
[37] Cf. Milgrom, *Leviticus 17-22*, 1832-34.

focus on the actions of the priest, the laity are also critical participants within the cultic drama.

Unlike Knohl's theory regarding the "sanctuary of silence," where the priests retreated behind the temple walls and distanced themselves from everyday life, the theology of Leviticus envisages communal participation where all of Israel plays its role.[38] Knohl contends that, "PT [Priestly Torah] attains a level of abstraction and loftiness unequaled in the Bible,"[39] in part due to the lack of anthropomorphic language. Yet Knohl neglects to take into account the physical role and presence of the layperson as well as the anthropomorphic language of burnt offerings being described as a "pleasing odor to the LORD" (Lev 1:9, 13, 17; 2:2, 9, et al.). Instead of an abstract deity, the priestly theology of Leviticus includes a whole cast of performers who are instrumental in performing ritual acts that are recognized and accepted by God who smells and accepts the offering as a pleasing sacrifice.

The drama of ritual in Leviticus is often violent, involving the death of an animal and the shedding of blood. The loss of animal life for the reconciliation and atonement of human life offers a vivid depiction for how Israel is reconciled to their God. Blood is never sprinkled on the offerer, but it is reserved for sprinkling on the altar or other parts of the tabernacle (Lev 4:5–7, 17–18; 5:9; 9:9).[40] This signifies that the guilt of the offerer is connected to the defilement of the altar, which must be cleansed through blood. The purification of the sanctuary is as significant as the purification of the sinner in Leviticus. At times this is explicitly stated

---

[38] Knohl, *Sanctuary of Silence*, 221–22.
[39] Knohl, *Sanctuary of Silence*, 222.
[40] Except in the case of the ordination of a priest or the cleansed leper. These rituals express the crossing of boundaries from the profane to differing grades of holiness.

(Lev 8:15; 16:33) to make clear that the priests atone for the altar and for the whole community of Israel.

Another ritual movement within the drama of sacrifice is the placing of a hand on the offering. The symbolic act has been widely debated in terms of its function and meaning.[41] The most likely explanation is that the gesture identifies the offering with the offerer. This is in effort to make the deity aware of who is presenting the sacrifice so that it can be received on their behalf. The placing of hands on the offering also provides the physical sensation of touch. The offerer is physically connected to the animal and then releases it from their possession to the possession of the Deity. This physical aspect cannot be overestimated in understanding how ritual generates knowledge concerning the relationship between God and humanity.[42] The act teaches the offerer that holiness, purification, and reconciliation require a physical release and sacrifice to God in order to maintain the purity of his sanctuary and the purity of the people (cf. Mal 1:8).

On the Day of Atonement, the ritual act of placing hands occurs again but this time in the context of an offering on behalf of the sins of all Israel. In this elaborate ritual, the high priest makes blood offerings for atonement, which is followed by laying two hands on the scapegoat. The high priest confesses all the sins of Israel and places them "on the head of the goat" before it is sent into the wilderness. The symbolic act takes place as the sins of the people are placed upon the goat who will "bear on itself all their

---

[41] See David P. Wright, "The Gesture of Hand Placement in the Hebrew Bible and in Hittite Literature," *JAOS* 106 (1986): 433–46; Milgrom, *Leviticus 1–16*, 151.

[42] Cf. Johnson, *Knowledge by Ritual*, 33–56.

iniquities to a barren region" (Lev 16:21-22). David Wright, however, argues

> Though this [double-hand-laying] ritual results in the placement of the sins on the goat's head, it should not be considered a transfer of sins in a strict sense. That is, the sins are not passed from Aaron through his hands to the goat. Aaron never carries or embodies these evils. Consequently, one cannot say that sins are *transferred*. Rather, the placement of the sins is effected by both the hand placement gesture which designates where the sins are to rest *and* the spoken confession which concretizes the sins which then fall on the head of the goat.[43]

However the hand placing gesture is to be understood, the ritual demonstrates the riddance of sin as it is carried away from the camp and into the wilderness.

Leviticus is not simply a clinical, technical manual on how offerings should be made (even though it does do this in some detail!). Instead, it engages the reader with the drama of sacrifice as a source of theological instruction that benefited both priest and the worshiping community. Through the drama of ritual, Israel was taught about sin, purity, sacrifice, worship, and thanksgiving. In a predominantly nonliterate culture, these physical acts served as powerful pedagogical tools that conveyed theological truths concerning Yhwh's holiness and how the people might approach his holiness. They also remind Israel what it means to live together as a covenant community where the priest takes the lead role as the intermediary who stands between the sacred and the profane to maintain this relationship and to ensure that it continues so that Yhwh's blessing might flow out to the people.[44]

---

[43] Wright, "The Gesture of Hand Placement," 436.
[44] See William K. Gilders, *Blood Ritual in the Hebrew Bible: Meaning and Power* (Baltimore, MD: Johns Hopkins University Press, 2004), 181–91.

THE LIFE IS IN THE BLOOD

Israelite beliefs concerning blood, the soil, and sacrifice date back to ancient traditions that can be found in the story of Cain (Gen 4:10–11)[45] and the offerings of Noah (Gen 9:4). Blood is intimately connected with the earth and has the power to appeal to the Deity if shed unjustly as in the case of Abel (Gen 4:10; cf. 1 *En.* 22:7). Blood must also not be consumed. The command given to Noah after the flood offers no explanation for why flesh and blood cannot be eaten together, but Genesis 9 alludes to an injustice being committed that incites Yhwh to respond with divine justice. The apparent parallel is made in the following verses (Gen 9:5–6) where human life is required if human blood is shed. The comparison points to the fact that all blood comes from God and the shedding of *any* blood, whether animal or human, requires some sort of reckoning. This does not prohibit sacrifice or eating meat, but if done inappropriately it amounts to homicide (cf. Lev 17:4).

Blood is at the forefront of theology in Leviticus because every aspect of life, whether human or animal, is considered a sacred gift from God.[46] The "life is in the blood" (Lev 17:11) and without blood there is no efficacy in the sacrificial system and there can be no forgiveness (cf. Heb 9:22).[47] Blood acts as the antidote and cleansing agent, or detergent to remove the stain of sin.[48] In other Pentateuchal texts, Israel is reminded why blood should not be

---

[45] See Mark W. Scarlata, *Outside of Eden: Cain in the Ancient Versions of Genesis 4.1–16*, LHBOTS 573 (London: T & T Clark, 2012), 131–56.
[46] Balentine, *Leviticus*, 148.
[47] The exception to this rule is Lev 5:11–13 where an offering of choice flour can be given as an atoning sacrifice.
[48] The same image is taken up by the author of Revelation where people are washed "white in the blood of the Lamb" (Rev 7:14).

consumed, but no particular theological reason is given (cf. Gen 9:4; Exod 23:18; Deut 12:16, 23). In Leviticus, however, we find a highly developed theology concerning the meaning of blood, how it can be used, and the penalties for its abuse.

In some cases, blood serves an apotropaic function. This is most clearly expressed in the Passover narrative where blood is smeared on the doorposts, which protects the Israelites from the death of their firstborn (Exod 12:12–13; cf. Exod 4:25–28; 2 Sam 24:18–25). In a similar protective manner, blood sprinkled on the mercy seat (*kappōret*) in the Holy of Holies allows the high priest to enter "without dying" (Lev 16:2) so that he can make atonement for the tabernacle and for the sins of Israel. Within the theology of Leviticus, however, the apotropaic function of blood is reserved for cultic use in the inner sanctum of God's dwelling.

Most ritual prescriptions in the priestly theology do not contain detailed explanations, which makes the explicit reference to blood, and its meaning, all the more striking in Lev 17:11: "For the life (*nepeš*) of the flesh (*bāśār*) is in the blood; and I have given it to you for making atonement for your lives on the altar; for, as life, it is the blood that makes atonement." A simpler account of blood is given in Deut 12:23, "For the blood is the life and you must not consume the life along with the flesh," but the detail of Leviticus demonstrates a "high[er] degree of theological reflection."[49] Leviticus builds and expands on ancient prohibitions related to blood and the consumption of meat, but it does so by creating stronger links between flesh, blood, life, and the altar.

If all life comes from God and that life is symbolically carried within the blood, then all blood (whether human or animal)

---

[49] Gerstenberger, *Leviticus*, 240.

belongs to God. But the blood/life that belongs to God has been given for expiation (*ləkappēr*). Levine argues that the phrase literally means "to serve as *kofer* (ransom) for your lives."[50] This relates back to the *ḥaṭṭā 't* as an example of a type of substitution. God accepts the life of animal blood as a cleansing agent for the death of sin that has stained the offerer and the tabernacle space. This explanation serves as a critical summary of the sacrificial system performed on the altar outlined in chapters 1–16. Blood is a gift from Yhwh that he has given to Israel *only for the sake of atonement on his authorized altar* by his priests and in his tabernacle. This stands in distinct opposition to blood use in other ancient Near Eastern cultures for ancestral worship, fertility rites, or magic.

Blood is, therefore, the *only* substance that carries the potency of life that has the power to purge death. Milgrom is correct to emphasize that though blood is the most sacred substance of life given for atonement, it is not the blood itself that atones for sin. Bloodless sacrifices such as flour given by the poor can also atone for sin (Lev 5:11–12). What is of central importance is the power of the altar to transform the offering into an efficacious sacrifice. Milgrom writes, "Blood is life. Hence it is powerful, but only God can activate it. This happens when the blood is sanctified; that is, when it is in contact with the altar and other sancta."[51] Blood is a

---

[50] Levine, *Leviticus*, 115; cf. Milgrom, *Leviticus 17–22*, 1474. However, Joshua M. Vis, "The Purgation of Persons through the Purification Offering," in *Sacrifice, Cult, and Atonement in Early Judaism and Christianity: Constituents and Critique*, ed. Henrietta L. Wiley and Christian A. Eberhart (Atlanta: SBL Press, 2016), 33–57, makes a strong argument that the use of *kipper* in the Day of Atonement rites are for the purging of sin from the people and not as only as a ransom.

[51] Milgrom, *Leviticus 17–22*, 1479.

divine gift in Leviticus that is given for expiation on the altar. It is as if God is saying, as Schwartz paraphrases, "It is not you who are placing the blood on the altar for me, for my benefit, but rather the opposite: it is I who have placed it there for you – for your benefit."[52] The offering of blood is only made possible through Yhwh's initiation to provide his people with a substance that will atone for their sin.

Leviticus presents a theology of blood that strips it of any magical power and yet there remains a mystery behind the life it carries, which has been given by God for atonement on the altar. The misuse of blood, possibly in reference to pagan practices or chthonic worship, is alluded to in the subsequent comment that Israelites were making offerings in the "open field" to "goat demons" (Lev 17:5, 7). This description could locate the command at various points during Israel's history. The specific reference to goat demons may come from the postexilic period when there was a rise in interest in different types of spirits.[53] Gerstenberger contends that the goat demon references are a projection of the Persian period authors into the past but had little relevance to their own worship.[54] Janowski, however, argues that the scapegoat elimination rite has ancient roots and is part of

---

[52] Baruch Schwartz, "The Prohibitions Concerning the 'Eating' of Blood in Leviticus 17," in *Priesthood and Cult in Ancient Israel*, ed. Gary Anderson and Saul Olyan, JSOTSS 125 (Sheffield: Sheffield Academic Press, 1991), 33-67 (51). Schwartz contends that the *kipper* action in 17:11 should be understood as a "ransom" (*kōper*) and not as expiation (55-61). His distinction between the two interpretations, however, is too rigid as, within the cultic offering, the cleansing of sin by blood (*kipper*) and the ransom (*kōper*) given are closely intertwined.

[53] Lester L. Grabbe, "The Scapegoat: A Study in Early Jewish Interpretation," *JSJ* 18 (1987): 152-67 (153-55).

[54] Gerstenberger, *Leviticus*, 237.

Sin, Sacrifice, and Atonement (Leviticus 1–7, 16)   59

the oldest core of the tradition based on similar Syrian rituals.[55] Though we may not be able to accurately date the reference to "goat demons," the theological message is clear – Israel is not to shed blood away from the shrine nor is the blood to be offered to anyone except Yhwh who is the only giver of life.

To connote the severity and weight of the commandments concerning blood, the priestly authors reiterate the maximum punishment "to be cut off" (*nikrətâ*) from the people, which was equivalent to the death penalty enacted by God (cf. Lev 20:5–6).[56] A similar use of the term is found in Psalm 37 where one could be "cut off" from the land and the promised inheritance (Ps 37:22). The sense of the punishment in Leviticus is that one might lose their standing as a citizen in Israel thereby forfeiting their rights to land and worshipping at the tabernacle/temple.[57] This extreme sanction for shedding any blood away from the altar reflects a situation where Jews must have had access to a regional shrine. If there was only a single place of offering at the Jerusalem temple then, according to Levitical laws, most families living beyond the Judean area could not eat meat from domesticated slaughter.

Just as blood atones for the life of the sinner and the cleansing of the tabernacle, so too can it be used to consecrate those who are

---

[55] Bernd Janowski, "Azazel," in *DDD*, 130; Nihan, *Priestly Torah*, 352–53. Milgrom, *Leviticus 17–22*, 1462, identifies goat demons with the Ugaritic god, Mot.
[56] Schwartz, "The Prohibitions Concerning the 'Eating' of Blood in Leviticus 17," 42–45.
[57] In Leviticus, the other offenses that result in being cut off are violating holy days (23:29), violations of certain purity laws (7:20–21; 22:3), prohibited sexual unions (18:29; 20:17–18), and other cultic offenses that defile the sanctuary (3:17; 7:25–27; 17:4, 9; 19:8; 20:3, 5–6). For detailed analysis of how *kārēt* ("cut off") is used throughout Scripture, see Milgrom, *Leviticus 1–16*, 457–60.

transitioning from the profane into the holy. This can be seen through the rituals associated with the consecration of priests and those with skin diseases who are brought back into the covenant community. In the ordination rite, the priests are smeared with the blood of the ordination ram on their right earlobe, right thumb, and right big toe (Exod 29:19–21; Lev 8:22–24). This symbolizes a full and complete covering with blood that has come in contact with the altar, which consecrates them and sets them apart for holy service. They have been removed from the profane world into the service of Yhwh's tabernacle. In a similar manner, those with skin diseases go through a related ritual to express their transition from outside the covenant community back into the fellowship of God's people (Lev 14:14). In both instances, the anointing of blood given at the altar symbolizes the power to move a person closer to the holiness of God.

Lastly, blood can also be a source of contamination. As blood is associated with life, so too is it associated with death when released from the body.[58] The blood of menstruation is one case where it is associated with death thereby making a woman ritually unclean, along with anything that she touches, for one week (Lev 15:19–24). A woman also becomes ritually unclean after birth where the bodily discharge of blood means that she cannot approach the sanctuary. After a period of forty days, for the birth of a boy, and eighty days, for a girl, the woman may present a purification offering for the sanctuary and for herself. No explanation is given in Leviticus regarding why the flow of blood makes a woman unclean (or why purification takes longer for girls than for boys!). Commentators have suggested various reasons from ancient taboos or beliefs that demons could attack

---

[58] Cf. Douglas, *Purity and Danger*, 7–29.

after birth. Leviticus only mentions the reason relating to the discharge of blood (Lev 12: 4, 5, 7) and not to the child itself. What is important to remember is that the woman's uncleanness caused by menstruation or childbirth is not a moral/ethical judgment against her.[59] The natural functions of life and the body around fertility and childbirth simply make her ritually unclean in relation to the tabernacle for a period of time.

In sum, the power of blood in the priestly theology cannot be overestimated. It is essential to the spiritual life of the community and to maintaining Israel's relationship with Yhwh. Blood is the cleansing agent for sin but it is also an agent that can bring about uncleanness in particular circumstances. Blood allows Israel to draw near to God's holiness but can also keep them away especially when handled improperly. With such great theological significance attached to blood, and stringent regulations in handling it, Leviticus entrusts its use only to authorized priests. This is to prevent Israel from sacrificing to any other gods/demons and preserving the sanctity of blood for atonement only on God's altar.

A THEOLOGY OF SIN AND ATONEMENT

Before we can comprehend the effects of blood and the notion of atonement, we must first understand the priestly concept of sin in Leviticus. Sin is not merely about private, spiritual disobedience against the Law. Sin has real effects in the physical world and on the tabernacle in Leviticus. Sin leads to disorder and chaos, it can

---

[59] See Klawans, *Purity, Sacrifice, and the Temple*, 53–56. Cf. Klawans, "Ritual Purity, Moral Purity, and Sacrifice in Jacob Milgrom's Leviticus," *RelSRev* 29.1 (2003): 19–28.

profane the land, or it can contaminate God's people and his sanctuary. We are not given specific details about how this happens in Leviticus, but the effects of sin in the material world are assumed in commands like those for the Day of Atonement. "Thus he shall make atonement for the sanctuary, because of the uncleannesses of the people of Israel, and because of their transgressions, all their sins; and so he shall do for the tent of meeting, which remains with them in the midst of their uncleannesses" (Lev 16:16). Somehow the *materia peccans* ("substance of sin") contaminates physical space, which must be cleansed, purified, and purged from the sanctuary to bring about holiness and the reordering of the world.

Sin also has social consequences that damage human relationships. Sin is as much a crime against God as it is against neighbor and reparation for sin must be made both horizontally in human relationships and vertically with the divine. Leviticus is concerned with justice among the people of Israel because if injustice is left unpunished or unatoned for, it can have a polluting effect on the tabernacle and on the community. Sacrifices for sin, therefore, are not efficacious or magical in their own right. The shedding of blood does not indicate immediate and full expiation of the sinner. The priestly theology of Leviticus, like the prophets, requires that ethical sins against one's neighbor be atoned for at the altar *and* offer reparation to the offended party (Lev 6:4–5).

One effect of sin is that it moves a person into a state of uncleanness. This can come about through moral/ethical disobedience but it can also be the result of certain diseases, bodily emissions, or contact with the dead. Ritual impurity has the potential to be as destructive as moral impurity in the theology of Leviticus because it produces the same result of uncleanness. It is probable that things like skin diseases, menstruation, or other things that caused ritual impurity were somehow associated with death, which must remain separate from God's presence.[60] Different processes were prescribed for different impurities such as ritual washings (Lev 15:1–32) but after a certain period of time the person could re-enter a state of cleanness before approaching God in his sanctuary. For Leviticus, the symbolism of washing in water and waiting indicated the appropriate purification of one's body before entering God's tabernacle. The allotted time differed for various grades of impurity but the sense is that, with the passing of time, the stain of sin would fade enough for a person to safely come before God's holiness without danger.

Finally, sin is a negative agent that causes a movement from order to chaos. We have seen the priestly theology of order in the design/creation of the tabernacle as a microcosm of God's creation of the cosmos (Genesis 1). When sin is introduced into that order, it breaks down established, natural boundaries and causes disorder that ultimately leads to death. Whether sin is committed knowingly or unknowingly, it produces a lethal situation where the offender may be destroyed in the presence of Yhwh's holiness (e.g., Nadab and Abihu). Therefore, to understand sacrifice and atonement and its various layers of meaning, it is critical first to understand the effects of sin in relation to both the physical and spiritual realms.

A common misunderstanding of the effects of sin in the Old Testament is an undue emphasis on God's anger and punishment upon the perpetrator. The picture of a perpetually angry judge seeking to strike down offenders to satisfy an insatiable desire for justice is not the picture Leviticus paints. There are, of

---

[60] Jacob Milgrom, "Rationale for Cultic Law: The Case of Impurity," *Semeia* 45 (1989): 103–9.

course, instances where sin arouses God's anger and incites a violent response of judgment. Stories in the Pentateuch such as the sin of the Golden Calf (Exod 32:1–10, 35), the rebellion of the sons of Korah (Numbers 16), the plague of the fiery serpents (Num 21:4–9), or idolatry with the Baal of Peor (Num 25:1–9) demonstrate this type of response from the divine, but this picture of appeasing a wrathful God is foreign to the theology of Leviticus.[61]

The only reference to God's "anger" (q-$ṣ$-p) in Leviticus is found in 10:6 when God warns Aaron not to mourn the death of his sons lest his anger break out against the people.[62] In this example, the wrath of God will only be incited if Aaron disobeys God's specific command not to mourn his sons. Since Aaron had just been consecrated as high priest, he was forbidden to come into contact with a dead body lest he become unclean and unable to perform his duties at the altar. The warning is not to fear God's wrath but, rather, to fear his holiness because, according to his words to Aaron, he will "show himself holy" (Lev 10:3) to all those who draw near to him. The implication is that the priests and Israelites must fear the awesome power of God's holiness, not his wrath, as they approach his divine presence in the sanctuary.

The seriousness with which the priestly authors take sin in the presence of the divine has less to do with God's anger and more to do with extreme reverence of his holiness for fear of death. Sacramental and ritual purity is of the utmost importance when

---

[61] Stephen B. Chapman, "God's Reconciling Work: Atonement in the Old Testament," in *T & T Clark Companion to Atonement*, ed. Adam J. Johnson (New York: Bloomsbury, 2106), 95–114 (104).

[62] In Lev 26:28, we read of God's "wrathful hostility" (*baḥămat-qerî*) against disobedient Israel who refuse to obey the commandments but, again, this is not within the context of atonement.

approaching the divine. Otto's reference to the *mysterium tremendum*, or "numinous dread," experienced before God's holiness offers an insight into Leviticus' theology of sacrifice and atonement.[63] It is not God's wrath that needs to be appeased but, rather, it is the power of his holiness and purity that must be approached with the utmost reverence and fear.

The underlying threat of sin and impurity, if it remains unatoned for, is the potential to drive out the divine presence so that Israel is left exposed to its enemies (Leviticus 26; cf. Ezek 10:18; 11:22-23). The link between God's divine presence and his protection of his people is seen throughout the exodus narrative and this defense of Israel continues as long as his divine presence remains in the tabernacle. Hundley contends that the priestly authors seek to create a divinely commissioned earthly dwelling for the transcendent deity (Yhwh) that is maintained by a strict, ritual system.[64] The intent of an integrated cultic system that includes both individuals and the sanctuary is to ensure that Israel keeps the divine presence, and therefore its link to heaven, on earth. With the threat of Yhwh abandoning his sanctuary, and abandoning his people, the priestly authors set in place the necessary rituals for atonement and purity that will enable his continued presence.

With this frame of reference, we can begin to understand the nature and function of atonement in Leviticus as a purging and purifying act that cleanses and maintains holiness in the sanctuary and among the people. In an effort to avoid Christian doctrines of

---

[63] Otto, *The Idea of the Holy*, 12-24.
[64] Michael B. Hundley, *Keeping Heaven on Earth: Safeguarding the Divine Presence in the Priestly Tabernacle* (Tübingen: Mohr Seibeck, 2011), 134-72.

atonement that have been read back into, and have often superseded, the Book of Leviticus, it is important to approach the text on its own terms. To do so we shall begin with a brief overview of the language of Leviticus and, in particular, the cultic terms that need to be defined within the context of the book in reference to atonement.

The Hebrew root *k-p-r* in the Piel stem (*kippēr*) is often translated as "atone" or "expiate." Both Levine and Milgrom[65] argue for the historical connection of the Hebrew with the Akkadian *kapāru* ("to wipe off") or *kuppuru* ("cleanse ritually," "rub off").[66] The sense is that something is wiped away as if an object or person is being purged or purified. In the sacrifices of Leviticus, this cleansing is often symbolized by the dabbing and sprinkling of blood on the sancta of the tabernacle as if wiping off or purging the effects of sin. This ritual could have had apotropaic overtones, similar to the smearing of blood on doorposts in the Passover rite, but the predominant meaning is that the blood acts as a purifying agent because the life in the blood (Lev 17:11) cancels out the death of sin and impurity.[67]

One type of offering for atonement is the *ḥaṭṭā't* and, as mentioned above, the Hebrew has often been translated as "sin offering" but should be rendered "purification offering" according to Milgrom's argument. Though Milgrom, at times, creates too sharp a distinction between the purgation of the sanctuary and the offerer, the *ḥaṭṭā't* signifies the expiation of an individual from

---

[65] Baruch Levine, *In the Presence of the Lord: A Study of Cult and Some Cultic Terms in Ancient Israel* (Leiden: Brill, 1974), 56–63, 121–27; Milgrom, *Leviticus 1–16*, 1078–83.

[66] In non-cultic use the Hebrew *k-p-r* can mean to wipe or smear as is the case in Gen 6:14 where Noah is commanded to cover the ark with pitch.

[67] See Hundley, *Keeping Heaven on Earth*, 186–89.

their guilty status *and* the purging of sin from the sanctuary.[68] The *ḥaṭṭāʾt* is, therefore, primarily about *purification* and not *propitiation* – the cleansing of sin rather than the appeasement of God's wrath.[69]

The *ḥaṭṭāʾt* was presented for transgressions against the commandments, but it was not limited to one's sin. It was also the offering for physical impurities (Lev 5:2–3) that had nothing to do with one's moral behavior. Two kinds of *ḥaṭṭāʾt* could be offered. One is prescribed in Lev 4:3–21, which consisted of a bull that was sacrificed for the sins of the high priest or the collective sins of the community. Specific acts of blood manipulation occurred within the tabernacle and no part of the sacrifice was consumed. Whatever was not offered on the altar was removed and burned outside the camp.[70] It is important to note that none of the blood from the bull was spread on the people. Its use was confined to the altar and instruments within the sanctuary.[71]

The second type of *ḥaṭṭāʾt* (Lev 4:22–5:13) is offered in the case of a ruler or other individuals who sin unintentionally. A goat or sheep is prescribed, but this could be substituted by birds or the non-blood sacrifice of grain for those who could not afford an animal. There are different varieties of this offering that cover

---

[68] Contra Milgrom, *Leviticus 1–16*, 441, who contends that purgation is for the tabernacle alone. He later modified his argument but was not convinced that atonement affected the offerer. See David Janzen, "Sin and Expiation," in *The Oxford Handbook of Ritual and Worship in the Hebrew Bible*, ed. Samuel E. Balentine (Oxford: Oxford University Press, 2020), 289–300.

[69] Cf. Joseph Lam, "On the Etymology of Biblical Hebrew: A Contribution to the 'Sin Offering' vs. 'Purification Offering' Debate," *Journal of Semitic Studies* 65.2 (2020): 325–46.

[70] Jacob Milgrom, "Two Kinds of *ḥaṭṭāʾt*," *VT* 26 (1976): 333–37.

[71] Cf. Andrew Rillera, *Lamb of the Free: Recovering the Varied Sacrificial Understandings of Jesus's Death* (Eugene, OR: Cascade Books, 2024), 81–84.

both moral sin and ritual uncleanness (Lev 5:1–13), which achieve the same result of purification/atonement (both for the individual and the sanctuary) and forgiveness (Lev 4:20; 5:13).

An important ritual linked to the *ḥaṭṭā't* was the hand leaning (*sāmak yād*) on the head of the animal before it was killed. The gesture of laying on hands can indicate the transfer of authority as in the case of Moses with Joshua (Num 27:18–23; Deut 34:9) or in the ordination of the Levites (Num 8:10). In Leviticus, there are various possibilities that include the identification of the offering with the offerer or the indication of ownership. These two options might convey the sense that the offerer's hand is a sign to the deity that they are linked to the sacrifice provided.[72] Milgrom, following Ibn Ezra, argues that the single hand placed on the animal cannot indicate the transference of sin since this is explicitly stated in the *Yom Kippur* rite where two hands are placed on the goat to pass on the transgressions of Israel (Lev 16:21).[73] If the transference of sin is reserved for the Azazel-goat rite on the Day of Atonement, then how does the single hand placing in the *ḥaṭṭā't* serve as a function of atonement and forgiveness?

Gese contends that the spirit (*nepeš*) of the person is identified with the *nepeš* of the animal as an offering of life for life. "The identification of the *nephesh* of the one making the offering with the sacrificial animal is presupposed (we saw that it is effected by the laying on of hands), and through the shedding of the animal's blood the life of the person who brings the sacrifice is symbolically offered up."[74] Thus atonement, or purification, comes through the

---

[72] David P. Wright, "The Gesture of Hand Placement in the Hebrew Bible and Hittite Literature," *JAOS* 106 (1986): 433–46.
[73] Milgrom, *Leviticus 1–16*, 151.
[74] Hartmut Gese, "The Atonement," in *Essays on Biblical Theology* (Minneapolis, MN: Augsburg, 1981), 107.

acceptance of the animal's *nepeš* in the form of its blood on the altar and its flesh transferred to the heavenly realms through fire and smoke. The result is that sin is both wiped away from the offerer and the substituted *nepeš* purges the sanctuary and is "bound up with the holy."[75]

If Gese is correct, then the theology of Leviticus expresses atonement partially through human *identification* with the blood and life of the animal. This identification gives life back to God (from whom all life comes) to allow for human life to be cleansed and allowed to draw near to his holiness. The animal's life and blood ascend through smoke and fire into Yhwh's presence, which symbolizes the offerer's union with the divine. The identification through the laying on of a hand in the *ḥaṭṭā't* is not for the transfer of the *materia peccans* but for the unity between offerer and offering that cause both to ascend symbolically to the heavens as a "pleasing aroma." This allows the one remaining on earth to be restored in right relationship with Yhwh because the blood of the offering has made atonement for sin and purges the altar.

Offerings for atonement, including the *ḥaṭṭā't*, were not understood in transactional terms. The symbolic identification of the offerer with the offering meant nothing without repentance and a commitment to live according to the justice and mercy expressed in the Mosaic laws. Though contriteness of heart is not specifically mentioned in Leviticus as part of the sacrificial offerings (cf. Ps 51:17), some type of acknowledgment of sin and repentance is assumed in the prescriptions. Sacrifices for atonement were not to appease God's wrath or simply a means to ensure that God did

---

[75] Gese, "The Atonement," 108. Cf. Nobuyoshi Kiuchi, *The Purification Offering in the Priestly Literature: Its Meaning and Function*, JSOTSS 56 (Sheffield: Sheffield Academic, 1987), 111–19.

not leave the sanctuary. Instead, they taught Israel the depth and gravity of sin in relation to God's holiness through ritual. Through the sacrificial laws, the people were taught that the holiness of God requires purification, atonement, and justice.[76] For the authors of Leviticus, the act of atonement needs more than blood sacrifice if holiness is to be achieved. The call to be holy as God is holy (Lev 19:2) required ritual offerings, but it also demanded upholding ethical precepts summed up in the command to love your neighbor as yourself (Lev 19:18). Ritual purity must be accompanied by moral purity and obedience to the Mosiac law if God's holiness and abiding presence would remain with his people.

Having discussed a theology of sin and atonement with a focus on the minor blood rite of the *ḥaṭṭā't* that purified the outer altar and the sancta in the inner court, we can now move into the major blood rite of the Day of Atonement to examine rituals that express both expiation and transference that are used to purge the innermost court of the Holy of Holies.

YOM KIPPUR

The Day of Atonement (Leviticus 16) constitutes the high point in Israelite cultic celebration as the tabernacle is purified and atonement is made on behalf of the whole congregation. This occurs through burnt offerings performed by Aaron, the high priest, on behalf of himself and his family as well as for the sins of all Israel. Incense is offered in the Holy of Holies where Aaron also sprinkles blood on the "mercy seat" (*kappōret*) that sits on

---

[76] John G. Gammie, *Holiness in Israel* (Minneapolis: Augsburg Fortress Press, 1989), 71–101.

top of the ark symbolizing the throne of Yhwh.⁷⁷ Blood is also placed on the horns of the altar. Following the purgation of the sacred space, the scapegoat ritual is performed whereby the sins of the people are placed "on the head of the goat" (Lev 16:21), which is then sent into the wilderness. After Aaron bathes again, he is clothed and offers up the rams of burnt offering and burns the remains of the bull and goat sacrifices outside of the camp.

Similar rites of purgation have been found among ancient Hittite and Babylonian cultures. According to one Hittite rite of purification for an epidemic or plague, an offering is made to the gods and the commanders place their hands on the rams to transfer the evil afflicting the people. The rams are then driven into the countryside away from the camp. This is followed by blood sacrifices to purge the camp of the epidemic.⁷⁸

In the Babylonian *Akitu* festival that occurred on the vernal and autumnal equinox, a similar rite of purgation was practiced in which a sheep's body and blood were used to "purify" (*kapāru*) the temple space and afterwards it was cast into the river.⁷⁹ Though not explicitly stated in the text, the animal seems to act as both a cleansing agent and an absorbent that soaks up the impurity in the space, which is then disposed of in the water. Both

---

77 Klaus Koch, "Some Considerations on the Translation of *kapporet* in the Septuagint," in *Pomegranates and Golden Bells: Studies in Biblical, Jewish, and Near Eastern Ritual, Law, and Literature in Honor of Jacob Milgrom*, ed. David P. Wright, David Noel Freedman, and Avi Hurvitz (Winona Lake, IN: Eisenbrauns, 1995), 65-75.

78 Billie Jean Collins, *The Hittites and Their World* (Atlanta: SBL Press, 2007), 186-88. Cf. Yitzhaq Feder, *Blood Expiation in Hittite and Biblical Ritual: Origins, Context, and Meaning*, WAWSup 2 (Atlanta: SBL Press, 2011); *COS*, 1:161-62.

79 Julye Bidmead, *The Akitu Festival: Religious Continuity and Royal Legitimation in Mesopotamia*, Gorgias Dissertations, Near East Series 2 (Piscataway, NJ: Gorgias Press, 2002).

examples demonstrate ancient practices of purging and disposing of uncleanness through blood and the transference of impurity on to the animal that is sent away.

In Leviticus, the symbolic movement of sin to the scapegoat takes place *after* the act of atonement is complete (16:14–20).[80] The sanctuary space must be purged from the cumulative effects of sin before those sins can also be disposed of in the wilderness. Janowski draws attention to the spatial aspects of the ritual and contends that the *kappōret*, representing the most holy space in Yhwh's throne room, is contrasted by the desert wilderness as the place of chaos. The atoning sacrifices cleanse the throne-room whereas the sins of the people both physically and symbolically depart from God's presence back into chaos and the world of death.[81] In this major rite, the tabernacle is purged from the *materia peccans* and Israel is restored to holiness through the blood of expiation and the process of concretizing and disposing of sin that is transferred to the goat.[82]

The scapegoat thus acts as the vehicle through which life is spared by substituting another life for the guilty as a ransom. This is summed up in the German concept of *Existenzstellvertretung*, meaning a vicarious offering of a life as an equivalent substitution for the ransom of another.[83] Within this ritual framework, the

---

[80] Wright, "The Gesture of Hand Placement," 436.
[81] Janowski, "Das Geschenk der Versöhnung," 20–21.
[82] David P. Wright, *The Disposal of Impurity: Elimination Rites in the Bible and in Hittite and Mesopotamian Literature*, SBLDS 101 (Atlanta: Scholars Press, 1986), 31–45; cf. Chapman, "God's Reconciling Work," 104.
[83] See Hartmut Gese, "Die Sühne," in *Zur biblischen Theologie: Altestamentliche Vorträge* (München: Kaiser-Verlag, 1977), 85–106; Bernd Janowski, *Sühne als Heilsgeschehen: Traditions- und religionsgeschichtliche Studien zur Sühnetheologie der Priesterschrift* (Neukirchen-Vluyn: Neukirchener Verlag, 2000). For the concept of *Existenzstellvertretung* in

Sin, Sacrifice, and Atonement (Leviticus 1-7, 16)

"substitution" does not bear the punishment, anger, or wrath of God but, rather, the offering acts as a ransom where sin is eliminated by being sent back into chaos so that the covenant relationship can be restored.[84]

If the scapegoat acts as a form of ransom, then to whom is the ransom paid? The scapegoat is not a blood sacrifice and so it provides no form of expiation or cleansing.[85] Instead, it remains alive after Israel's sins have been purged from the tabernacle and only then are Israel's iniquities transferred to it before it is sent into the wilderness to Azazel. It is unclear who Azazel is since the name only occurs in Leviticus (16:8, 10, 26), but the etymology suggests something like "strong god" or possibly represents the name of a demon or the geographical location where that demon resides.[86] Janowski contends that the Azazel-rite stems from ancient tradition and that the process of demonization occurred in later Judaism (cf. 1 *En.* 8:1; 9:6; 10:4-8; 13:1).[87] Blair, however, argues that Azazel does not likely represent a demon but, rather, was a deity that symbolizes chaos and the forces that disrupt creation.[88]

---

dialogue with the theology of Karl Barth, see Matthias Grebe, *Election, Atonement, and the Holy Spirit*, PTMS 214 (Eugene, OR: Pickwick, 2014), 66-99.

[84] Gese, "The Atonement," 95-96.

[85] Cf. Roy Gane, *Cult and Character: Purification Offerings, Day of Atonement, and Theodicy* (Winona Lake, IL: Eisenbrauns, 2005), 251; Lester Grabbe, "The Scapegoat Tradition: A Study in Early Jewish Interpretation," *JSJ* 18 (1987): 152-67; Robert Helm, "Azazel in Early Jewish Tradition," *AUSS* 32 (1994): 217-26; Dominic Rudman, "A Note on the Azazel-goat Ritual," *ZAW* 116 (2004): 396-401; Ilona Rashkow, "Azazel: The Scapegoat in the Bible and Ancient Near East," *The Jewish Bible Quarterly* 51.2 (2023): 85-90.

[86] Janowski, "Azazel," in *DDD*, 128.

[87] Janowski, "Azazel," 130; cf. Milgrom, *Leviticus 1-16*, 1021, 1042, 1072.

[88] Judit M. Blair, *De-Demonising the Old Testament: An Investigation of Azazel, Lilith, Deber, Qeteb and Reshef in the Hebrew Bible*, FAT 2.37 (Tübingen: Mohr Siebeck, 2009), 55-62.

Whether demon or deity, Leviticus 16 offers a symmetry between the two goats – one given as a blood sacrifice for expiation in the Holy of Holies and the other sent away alive back to the chaos of the wilderness bearing the sin of the people. It seems likely that Azazel represents a god or demon in the wilderness and that the goat-rite is the mirror opposite symbol of returning the evil that contaminated Israel to its rightful place/owner. The ransom is not an appeasement but a reordering of the world where the disorder of sin is removed from God's people and sent back to its place of origin in the symbolic place of chaos in the wilderness.

The theology of atonement in *Yom Kippur* is one that expresses identification, expiation, and substitution that results in the atonement of all Israel's sins. New life, holiness, and reconciliation come through purging the sanctuary with blood. Here we find the positive connotations of atonement through identification, expiation, and cleansing. The Holy of Holies is purified, but the sins of the people must also be removed. The negative act of transferring sin to the Azazel-goat does not suggest the insufficiency of the blood rites. Instead, the goat is a symbol and an annual reminder that the forces of chaos and sin are ever corrupting God's holy people.[89] This pollution must be expelled so that

---

[89] Christian A. Eberhart, "To Atone or Not to Atone: Remarks on the Day of Atonement Rituals According to Leviticus 16 and the Meaning of Atonement," in *Sacrifice, Cult, and Atonement in Early Judaism and Christianity: Constituents and Critique*, ed. Henrietta L. Wiley and Christian A. Eberhart (Atlanta: SBL Press, 2016), 197–231, argues that a more holistic view of atonement is needed beyond just the blood rites and that atonement can also come through other rituals and elimination rites. Though the Day of Atonement has multiple layers of symbolism, Leviticus places a consistent emphasis on blood shed at the altar for atonement and it is difficult to see the scapegoat rite achieving atonement on its own.

order might be restored and that Israel might continue to live in the presence of Yhwh's holiness (cf. Isa 62:5; Jer 2:2).

The cultic rites in Leviticus consolidate and standardize Israelite sacrificial tradition in written form. They offer a guide for both priest and layperson for the basic types of offerings and how they are to be performed. By committing ritual practice to the written word, Leviticus, in some ways, demystifies what might have been considered esoteric knowledge intended only for priests. Instead, the instructions clarify how all Israelites are to approach Yhwh's holy presence whether by offering sacrifices of praise and thanksgiving or making atonement for sin.

The cultic rites also have a didactic effect through the drama of liturgy and ritual. Through the symbols of blood, sacred space, and the participation of both layperson and priest, Israel is taught key concepts regarding sin, atonement, purity, and the holiness of the God who dwells in their presence. These lessons involve the inclusion of every Israelite home so that the whole covenant people may comprehend the nature of sin, sacrifice, and their responsibility in maintaining the holiness of the tabernacle. Purity and holiness in the theology of Leviticus are not attributes reserved only for the priests. Instead, Leviticus presents a vision for an entire community, including the land, that is being consecrated and is restoring the order of creation. The divine drama invites the Israelites to participate in the ongoing work of redemption, reconciliation, and praise for the God who delivered them from the death of Egypt and will plant them in the promised land.

ANSELM, ATONEMENT, AND LEVITICUS

To understand a theology of atonement in Leviticus, the reader is required to take into account every aspect of ritual sacrifice and not merely one or two distinct points. When considering the entire ritual system for atonement we discover prominent features that might be summed up in the following: (1) God is holy and cannot tolerate moral or ritual impurity in his presence. (2) Sin has both physical and metaphysical properties. It damages the capacity for communion with God and with others human beings, but it also causes a type of stain where the *materia peccans* covers both sinner and the sanctuary. (3) The *materia peccans* must be cleansed and/or eliminated from sinner and sanctuary for Yhwh to dwell amidst his people. (4) To cleanse sinner and sanctuary, the lifeblood, given by God, must be used by authorized persons according to strict regulations to bring about expiation and purification thereby ensuring Israel's ongoing communion with Yhwh.[90]

Over the centuries, Christian interpretations concerning the nature of atonement in the Old Testament, and how it pertains to Christ's sacrifice on the cross, have often been driven by certain doctrines that are subsequently read back into the cultic rituals of Leviticus. The largely Western Christian notion of "substitutionary atonement" as ransom and satisfaction for sin has had a significant influence on Christian theologies of atonement. This doctrine was astutely articulated by the Benedictine abbot and theologian Anselm of Canterbury (1033–1109) in his *Cur Deus Homo*.[91] Though different variants of Anselm's doctrine of atonement in Christ have developed, we can describe some of

---

[90] For more views on atonement, see Christian A. Eberhart, "Introduction," in Henrietta L. Wiley and Eberhart, ed. *Sacrifice, Cult, and Atonement in Early Judaism and Christianity Constituents and Critique* (Atlanta: SBL Press, 2017), 12–24.

[91] See David Brown, *God in a Single Vision: Integrating Philosophy and Theology* (London: Routledge, 2016), 125–41.

his general theological points to see how they stand in relation to what has been discussed above.[92]

Anselm understood original sin according to Augustine's doctrine that all human beings are born into sin. Since all humans have an obligation to worship God but fall short because of sin, they owe a debt to God that can never be fulfilled. Sin is an offense to God that incurs some type of penalty that humanity cannot pay, nor can God cancel. Anselm places an emphasis on the intolerable burden of sin that builds up in each person, which, like a debt, must be satisfied or repaid.[93] For God to arbitrarily forgive this debt would be incompatible with his nature and would violate his justice so sin cannot go unpunished. Therefore, God's wrath is constantly directed against his people because of the penalty they deserve and the debt that they cannot repay.[94]

Yet Anslem also argued that humanity was created for salvation and so what was needed was something that could pardon human debt from sin and satisfy God's justice. Since only God could achieve what humans were incapable of achieving, God sent his Son to offer his life for the satisfaction of sin. This reasoning is central to answering the question and title of his book "Why God [became] Human?" (*Cur Deus homo*). Within Anselm's interpretative framework, Christ pays humanity's debt in full by suffering

---

[92] For more on the different Christian doctrinal approaches to atonement, see Joshua M. McNall, *The Mosaic of Atonement: An Integrated Approach to Christ's Work* (Grand Rapids, MI: Zondervan Academic, 2019).

[93] Katherine Sonderegger, "Anselmian Atonement," in *T & T Clark Companion to Atonement*, ed. Adam J. Johnson (New York: Bloomsbury, 2016), 175–94 (179).

[94] For a concise analysis of Anselm's debt-repayment doctrine, see Rachel Cresswell, "Reframing Anselm and Aquinas on Atonement," *New Blackfriars* 104.1109 (2023): 39–56.

and dying on the cross. His once-for-all sacrifice appeases God's anger against human sin and allows for them to be brought back into a right relationship with him.[95]

Whether intentional or unintentional, Anselm's juridical framework was often interpreted as God being a ruthless overlord who is committed to abstract principles of justice above all else and who is willing to submit an innocent substitution (Christ) to violent punishment as payment for sin.[96] Over the centuries, others have applied Anselm's doctrines to further the idea of God as cosmic Judge whose justice is only satisfied through the punishment of the sinless and innocent offering of Christ. Rather than an offering of *expiation*, Christ's sacrifice is seen as a *propitiation* that satisfies God's demand for justice and appeases his wrath against humanity.[97]

The difficulties with these doctrines of atonement are many, but here we may note their discord with the theology of atonement expressed in Leviticus. Nowhere in the language of Leviticus do we find God presented as Judge in need of appeasement or

---

[95] It is important, however, to stress that Anselm did not advocate a doctrine of "penal substitutionary atonement". Instead, he emphasized the free offering Christ gave on behalf of humanity. "God the Father did not treat that man as you apparently understand him to have done; nor did he hand over an innocent man to be killed in place of the guilty party. For the Father did not coerce Christ to face death against his will, or give permission for him to be killed, but Christ himself of his own volition underwent death in order to save mankind." *Cur Deus Homo* 1.8. Translation from Anselm, *Anselm of Canterbury: The Major Works*, eds. Brian Davies and G. R. Evans (Oxford: Oxford University Press, 1998), 275.

[96] Cf. Kathryn Tanner, *Christ the Key* (Cambridge: Cambridge University Press, 2010), 247–73; Stephen Sykes, ed., *Sacrifice and Redemption* (Cambridge: Cambridge University Press, 1991).

[97] For more perspectives on atonement from an analytical theological perspective, see Eleonore Stump, *Atonement* (Oxford: Oxford University Press, 2019).

Sin, Sacrifice, and Atonement (Leviticus 1–7, 16) 79

satisfaction. The emphasis concerning the cult is God's divine holiness rather divine justice. The predominant symbolism of sacrifice is for the expiation and purging of sin and not for appeasement to avoid punishment (even though that fear may be lingering in the background). We are presented with a holy God who desires purity and cleanness in his tabernacle and in his people whom he has redeemed so that he might remain in communion with them. The goal of sacrifice is understood primarily within the relational spheres of union with God the Father and not in the juridical setting of God the Judge.

It would be foreign to the priestly authors to think of a penalty inflicted on an innocent animal as merely a way of being freed from debt or divine wrath. Unlike Girard's theory that reduces animal sacrifice to the infliction of human violence on to a "surrogate victim" in order to contain or limit social violence,[98] Leviticus offers no sense of killing animals with violent intent to somehow satisfy God's need for justice. This is not to say that the priestly theology was unconcerned with God's justice. The opposite is true. Leviticus is very clear that God is holy *and* just and that he will judge the people according to their sins (cf. Lev 26:14–39). What is equally clear is that the cultic system of sacrifice was not a vehicle for averting God's punishment but, rather, it was to offer ritual acts that represent expiation, cleansing, and purification from the effects of sin.

Another obstacle with the doctrine of penal substitution is that it is unclear how the penalty paid through the sacrifice offers any ongoing mediation between God and his people. If the primary good of atoning sacrifices is that punishment has been evaded,

---

[98] Girard, *Violence and the Sacred*, 85, 92–93. For a critique of Girard, see Klawans, *Purity, Sacrifice, and the Temple*, 22–26, 44–47.

then the atoning work is limited to the individual or the community. In Leviticus, however, when sin is expiated through the blood of an individual's offering the primary result is the cleansing of the tabernacle, which creates a possible future for priestly sacrifice to take place. Though sin is expiated for the individual and the community, the force of the offering is to maintain the holiness of God's tabernacle and altar for the benefit of Israel and all of creation. If atonement is primarily about evading punishment, then we lose the cosmic significance of the purity of the tabernacle on earth as a microcosm for God's heavenly temple.

Animal sacrifices that appease an offended deity in order to avoid the penalty of sin is far from Leviticus' theology of atonement where the emphasis remains on the holiness of God and his desire to remain in relationship with his people. God is Father to Israel, his firstborn son, and he is their deliverer (Exod 4:22-23). Though he is just and judges according to his commandments, Yhwh also reveals himself to Moses as, "merciful and gracious, slow to anger, and abounding in steadfast love and faithfulness" (Exod 34:6).[99] The rituals and sacrifices concerning atonement are not given to appease his wrath but, instead, they create a positive movement toward expiation, the removal of sin and guilt, and the restoration of communion with a holy God who longs to be in relationship with his people.

---

[99] See Brent A. Strawn, "'Israel, My Child': The Ethics of a Biblical Metaphor," in *The Incomparable God: Readings in Biblical Theology*, ed. Collin Cornell and M. Justin Walker (Grand Rapids, MI: Eerdmans, 2023), 189–224; Brent A. Strawn, "Yhwh's Poesie: The Gnadenformel, the Book of Exodus and Beyond," in *The Incomparable God: Readings in Biblical Theology*, ed. Collin Cornell and M. Justin Walker (Grand Rapids, MI: Eerdmans, 2023), 26–44.

The focus of a priestly theology of the cult is on holiness, purity, and being purged of sin so that relationship is restored – the relationship between God and his sanctuary and the relationship between God and his people. Atonement moves God's people from estrangement to reconciliation.[100] Atonement is not fundamentally about avoiding punishment or retribution (though, at times, it does achieve this), but it is about cleansing, purgation, and restoration. The *telos* of atonement in the theology of Leviticus is wholeness and purity that enables ongoing communion with Yhwh. As Gese argues, "Atonement is the sacrifice of life for the sake of making life whole. It brings the abyss of human life into union with the highest divine *doxa*."[101]

Having discussed atonement and blood sacrifice, it is important to recall that the cultic rites of Leviticus are not only about atonement. Though the purgation of sin was critical for the purity of Israel and the tabernacle, the Day of Atonement was performed once a year and other atoning sacrifices, such as the ḥaṭṭā 't and 'āšām, were offered occasionally. The heart of sacrificial rituals in the theology of Leviticus is to worship and draw near to God.[102] Yhwh has delivered his people from slavery and death in Egypt and now at Mt. Sinai he invites them to "draw near" (qārab) to worship him and to come into his holy presence.

Sacrifice in Leviticus is about celebrating the God who saves and provides times and seasons for festive communal gatherings. The altar was not merely a place to deal with the negative consequences of sin and impurity but, rather, it was a place of joy where Israel could give thanks for God's provision in the harvests of

---

[100] Janowski, "Das Geschenk der Versöhnung," 16, 25–27.
[101] Gese, "The Atonement," 115.
[102] Cf. Janowski, *Sühne als Heilsgeschehen*, 358–59.

grain, wine, and olives. They could rejoice in times of peace when families were enlarged, when there were wedding feasts, and communal celebrations. As Alfred Marx argues concerning the ancient sacrifices of Israel, "The sacrifice is a festive meal to which the faithful invite Yhwh and which they offer in order to honor him and pay homage to him."[103] Blood rites and atonement are central to understanding the theology of Leviticus, but they should not overshadow the primary purpose of Israel's cult, which was to worship and draw near to the holy God so that they too might become a holy people.

---

[103] Alfred Marx, *Les systèmes sacrificiels de l'Ancien Testament: Formes et fonctions du culte sacrificiel à Yhwh*, VTSup 105 (Leiden: Brill, 2005), 221. My translation of the French, "Le sacrifice est un repas festif auquel les fidèles convient Yhwh et qu'ils offrent en vue de l'honorer et de lui rendre hommage."

CHAPTER 3

Purity and Impurity (Leviticus 11–15)

DEFINING BOUNDARIES

As was demonstrated in Chapter 2, the source of all life in Leviticus is the tabernacle. Within this holy space, we found the priest as the agent who is set apart from the community to order, create boundaries, and maintain divisions according to Yhwh's command. The priest is the locus of stability and sustainability within God's sanctuary for the sake of Israel. Thus, the priests are charged with the command, "You must distinguish between the holy and the profane, and between the unclean and the clean" (Lev 10:10). The priestly role is to establish and maintain distinct divisions between the sacred and the profane so that they might preserve their own lives ministering in the tabernacle and preserve the life and purity of God's people.

Defilement or pollution in Leviticus moves things/people into a state of uncleanness, which in some cases is a natural part of life and cannot be avoided. It is often the priest's duty to purify, wash, and sanctify those things/people to move them back into a state of purity so that they may draw near to the holiness of God's presence. Holiness is not a static state in the theology of Leviticus. Life ebbs and flows between the profane and the sacred where purity and impurity are in constant tension.

With the priestly role established and the altar consecrated, Leviticus 11–15 shifts its focus to everyday living in the Israelite home where the potential for impurity exists. The various defilements are described with a view toward maintaining the holiness of God's altar and who may approach his tabernacle. Though the purity laws govern circumstances within the Israelite homes, the summation of these rules emphasizes the end goal of keeping Yhwh's home free from contamination. "Thus you shall keep the people of Israel separate from their uncleanness, so that they do not die in their uncleanness by defiling my tabernacle that is in their midst" (Lev 15:31). Leviticus offers a theology of physical space that has spiritual/metaphysical connections with regard to purity and holiness. The bond between the Israelite tent and Yhwh's tent, though located in different physical places, is one that is completely united in the spiritual realms. If impurity exists in the Israelite home, then it will contaminate Yhwh's home.

Leviticus uses a variety of terms to describe the boundaries between what is holy/common (*qôdeš/ḥōl*), clean/unclean (*ṭāmē'/ṭāhôr*), and sanctified/defiled (*qiddēsh/ḥillēl*). Before looking at precise definitions, however, it is important to remember that the priestly theology of Leviticus is rooted in the divine order and boundaries established in creation. These divisions were necessary to bring an abundance of life out of chaos and allow all things on earth to be fruitful and multiply. As Ellen Davis argues, "Leviticus articulates, perhaps more fully than anywhere else in Scripture, a theologically profound vision of the complexity and interdependence of the created order."[1] The commands of Leviticus take their cue from the patterns already set in creation so

---

[1] Ellen F. Davis, *Scripture, Culture, and Agriculture: An Agrarian Reading of the Bible* (Cambridge: Cambridge University Press, 2009), 83.

that the priests might maintain its integrity and keep the world from sliding back into chaos.

The technical categories used by Leviticus pertaining to different aspects of life are not the result of pedantic, neurotic priests who were only concerned with a highly developed legalism.[2] At the heart of the priestly theology is the desire to maintain holiness and purity so that Israel and the world might experience the blessing of God's presence. If specific classifications were crossed or boundaries breached, the results could be catastrophic with the possibility that Yhwh would leave his dwelling. Such a tragedy is recounted later through the prophet/priest Ezekiel. God condemns the priests in Jerusalem because they "have done violence to my teaching and have profaned my holy things; they have made no distinction between the holy and the common, neither have they taught the difference between the unclean and the clean ... so that I am profaned among them" (Ezek 22:26). The blurring of boundaries between the holy and the profane had the potential to lead Israel, and creation, back toward a state of chaos. The integrity and wholeness of the world, and the holiness of Yhwh's name, was to be maintained through right priestly action and instruction.

Many of the purity laws will seem like odd, ancient superstitions to the modern reader. Why would an Israelite wearing a garment made of linen and wool be hazardous to the order of the world? How can principles categorizing animals be applied to gender boundaries or reproductive activity? Things like incest, bestiality, or other sexual relationships are equally thought to

---

[2] See Jacob Milgrom, "Rationale for Biblical Impurity," in *Numbers*, JPS Torah Commentary (Philadelphia: Jewish Publication Society, 1990), 346–48, 444–47.

transgress the natural order of life in Leviticus. Everything is to be classified "according to its/their kind" (Lev 11:14, 15, 16, 19, 22, 29) because this follows the pattern of the creator God's design within creation.³

To touch a dead animal or to have a bodily discharge is not to commit a moral sin in most cases. Instead, these things represent a movement from order to disorder, from cleanness to uncleanness. To try to explain the purity laws as if they formed some rational system according to modern standards is to misunderstand what is at the heart of the priestly theology in Leviticus. These were not a "rational" set of commandments according to modern scientific practice or purely objective thinking. The priestly rationale was not based primarily on empirical evidence but on a sacramental understanding of God's holiness and how that is reflected in the world. Though there is an inner logic to the purity laws, it is one that is held together by the culture and beliefs of an ancient people that may not make sense to the modern reader.

The divisions between clean and unclean are not always consistent in Leviticus. In many instances, bodily discharges can lead to uncleanness, but not all bodily secretions make a person impure. Blood spilt from a wound was unlike the blood shed by murder (Lev 17:4) or menstrual blood (Lev 18:19). In a similar manner, the division between clean and unclean birds or animals does not seem to follow a consistent pattern.⁴ Insects that hop can be eaten but ones that fly cannot (Lev 11:20-24). These systems of

---

³ See Mary Douglas, *Purity and Danger: The Analysis of Concepts of Pollution and Taboo* (London: Routledge, 1966; 2002), 7-29; Milgrom, *Leviticus 1-16*, 934-35.
⁴ See Peter Altmann, *Banned Birds: The Birds of Leviticus 11 and Deuteronomy 14* (Tübingen: Mohr Ziebek, 2019).

division have often been interpreted as "symbolic" where rules are determined not by a logical pattern but according to the inner logic and social order of the culture. Douglas argues that these symbols express "the relation between parts of society, as mirroring designs of hierarchy or symmetry which apply in the larger social system."[5]

The divisions between clean and unclean can change over time in cultures, but symbolic structures are often maintained. If we try to extract one law to examine its original intent (e.g., do not wear fabric made of wool and linen [Lev 19:19]), we have already lost the point. Systems of belief that are inherited function within a broader scope of belief and do not often ask the question why. Rather, they offer an action or prohibition that is tied to a broader cosmology of order within the world.

EATING OUR WAY TO HOLINESS

The dietary regulations of Leviticus 11 are the most extensive in Scripture and sit virtually at the center of the Pentateuch. Laws around what one can or cannot eat are established as a guide to holiness and connect Israel's table to Yhwh's table, the altar. How Israel ate reflected how they lived in relationship with creation, how they treated their neighbor, and how they honored a holy God. The dietary restrictions of Leviticus 11 stand as much in relation to the sexual injunctions of chapters 18 and 20 as they do to the moral code of chapter 19 or the ritual regulations of chapter 17. Israel is set apart as holy and as a result they are to strive toward the ideal goal of holiness in everyday activities in the home like eating as well as in their ethical behavior in political, social,

---

[5] Douglas, *Purity and Danger*, 4.

and economic affairs. Thus, we see a deeper consistency between the commands for holiness in Leviticus 1–16 and 17–26, which focus on the purity of the tabernacle, and how that relates to purity within the home and the broader covenant community.[6]

The detail of this chapter might seem pedantic or boring to the modern reader, but Leviticus draws attention to one of the most significant disciplines of faith that is often lost in the modern Western world: to grow in holiness is to consider one's relationship to creation and to God through what we eat. Holiness in Leviticus requires an attentiveness to physical appetites and the intimate connections we share with the ecosystems in which we live. In the priestly theology of Leviticus, thoughtful and prayerful consideration goes into everything that enters one's mouth because eating is a sacrament that shapes who we are as human beings.[7] Eating meat is also connected to the holiness of Yhwh's altar since all meat was offered there first before being consumed in the home.

To eat is also to practice covenant fidelity. As Wenham writes, "Through this system of symbolic laws the Israelites were reminded at every meal of their redemption as God's people."[8] When food was consumed in the home at the table it acted as a reminder of God's salvation from Egypt, his call to holiness, and his promise of blessing in the land. To refrain from eating particular things was a form of ritual that taught the Israelites what it meant to be set apart as a holy people, to be different from those around them, and to be sanctified by God. Douglas rightly argues,

---

[6] This is despite arguments that Lev 11:43–45 belong to the Holiness stratum. Cf. Milgrom, *Leviticus 1–16*, 13–14, 696; Walter Houston, *Purity and Monotheism: Clean and Unclean Animals in Biblical Law* (Sheffield: Sheffield Academic Press, 1993), 248; Knohl, *The Sanctuary of Silence*, 69.
[7] Cf. Feder, *Purity and Pollution*, 131–44.
[8] Wenham, *Leviticus*, 170.

"the dietary laws would have been like signs which at every turn inspired meditation on the oneness, purity and completeness of God. By rules of avoidance holiness was given a physical expression in every encounter with the animal kingdom and at every meal."[9] Every time the Israelites sat around the table to eat, or made offerings at the altar, they were reminded of their covenant with God and their call to be a holy people.

The symbolic interpretation of the dietary laws is found as early as *The Letter of Aristeas* (ca. 150 BCE). The author contends that the natural divisions seen in food restrictions were given by Moses "for the sake of righteousness to aid the quest for virtue and the perfecting of character" (*Aristeas*, 144). Each law demonstrates an example of wisdom that teaches Israel how to live. The author writes of cultivating a spirit of nonviolence by not eating birds of prey that terrorize other creatures and thus eating defiled blood. Instead, one should eat of the prescribed birds who feed on grains and live peaceably (*Aristeas*, 145–48). Therefore, the moral and ethical behavior of a creature somehow influences the person who consumes it and those traits may become part of that person's life. Israel can only remain holy if they eat those creatures that reflect the holiness found in the natural order of God's creation.[10]

---

[9] Douglas, *Purity and Danger*, 58.
[10] A similar type of interpretation can be found in Philo who argues that fish with fins and scales symbolize endurance and self-control like the soul that is devoted to perseverance and temperance (*Spec. Leg.* 4:110–12). Philo also identified the blood of the creature with its *psyche*, a semi-material substance given to an animal by God, which was the same way God breathed his divine spirit into human beings (Gen 2:7, 12). Thus, the blood of an animal should be given back to God as his possession. Cf. Walter Houston, "Towards an Integrated Reading of the Dietary Laws of Leviticus," in *The Book of Leviticus: Composition and Reception*, ed. Rolf Rendtorff, Robert Kugler, and Sarah Smith Bartel (Leiden: Brill, 2003), 142–61 (146–47).

Following early rabbinic interpretations, Milgrom contends that dietary laws enforce ideas of social justice and form an ethical system.[11] At the forefront of the system is the foundational idea that the life is in the blood and that humanity is prohibited from handling it improperly. Milgrom argues, "The human being must never lose sight of the fundamental tenet for a viable human society. Life is inviolable; it may not be treated lightly. Mankind has a right to nourishment, not to life. Hence the blood, the symbol of life, must be drained, returned to the universe, to God."[12] From this principle, Milgrom contends that humanity has a moral/ethical responsibility in how it treats creation because they are to mirror the justice and compassion of the creator. Dietary laws were, therefore, a way to instill in God's people a reverence for life and their place within the order of creation by limiting the number of animals for consumption, not partaking of their blood, and requiring that slaughter take place only at the altar.[13]

The noted anthropologist Mary Douglas offered her initial understanding of the dietary laws in her classic work *Purity and Danger*, which she expanded on in later writings. Douglas contends that the classification of animals in the dietary laws reflect the organization of social and religious life in Israel. She identifies

---

[11] Milgrom, *Leviticus 1–16*, 704–42. Cf. David P. Wright, "Observations on the Ethical Foundations of the Biblical Dietary Laws," in *Religion and Law: Biblical-Judaic and Islamic Perspectives*, ed. Edwin Brown Firmage, Bernard G. Weiss, John Woodland Welch (Winona Lake, IN: Eisenbrauns, 1990), 193–98.

[12] Milgrom, *Leviticus 1–16*, 713.

[13] Jacob Milgrom, *Studies in Cultic Terminology and Theology*, SJLA 36 (Leiden: Brill, 1983), 104–18; cf. E. B. Firmage, "The Biblical Dietary Laws and the Concept of Holiness," in *Studies in the Pentateuch*, ed. J. A. Emerton, VTSup 41 (Leiden: Brill, 1990), 177–208.

a tripartite division between creatures that inhabit the air, land, and water. Unclean animals for Israel are those that act unnaturally within their specific classifications. Within this interpretative framework, Douglas contends that a creature's natural means of movement is one measure of whether something is clean or unclean. For example, in the spheres of air, land, and water, the natural movement is to fly, walk, and swim. Creatures that "walk" in the water (Lev 11:10-12) cross a natural boundary and so must not be eaten unlike fish with fins and scales that swim naturally in water and are permitted to be eaten.[14] Within these categories unclean animals symbolize imperfection and a movement toward disorder or chaos, whereas clean animals signify wholeness, purity, and completeness.

Like Milgrom, Douglas also found ethical overtones in the dietary laws. She later argued that one of the main issues in dietary regulations had to do with the predatory nature of certain animals.[15] In the priestly vision of Genesis 1, the order of creation was originally vegetarian (Gen 1:29-30) where there was peace in the animal kingdom. This is the eschatological vision of Isaiah for a future time of restoration when carnivores and herbivores will lie down together (Isa 11:6-7). Douglas contends that the justice and righteousness of Yhwh permeate both the covenant and creation. To care for the poor and vulnerable are central tenets of the law. This is reflected in prohibitions against eating vulnerable species because they represent victims of other predators.[16] She concludes that holiness and

---

[14] Douglas, *Purity and Danger*, 56-57.
[15] Mary Douglas, "The Forbidden Animals in Leviticus," *JSOT* 59 (1993): 3-23.
[16] Douglas, "The Forbidden Animals in Leviticus," 22-23.

purity are incompatible with any creature that preys on the weak or has no means to defend itself.

In her later work, Douglas focuses on the dietary laws and creatures of abomination in relation to the covenant and what does or does not belong at God's table.[17] She understands Israel's relationship to their flocks as a parallel to their covenant with God. Animals that can be eaten are similar to those used in offerings and so we see a connection between the Israelite table and God's table. She argues that the table at home represents God's table in the tabernacle, all under the same laws of holiness. "Body for altar, altar for body, the rules which protect the purity of the tabernacle are paralleled by rules which protect the worshipper. What he can eat without contracting impurity and what can be offered to God in sacrifice are the same."[18]

Though Douglas' categories concerning clean and unclean animals at times lack consistency,[19] her interpretations concerning the systems underlying purity regulations have offered the most comprehensive and coherent approach to Israel's food laws. Other arguments suggest that Israel's dietary laws were established to distinguish themselves from Canaanite cultic practices. Some contend that food restrictions were concerned primarily with hygiene.[20] Though these approaches may account for some

---

[17] Douglas, *Leviticus as Literature*, 134–75.
[18] Douglas, *Leviticus as Literature*, 138–39; cf. Houston, *Purity and Monotheism*, 114–20, 230–34. The only exceptions to this statement are things that are not offered at Yhwh's altar but can be eaten such as fish, other types of birds, and other mammals. See also Brent A. Strawn, "The X-Factor: Revisioning Biblical Holiness," *ATJ* 54 (1999): 73–92.
[19] Houston, "Towards an Integrated Reading of the Dietary Laws of Leviticus," 150–57.
[20] See Roland K. Harrison, *Leviticus* (Downers Grove, IL: Intervarsity Press, 1980), 121–26.

possible prohibitions, they fail to offer a comprehensive framework regarding dietary laws.[21]

Having discussed different theories regarding Israel's categorization of unclean animals, we can now address why the priestly authors felt it necessary to divide different species into classes of pure and impure. Dietary restrictions are mentioned in Exod 22:31; Lev 11:44-45; 20:26; Deut 14:2, 21, which all point to Israel as a consecrated people. Holiness in the theology of Leviticus extends to every aspect of life. The act of eating, the most basic of human needs, becomes an act of worship for Israel in their covenant with Yhwh. The created world has not changed, but Israel has changed in their relationship to God. Apart from global prohibitions on blood, the patriarchs had no dietary restrictions even though they were under the covenant promise.[22] The most important difference with the advent of the Mosaic covenant is that God's permanent presence now resides in the tabernacle. Yhwh's holiness made manifest on earth precipitates the need for a distinction between what is "clean" and "unclean." In the light of holiness, then, certain parts of God's good creation become unfit for those in proximity to his divine presence. Milgrom contends that unclean animals act as "forces of death,"[23] and though this is true in relation to the sanctuary, it does not mean that God suddenly despises the beauty of his created order. Certain animals, insects, or birds are not inherently evil even though English translations of some creatures as "detestable, abomination" (šeqeṣ)

---

[21] Cf. Wenham, *Leviticus*, 166-71.
[22] The only other specific prohibitions in Genesis are the fruit tree in the Garden of Eden (Gen 2:17) and the sinew of the thigh associated with Jacob's injury when wrestling at the ford of the Jabbok (Gen 32:33).
[23] Milgrom, *Leviticus 1-16*, 733.

makes it seem like they are. How can those parts of creation deemed "good" by God suddenly become an abomination?

Any interpretation must consider divine order in creation and the particular relationship Yhwh has established with Israel since his manifestation in the tabernacle. If the abiding presence of holiness causes a reordering and reclassification in the world, then new regulations are required for how one draws near to that holiness and maintains the purity and sanctity of God's holy abode. Those creatures classified as "detestable" for Israel's diet are still part of God's good creation, but they are banned from consumption because their particular characteristics will cause uncleanness to be present in Yhwh's tabernacle. The use of the noun *šeqeṣ* is almost exclusive to Leviticus 11 and might be more accurately translated with the sense of "you shall completely ban" or "you shall completely reject" consuming these specific creatures.[24] The description is not a commentary on the creatures themselves but, rather, on their uncleanness in relation to the Israelites and to the tabernacle.[25]

---

[24] Douglas, *Leviticus as Literature*, 166–69. Douglas contends that the commands demonstrate God's protection for the "detestable" water and swarming creatures because of their vulnerability and potential for fertility. She argues that these cannot be sacrificed on the altar and thus cannot be eaten, but this does not account for fish that can be eaten and not sacrificed. The fact that they have fins and scales does not make them any less vulnerable as prey. Nicole Ruane, *Sacrifice and Gender in Biblical Law* (Cambridge: Cambridge University Press, 2013), 226, however, argues that swarming creatures represent an uncontrolled chaos and not the potential for fertility. She contends that fertility is a neutral concept in the Old Testament and that it is "controlled and optimal" fertility that is considered a blessing. Cf. Nicole Ruane, "Pigs, Purity, and Patrilineality: The Multiparity of Swine and Its Problems for Biblical Ritual and Gender Construction" *JBL* 134 (2015): 489–504.

[25] Cf. *Wisdom of Solomon* 11:24. "For you love all things that exist, and detest none of the things that you have made, for you would not have made anything if you had hated it."

The reason for the legislation is summed up in Lev 11:43–45. Israel must not become "detestable" by eating anything unclean lest they become defiled. Houston argues that verbal form š-q-ṣ ("detest, abhor") is being used in a deprecatory manner, but this misunderstands the context of the command.[26] The noun šeqeṣ is found nine times in Leviticus with the only other two occurrences in the prophets (Isa 66:7; Ezek 8:10) and in no instance is the term used pejoratively. Instead, šeqeṣ is used to describe an unclean creature that cannot be touched or consumed by the Israelites. The description does not express contempt or disdain for certain parts of God's creation but, rather, it expresses a new reality of holiness in the physical realms relating to one's proximity to Yhwh's dwelling. To be holy, and to draw near to his holiness, means that Israel must be obedient to his command. The restrictions around eating provide Israel with a paradigm that maps and classifies what can and cannot be used to satisfy their physical appetites if they are to be holy people. These classification are not a comment on the goodness of God's creation but, instead, they underscore that a holy people must not freely devour anything that God has brought into being. As God's chosen people, Israel should recognize their place within the wider ecology of creation and consume only those things that Yhwh allows.

As proposed by Douglas, the categories of clean and unclean creatures are, in part, based on how they function within their particular class. Sacrificial animals such as oxen, sheep, or goats function properly within their classification. They all have cloven hoofs and are ruminators that chew their cud. The distinction made with the camel, rock hyrax, and hare is that though they are ruminators (or look like ruminators), they do not have cloven

---

[26] Houston, "Towards an Integrated Reading," 155–56.

hoofs. They stand in contrast to their normal classification in their behavior and physical form and must not be eaten (Lev 11:4–8). In a similar manner, the pig is prohibited because though it has a cloven hoof, it does not chew the cud. The impermissibility placed on these animals means that they deviate from "normal" domesticated animals within their classification (ruminants) and so they were off limits to God's holy people.[27]

The same is true for creatures in the sea. If they naturally swim with fins and scales, then they are fine for consumption (Lev 11:9–12). This is the "natural" way to move through the waters, but the unnatural way was to walk and so scavengers and bottom-dwellers were unclean. In reference to particular birds that are banned from consumption (Lev 11:13–19), the reason is likely that they feed on dead animals and consume the blood with the flesh. Birds that act "naturally" within their class feed on grains or insects.

In the examples of things that "swarm" (*šereṣ*), Douglas holds to her categories of natural classifications and argues that insects and creatures that creep have no defined form of movement. Swarmers break classifications because they can travel in land, sea, and air. Douglas argues that they have no particular motion that identifies them with any one sphere and so they are considered unholy.[28] A similar case arises with locusts. Those that are considered clean are those that have legs to hop even though they have wings. Any locust that flies (like a bird) or crawls (like a swarmer) is unclean, but those that hop are fine. This may seem

---

[27] Milgrom, *Leviticus 1–16*, 727–28, notes six anomalous animals: the camel, hare, rock badger, pig, hippopotamus, and the llama. He contends that the criteria for the classifications came first and then after the anomalies were found.

[28] Douglas, *Purity and Danger*, 57.

like a strange rule to readers today but within a possible ancient understanding of natural movement and classification within the created order, it begins to make sense within the symbolic world of Leviticus.

The dietary laws of Leviticus 11 are not meant to provide a comprehensive list of what can or cannot be eaten. Like other biblical laws, the prohibitions on certain foods are meant to be paradigmatic. There was no need for the priestly authors to list every unclean food because they were offering a model for eating based on natural patterns revealed in creation. These commandments were not merely examples of "detailed casuistry" as Rainer Albertz suggests but, rather, they offered the Israelites a paradigm that linked everyday acts of eating with covenant faithfulness and the pursuit of holiness.[29] Reverence for Yhwh's creation through obedience expressed in one's diet was a constant reminder of what it meant to be a holy people and how one lived within the wider ecology of creation.

When considering the dietary laws, it is also important to recall that the ancient Israelite diet was not as expansive as many cultures enjoy today. Subsistence farming meant that eating meat was a rare occurrence for the average person. Livestock was mainly used for heavy labor and would not have been as common on small farms due to their significant consumption of water and pasturage. Boer argues that in smaller villages sheep and goats would have been the primary domesticated animals because they required fewer resources.[30] They could be culled at an early age

---

[29] Rainer Albertz, *A History of Israelite Religion in the Old Testament Period*, trans. John Bowden (London: SCM, 1994), 408.
[30] Roland Boer, *The Sacred Economy of Ancient Israel* (Louisville: Westminster John Knox, 2015), 60–64.

and used for their meat and skins. This means that the main sources of nourishment were fruits, grains, and dairy products, which are virtually absent from the dietary laws.[31] Meat from domesticated animals was a rare meal that was served only on special occasions or to show hospitality.[32] Instead, the Israelites likely lived on the "Mediterranean triad" of grain, wine, and olive oil with the bulk of their calories coming from bread or grain-based foods such as porridge.[33]

Dietary restrictions, however, also influenced the social structures associated with food, family, and the animal kingdom. In most instances, domestic animals were considered part of the larger household in ancient Israel where animals lived in close proximity to the family and could often outnumber family members.[34] The fact that the biblical laws address both men and women who commit sexual acts with domestic beasts (Exod 22:19; Lev 18:23; 20:15–16; Deut 27:21) is possibly an indication of what went on inside the privacy of the home.

The theology of Leviticus expresses an intimate bond between spirituality, covenant fidelity, and the act of eating. Israel's relationship to the land and the animals they keep are symbolic of their relationship to Yhwh. What they eat is a sign of how they care for one another and how they tend to the land and animals

---

[31] Cf. Carol Meyers, "Having Their Space and Eating There Too: Bread Production and Female Power in Ancient Israelite Households," *Nashim* 5 (2002): 14–44 (22).

[32] Cynthia Shafe-Elliott, *Food in Ancient Judah: Domestic Cooking in the Time of the Hebrew Bible* (Sheffield: Equinox, 2013), 21–22. Cf. Nathan MacDonald, *Not Bread Alone: The Uses of Food in the Old Testament* (Oxford: Oxford University Press, 2008), 47–69.

[33] MacDonald, *Not Bread Alone*, 61–62.

[34] Boer, *The Sacred Economy*, 90–94.

that have been placed under their care. If all good things come from God, then the theology of Leviticus conveys the humility and gratitude with which Israel should receive those gifts. Ignoring the commands is tantamount to idolatry as one turns the gift of food and daily dependence on God into the exertion of human power and will. To devour creation recklessly and without restraint is to reject God's word in order to satisfy one's appetite. As the first garden dwellers disobeyed the command and ate from the tree of knowledge (Gen 2:17), Israel is now given the chance to reverse the consequences of Eden and draw near to God in holiness by obedience through what they eat.

Natural appetites require all human beings to consume part of God's good creation in order to survive. How one disciplines those appetites is critical to a theology of holiness in Leviticus. The commands offer a framework for consumption that mirrors the holiness of Yhwh and the purity of his altar. This vision rejects the commoditization of animals or treating creation as anything less than a gift from God. Care and consideration must be displayed in how one lives and works for the well-being of the community and the natural world. Holiness requires Israel to act as a contributing member to the community of creation through responsible consumption. Eating is a necessity of life, but for Leviticus it is also a path to holiness.[35]

Some of the earliest followers of Christ largely abandoned Jewish dietary regulations as a result of the mission to the gentiles. All foods were declared clean by Christ (Mark 7:19) but the prohibition against eating blood with meat was retained

---

[35] See Ellen Davis, "Identity and Eating: A Christian Reading of Leviticus," *Studies in Christian Ethics* 30 (2017): 3–14.

(Acts 15:29).[36] St. Paul offered detailed instructions to the churches in Corinth regarding meat sacrificed to idols in the marketplace (1 Corinthians 8–10) and concluded that all meat was edible by quoting Ps 24:1, "the earth and its fullness are the Lord's" (1 Cor 10:26). He goes on to say that "whether you eat or drink, or whatever you do, do everything for the glory of God" (1 Cor 10:31). The apostle was concerned with breaking down barriers between Jew and gentile to be united in Christ (Eph 2:11–22) especially when it came to dietary restrictions.

Much of our contemporary meat consumption, however, might be judged by first-century Christians and Jews as a violation of Levitical principles. Today the production of meat, fish, and poultry is treated as business based on profitability and commoditization. Animals are bred not in their natural habitats and ecosystems but unnaturally with growth-inducing hormones, antibiotics, and artificial light. Industrialism in the Western world has been characterized by a willingness to ignore anything that does not lead to cheap production and profit gains. Wendell Berry laments that modern Christianity has "stood silently by, while a predatory economy has ravaged the world, destroyed its natural beauty and health, divided and plundered its human communities and households."[37] This commoditization of God's world stands in

---

[36] There is an alternative argument that Jews who followed Christ continued to maintain the food restrictions of Leviticus and that Jesus' contention here is against the Pharisee's notion that food becomes unclean if touched by unwashed hands. See David J. Rudolph, "Jesus and the Food Laws: A Reassessment of Mark 7:19b," *EQ* 74 (2002): 291–311; Richard Bauckham, ed. "James and the Jerusalem Church," in *The Book of Acts in Its Palestinian Setting* (Grand Rapids, MI: Eerdmans 1995), 415–80.

[37] Wendell Berry, "Christianity and the Survival of Creation," *Cross Currents* 43 (1993): 149–63 (162). Cf. Wirzba, *Food and Faith*, 71–109.

stark antithesis to the vision of Leviticus that views all life as a sacred gift to be treated with wisdom, justice, and righteousness.

Holiness in Leviticus is incompatible with human exploitation of creation. Holiness requires the daily preservation of life and not its destruction for humanity's benefit. Holiness seeks the increase of fertility in the world not for excessive consumption but to allow creation to flourish in abundance. To be holy is to sustain, to bless, to bring forth life, and to cause all creation to flourish. Berry sums this up when he writes, "The Bible leaves no doubt at all about the sanctity of the act of world-making, or of the world that was made, or of creaturely or bodily life in this world. We are holy creatures living among other holy creatures in a world that is holy."[38]

The dietary laws of Leviticus are interwoven with the moral/ethical code for holy living where concepts of justice and righteousness are connected to the food we eat. The priestly theology of Leviticus expresses a wholistic idea of holiness where all life is sacred and treated as a gift from God. Norman Wirzba writes of this agrarian approach to life and faith. "The divine command to serve and protect the sources of life, first given to Adam in the Garden of Eden, has not been eclipsed. It cannot ever be eclipsed, because care and celebration of each other and our places is our most blessed way of participating in the nourishing, sustaining, and healing love of an agrarian God."[39]

Many modern Jews continue to practice *kashrut*, or a kosher diet, today despite the fact that there is no longer a temple or

---

[38] Berry, "Christianity and the Survival of Creation," 152. On the issue of genetically modified crops, see Davis, *Scripture, Culture, and Agriculture*, 87–88, 90.

[39] Norman Wirzba, *Agrarian Spirit: Cultivating Faith, Community, and the Land* (Notre Dame, IN: University of Notre Dame Press, 2022), 29.

animal sacrifices. Food restrictions remain an important identity marker for Jews and continue to act as a guide to holiness and how one lives ethically and responsibly within the world. Though dietary laws were abandoned by the Christian church, the Levitical commands still offer an analogical model for how one lives and what one consumes within the community of creation.

PURIFICATION AND CHILDBIRTH

The purity laws of Leviticus 12–15 shift the focus from what goes into our bodies to what comes out of our bodies. Infectious diseases, childbirth, menstruation, and other processes cause bodily discharges. For the priestly authors of Leviticus, these natural physical occurrences are intimately connected to the holiness of the sanctuary. Leviticus offers no clear explanations regarding how these things are interconnected, but the range of possibilities for contamination and purification are given in varying detail.

With the purity laws, we find that contamination often varies in intensity. Any impurity within the camp must be cleansed for fear that it will ultimately contaminate the tabernacle. Milgrom separates the purity laws according to their contagion factor, type of impurity, relevant purification rituals, and the holiness of the sanctuary.[40] Contamination levels can reach critical status if not addressed appropriately through sacrifices and purification rites. In theory, if impurities are not addressed in the camp, a point could be reached where the purification of the sanctuary is no longer possible and preservation of Yhwh's presence would be impossible.

---

[40] Milgrom, *Leviticus 1–16*, 984–85.

There is still some ambiguity, however, regarding contamination and its exact relationship to the areas of the sanctuary. In the case of Nadab and Abihu, we find disobedience and "strange fire" purged by God's holiness in the form of his fire from heaven (Lev 10:1-3). In this instance, any potential threat of contamination is immediately destroyed by Yhwh himself. Aaron and his other sons then eat the grain offering at Moses' command but are chastised for failing to eat the meat of the purification offering (Lev 10:16-20). The sense of the passage is not that specific atonement needs to be made for Nadab and Abihu's transgressions in the holy space but, rather, the general purification offerings must be completed even though Aaron fails to do so properly because of his fear (Lev 10:19-20). This particular narrative highlights the fact that not all contamination affects the tabernacle. In some instances, we see that the purifying power of Yhwh's holiness can directly destroy the threat of contamination or the forces of death that lie behind, or within, them.

In Leviticus 12, however, the possible threat for contamination of the holy space is related to the most natural of event of childbirth. The brief chapter describes the ritual practices a woman must go through before she is fit to draw near the tabernacle after giving birth. The command that she "not touch anything holy, nor come in the sanctuary" (Lev 12:4) assumes that women participated in sacrificial rites. In the Second Temple period, Jewish women would be isolated in their own court away from the males; but within the priestly theology of Leviticus, the altar is open to all who are ritually clean, male or female. Though service in the holy courts and at the altar were reserved for Aaron and his sons, men and women of Israel were equally called to draw near to Yhwh with sacrifices for worship.

The process of purification after parturition is explained clearly. If a woman gives birth to a male child, she is ritually unclean for seven days and should have the child circumcised on the eighth day. Then she continues her time of purification for thirty-three days. If she bears a female child, the days of impurity/purification double so that she is unclean for fourteen days and goes through her purification for sixty-six days (Lev 12:1-5). When the purification period is complete, she can return to the sanctuary to offer a lamb for her atonement or two turtle doves or pigeons if she cannot afford a lamb (vv. 6-8). The command is straightforward but since this is the only place in the Old Testament that prescribes specific rites around childbirth and female purification, there are several questions that might be raised.

Scholars have approached the text through anthropological comparisons, ancient Near Eastern literary parallels, and feminist readings.[41] Milgrom provides a detailed summary of both ancient and modern cultures that offer diverse ritual approaches to parturition. He concludes that the wide range of traditions indicate that ancient Israel shares in a universal response to the mystery of childbirth that exists deep in the human psyche.[42] Balentine rightly notes that we cannot consider the Levitical prescriptions overly burdensome or unreasonable for menstruants and parturients but,

---

[41] See, e.g., Kristin De Troyer, Judith A. Herbert, Judith Ann Johnson, and Anne-Marie Korte, eds., *Wholly Woman, Holy Blood: A Feminist Critique of Purity and Impurity* (Harrisburg: Trinity Press International, 2003); Tarja S. Philip, *Menstruation and Childbirth in the Bible: Fertility and Impurity* (New York: Lang, 2006); Elizabeth W. Goldstein, *Impurity and Gender in the Hebrew Bible* (Lanham, MD: Rowman & Littlefield, 2015); Jonathan Klawans, *Impurity and Sin in Ancient Judaism* (Oxford; New York: Oxford University Press, 2000), 41-42.

[42] Milgrom, *Leviticus 1-16*, 763-65. For parallel Hittite rituals, see Gary Beckman, *Hittite Birth Rituals*, StBoT 29 (Wiesbaden: Harrassowitz, 1983).

rather, these laws demonstrate the priestly desire for all critical aspects of life to come under the holy prescriptions of Yhwh.[43] Rather than being seen as means of diminishing a woman's status within the covenant community, these prescriptions highlight the power of the feminine in relation to the holiness of the sanctuary. The discharge of blood and the ability to create human life are not an indication of a woman's inferior status. Instead, the female capacity to bring life into the world is reverenced by the authors of Leviticus, which is demonstrated by the very fact that women are given their own purification requirements.

The process and time of purification for male and female children might also be seen as a devaluation of women (cf. Lev 27:2–7). The sixty-six days, however, need not be interpreted as diminishing female worth but could have been additional protection for the vulnerable mother and daughter. This may have been because postnatal discharge was longer after the birth of a girl or because that girl will also grow up to be a menstruant. There was also an ancient belief that the female embryo takes longer to form than the male and thus requires a longer purification period.[44] It is unlikely that the inferiority of a daughter is being expressed in the command because the length of time for purification within Leviticus does not reflect a person's moral or ethical status before God. It may have been that the healing of the woman's body was the concern. It is also possible that a female child, who is endowed with the capacity to create life from the womb as a reflection of divine creativity, needs double the time to be purified. A woman bringing a female child into the world could have been seen as an event so charged with the life/death associated with parturition that extra time was needed before approaching God's holiness.

---

[43] Balentine, *Leviticus*, 102.
[44] Milgrom, *Leviticus 1–16*, 750.

It is important to recall that a woman's cultic impurity has nothing to do with her ethical behavior.[45] She enters a state of uncleanness as a natural part of life as she participates in the blessings of fertility given by Yhwh (cf. Psalm 128). The text alludes to this by the unusual use of the Hiphil form of the root z-r-ʿ ("sow") in Lev 12:2 (NRSV translates "conceives"). The only other occurrences of the verb in the Hiphil are in Gen 1:11–12 in reference to the fruit-bearing trees and seed-bearing grasses. Females "bear seed" or bring forth new life as part of their unique role within creation even if that process renders a woman ritually unclean for a certain time.

Other linguistic features of the text on purification for parturition occur only in Leviticus. Verse 4 speaks of the time of the woman's "blood purification" (*bidmê ṭahŏrâ*) and her "days of purification" (*yəmê ṭohŏrāh*). Translations vary in their rendering of the first phrase as "the blood of her purifying" (RSV, ESV), "purified from her bleeding" (NIV), or "a state of blood purification" (JPS). The literal sense is that the woman will remain "in the blood" that will cause her to become pure.

The common cycles that occur after childbirth are three stages of lochia, or blood discharge (rubra, serosa, and alba). The initial stages are marked by a heavier flow of dark brown and red discharge, which moves toward darker brown with lighter pink blood and ends with a paler, creamy white blood loss.[46] The process indicates a natural purification of the body, which may have been taken into account by the priests since the parturient is not instructed to perform any ceremonial washing before she

---

[45] See Klawans, *Impurity and Sin in Ancient Judaism*, 22–26.
[46] S. Tamar Kamionkowski, *Leviticus*, Wisdom Commentary Series (Collegeville, MN: Liturgical Press, 2002), 108–11.

presents her offering at the altar, which is somewhat strange considering that males are always prescribed to wash after an impurity.[47] After she presents her purification offering, the priest makes atonement for her and she is made clean (Lev 12:8). The atoning sacrifice is not for the forgiveness of moral sin but for the cleansing of ritual uncleanness so that the woman is brought back into full relationship with Yhwh and the covenant community.[48]

Purity regulations around childbirth are likely to seem archaic to the modern reader, but Christians throughout the centuries have used Leviticus 12 to shape doctrines and rituals in the church. In an effort to understand how the impurity of childbirth in ancient Israel related to the Christian church, Origen argued that all childbirth in the flesh is marked by sin and results in impurity (*Homilies* 8).[49] He interprets the purification offering prescribed in Lev 12:6-7 as a propitiation for the parturient's sin and appeals to other biblical texts like Job and Jeremiah cursing the days of their birth or the psalmist lamenting that they were conceived in sin (Ps 50:7). Augustine argued that the sin associated with childbirth (and sex) was linked to original sin and proved the need for infant baptism. He also contended that there was no sexual sin associated with Mary's conception of Christ and so the virgin birth required no purification even though Mary, according to the law, made her offerings at the temple (Luke 2:22-24). Ambrose, who also extolled virginity and sexual purity,

---

[47] Cf. Milgrom, *Leviticus 1-16*, 756-57.
[48] Dorothea Erbele-Küster, *Body Gender Purity in Leviticus 12 and 15*, LHBOTS 539 (London: T & T Clark, 2017), 117-37.
[49] For medieval Jewish links between childbirth and original sin, see Alan Cooper, "A Medieval Jewish Version of Original Sin: R. Ephraim of Luntshitz on Leviticus 12," *HTR* 97 (2004): 445-59.

built his doctrine of impurity and childbirth around the Levitical prohibitions against the unnatural mixing of different kinds, which he applied to the joining of male and female in intercourse.[50]

These types of doctrines influenced rituals in the Roman Catholic Church that performed a similar ritual of washing and purification for women after childbirth. During the medieval period, rites of purification were to cleanse the woman of sin and every impurity of the heart as well as the sexual sin associated with the conception of the child in line with the doctrines of Augustine and Ambrose. Some rituals required washings and being sprinkled with holy water by the priest.[51] In 1614, the church adopted the rite of the "churching of women after childbirth," which shifted the language of purification from sin to joyful celebration. The postpartum woman would wait at the entrance of the church with a lighted candle and would be met by the priest who sprinkled her with holy water while reciting Psalm 24. He would then extend the left end of his stole to lead her into the church.[52] A similar rite is retained in the Anglican 1662 Book of Common Prayer with the additional title "The Thanksgiving of Women After Childbirth." The woman enters the church on her own "decently appareled" and is met by the priest who recites a psalm (116 or 127), which is followed by a prayer and the

---

[50] Peter Brown, *Body and Society: Men, Women, and Sexual Renunciation in Early Christianity* (New York: Columbia University Press, 1988), 351–55.

[51] Paula M. Reider, *On the Purification of Women: Churching in Northern France 1100–1500* (New York: Palgrave Macmillan, 2006), 61–80, 105–21.

[52] Susan K. Roll, "The Old Rite of the Churching of Women after Childbirth," in *Wholly Woman, Holy Blood: A Feminist Critique of Purity and Impurity*, ed. Kristin De Troyer, Judith A. Herbert, Judith Ann Johnson, and Anne-Marie Korte (Harrisburg: Trinity Press International, 2003), 117–41.

"accustomed offerings" made by the woman. The Protestant rite clearly moves away from the purification of sin but maintains the Levitical prescription of the new mother making offerings to God after giving birth.

PURIFICATION, SKIN DISEASE, AND BODILY DISCHARGE

Leviticus 13–15 deal with external signs of uncleanness that are potentially contagious and could bring disaster upon the whole community. These outward signs are called ṣāraʿat ("skin disease"), which is a general term for any kind of skin disfiguration that can be healed and is not to be confused with a reference to modern leprosy (Hansen's disease). The common English translation "leprosy" is derived from the LXX rendering of the Hebrew as lepra ("skin disease"). These types of skin diseases were thought to be transmittable, so it was necessary to isolate those infected from the rest of the community. They were likely some form of psoriasis or fungal infections that included discoloration and peeling or flaking of the skin.[53]

Contagious diseases and the need to isolate the sick were not uncommon occurrences in the ancient world. Communications from Mari in the eighteenth century BCE tell of epidemics that required the quarantine of particular areas. "The god is striking in the upper district ... my lord should give orders that inhabitants

---

[53] E. V. Hulse, "The Nature of the Biblical 'Leprosy' and the Use of Alternative Medical Terms in Modern Translations of the Bible," *PEQ* 107 (1975): 87–105. NRSV, ESV, NASB, NKJV, JPS, all translate "leprous/leprosy". For the language used around skin disease see Yitzhaq Feder, *Purity and Pollution in the Hebrew Bible* (Cambridge: Cambridge University Press, 2022), 59–106.

of the towns, as soon as they have been touched, must not enter into untouched towns. (Otherwise,) it could well happen that they infect ('strike') the whole country."⁵⁴ The language of the god "touching" or "striking" people with disease in the Mari text was a sign of divine punishment. This anthropomorphism may have influenced the Hebrew phrase *lənega' ṣāra'at*, which can be translated literally as "to touch/strike with skin disease." In addition to the physical suffering of the disease, the Hebrew likely alludes to the fact that the person has somehow been cursed by God, which is a common motif throughout the Old Testament. Though Leviticus does not expressly state such a theology, the consequence of being cut off, alone, and living "outside the camp" (Lev 13:46) reflects a death-like state in relation to the life and blessing of being in the covenant community.⁵⁵

The structure of the chapters is neatly divided into three sections. The first deals with serious skin diseases, how they are diagnosed by the priests, and the appropriate treatment (Lev 13:1–59). The last portion is concerned with fabrics that have become infected and how to treat them. The second section prescribes the ritual cleansings necessary after a skin disease has been cured (Lev 14:1–32); and the third section addresses how to

---

[54] Walther Farber, "How to Marry a Disease: Epidemics, Contagion, and a Magic Ritual against the 'Hand of a Ghost,'" in *Magic and Rationality in Ancient Near Eastern and Greco-Roman Medicine*, ed. Herman F. J. Horstmanshoff and Marten Stol (Leiden: Brill, 2004), 119–20, n. 21.

[55] Direct divine infliction of skin disease is more clearly represented in Miriam's hand turning white (Num 12:10), Job's skin outbreak (Job 2:7; 7:5), Gehazi's punishment (2 Kgs 5:27), and king Azariah (2 Kings 15:5) and king Uzziah's being struck with skin disease (2 Chron 26:19). Outside of Israel, only Naaman the Syrian (2 Kgs 5) is said to have had *ṣāra'at*, which did not prevent him from functioning as a successful military general as a gentile.

deal with this infectious disease when it has contaminated houses (Lev 14:33-57).[56] The lengthy legislation indicates the importance of maintaining the physical purity of the camp and preventing any infectious disease from spreading or coming into contact with the tabernacle. Why skin diseases are specifically identified in Leviticus, and not other types of infection, may be due to the prevalence of these diseases in ancient Israel or possibly because of the visible signs of this particular contagion. Whatever the reason, the detailed commandments offer the most explicit and extensive instructions in the Old Testament on how Israel should treat infectious disease.

What the prescriptions regarding skin disease and infection reveal is Leviticus' theology of purity and place where an inseparable physical and metaphysical link exists between Yhwh's tent/tabernacle and Israel's tents. The necessity for the purification of the people in the home reflects the purity of the priests who serve in the sanctuary. The fabrics of the home must be pure because they parallel the fabrics of the tabernacle. The stones of the Canaanite dwellings that Israel will inherit in the land must be cleansed (Lev 13:34-53) because they reflect the future stones of Yhwh's temple. Whether tent or stones, the Israelite home must be cleansed and purified if they are to dwell in the holy land and live in proximity to Yhwh's holiness.

The language describing diseases as "impure" (*ṭāmē'*) also indicates that physical infection is directly linked to the purity of the tabernacle. Suffering from skin ailments was a sign of ritual impurity that needed to be cleansed before the afflicted could become "pure" (*ṭāhôr*). All aspects of life are somehow connected to the purity and holiness of God's people in relation to his holy

---

[56] See Wenham, *Leviticus*, 193-94, for further possible divisions.

abode in Leviticus. The priest's role in distinguishing "between the clean and the unclean" (Lev 10:10) was not restricted to those things that took place within the tabernacle. They were also in charge of discerning how physical diseases could potentially defile the wider community.

In these chapters, Leviticus presents the priestly role as physician. This is not in the sense of curing the sick but being responsible for diagnosing and restoring those who have been healed. The priests are the only authorized power in Leviticus to welcome or exclude people from the covenant community. This adds a significant level of social power to the priestly role over those with infectious diseases as he becomes the "the priest who cleanses" or more literally, "the priest, the purifier" (Lev 14:11).

Physical decay and disease were outward signs of the forces of death that could not come into contact with the purity and life of the tabernacle. In some instances, the carriers of contagion threatened the whole community and needed to be separated until restored. The priests in Leviticus were authorized to make decisions among the Israelites, even in medical and ritual diagnoses, to ensure that holiness was preserved among the people. The details of Leviticus 11–15 reveal the symbols and beliefs of a culture that was aware of the destructive forces of death and disease that could penetrate and destroy the community of faith.

The purity laws of Leviticus 11–15 are a remarkable collection of rules that offer further insights into the world of ancient Israel and their theological beliefs in relation to impurity in everyday life and its connection to the tabernacle. Separation, washings, and time are prescribed for anyone/anything that needs to be purified and given permission to come back into Yhwh's presence. Though at times the purity laws may be viewed as exclusionary, they were also for the physical protection of the people. We are reminded of the fear that comes with infectious disease after the Covid-19 global pandemic. Most countries experienced complete lockdowns despite the technological and medical advances society enjoys today. We can imagine the anxiety of an ancient people without vaccines or medicines in the face of contagious diseases. This might help us begin to understand some of the purity laws in Leviticus and develop a further appreciation of how an ancient people placed such great emphasis on cleanness when approaching the divine.

CHAPTER 4

Inhabiting Sacred Space (Leviticus 8–10, 24–27)

A PRIESTLY THEOLOGY OF SPACE: THE TABERNACLE

The tabernacle is the center of all life in Leviticus and contains a divine potency that could be likened to a nuclear power plant. To maintain the site safely, the ordering and delineation of space is critical. This is reflected in the grades of holiness that can be seen most clearly in the instructions for the tabernacle given by God to Moses (Exodus 25–31, 35–40). The detailed blueprint for the sanctuary reflects a microcosm of the broader cosmic order established in creation. George argues that the descriptions found in the tabernacle instructions, "express a social configuration and Priestly understanding of Israelite society, social organization, and Israel's role in the divine creation."[1] Thus, the tabernacle becomes the key physical space through which Israel relates to God, to one another, and to the world. The ordering of space for worship provides an archetypal pattern for the social order of Israel, their homes, and all of humanity.[2]

---

[1] Mark K. George, *Israel's Tabernacle as Social Space*, SBL Ancient Israel and Its Literature 2 (Atlanta: SBL Press, 2009), 8.

[2] There is not space to offer a detailed description of the tabernacle and its elements here. For a description of its construction, see Scarlata, *The Abiding Presence*, 185–209.

The links between the tabernacle and the priestly account of creation have been noted by scholars.[3] Eliade contends that every plan for temple building "has the cosmogony as paradigmatic model. The creation of the world becomes the archetype of every creative human gesture, whatever its plane of reference may be."[4] Israel is no different and the divine instructions provide a microcosm of the universe where the heavenly throne of God is the source of all holiness that radiates outward. The concentric zones of holiness move from the heavens creating various degrees of holiness based on proximity to the divine presence. The zones of the tabernacle follow a similar pattern by reflecting different "grades" of holiness in its division as well as in the objects and people who occupy the space.[5]

Later Jewish interpreters as early as Josephus saw similar patterns in the tabernacle. He argues that the threefold division of space represents the waters, the earth, and the heavens and that the seven-branched candle signifies the division of the planets.

---

[3] Joseph Blenkinsopp, "The Structure of P," *CBQ* 38 (1976): 275–92; Jon D. Levenson, "The Temple and the World," *The Journal of Religion* 64: 275–98; Jon D. Levenson, *Creation and the Persistence of Evil: The Jewish Drama of Divine Omnipotence* (Princeton: Princeton University Press, 1994), 86; Dan Lioy, *Axis of Glory: A Biblical and Theological Analysis of the Temple Motif in Scripture*, SBL 138 (Oxford: Peter Lang, 2010), 5–15.

[4] Mircea Eliade, *The Sacred and the Profane: The Nature of Religion*, trans. Willard R. Trask (London: Harcourt, Brace, 1959), 45.

[5] Menahem Haran, *Temples and Temple-Service in Ancient Israel: An Inquiry into the Character of Cult Phenomena and the Historical Setting of the Priestly School* (Oxford: Clarendon, 1978), 172 n. 50. Concerning the material of the tabernacle see pp. 158–65, and for grades of access, see pp. 175–88. See also Philip Jenson, *Graded Holiness: A Key to the Priestly Conception of the World*, JSOTSS 106 (Sheffield: JSOT Press, 1992), 91–92. On graded material and access see pp. 101–9. For an argument against holiness as the organizing principle of the tabernacle, see George, *Israel's Tabernacle as Social Space*, 110–11.

The fabrics and materials used inside the tabernacle also symbolize the elements of soil, fire, water, and air (*Ant.* 3.179–87). The author of the epistle to the Hebrews (9:11) similarly sees the cosmology represented in the sanctuary referring to the earthly abode and its furnishings as "copies of the heavenly things" while arguing for the "greater and more perfect tabernacle" of the heavens that was "not made with human hands" (Heb 9:23).

Eden also represents the first sanctuary where God's presence was made fully manifest. In Gen 2:15, we hear resonances of the tabernacle in the command for the first garden dwellers to "till and keep it [the earth]." The Hebrew verbs for "till" (ʿ-b-d) and "keep" (š-m-r) can also be rendered with the sense of "service/worship" and "guard/protect." Similar language is often used to describe priests performing their duties in the sanctuary.[6] The sacerdotal responsibilities in the garden-sanctuary of Eden offer a type for the tabernacle/temple as the place of creation, abundance, life, and the fullness of God's presence.

Milgrom offers a detailed account of sacred space in the tabernacle and considers the whole site as holy while pointing out various distinctions between priestly and non-priestly space.[7] In the center is the most holy place that receives purgation yearly. This is the place where God's holiness radiates outward toward the priests, the people, and the land. The space of the tabernacle, arranged around his holiness, obligates Israel to be a holy people.

The divine court containing God's presence is called the "holy place" (*miqdāš*) (Exod 25:8; Lev 12:4), which refers to the entire

---

[6] Cf. Num 3:7–8; 8:25–26; 18:5–6; 1 Chron 23:32; Ezek 44:14; von Rad, *OTT* 1962: 241–42.
[7] Jacob Milgrom, "The Compass of Biblical Sancta," *JQR* 65 (1975): 205–16; Milgrom, *Leviticus 1–16*, 182–83, 392–95, 401–8.

compound of the tabernacle space.⁸ In Leviticus, however, the language used to demarcate the different areas of the tabernacle are not always consistent with other priestly descriptions. In chapter 16, the inner sanctuary, often called the "most holy place," is simply named "the holy place" (*haqqōdeš*) (Lev 16: 2, 3, 16, 17, 20, 23, 27), while the outer sanctuary is referred to as "the tent of meeting" (vv. 16, 17, 20, 23, 33). Milgrom attributes this to the priestly writers incorporating an earlier account but using different terminology.⁹ Hundley, however, contends that the priestly authors only employ two terms ("holy" and "most holy") to designate particular gradations of space and these are often used indiscriminately throughout. He argues that the priestly authors are concerned with separating the divine space according to a consistent hierarchy to stress privileged access and warning so that boundaries would not be transgressed.¹⁰

Eliade describes the power of sacred space and how humanity responds to encounters with the holy: "For religious man, space is not homogeneous; he experiences interruptions, breaks in it; some parts of space are qualitatively different from others .... There is, then, a sacred space, and hence a strong, significant space; there are other spaces that are not sacred and so are without structure or consistency, amorphous."¹¹ Eliade's emphasis on the real presence of the divine and its manifestation in a particular locale is important in understanding the distinction between sacred and profane space and how Leviticus presents Yhwh's holy abode.

---

[8] Milgrom, *Leviticus 1–16*, 754–55; Haran, *Temples and Temple Service*, 14–15.
[9] Milgrom, *Leviticus 1–16*, 408, 1013, 1063.
[10] Michael Hundley, "Sacred Spaces, Objects, Offerings and People," *JBL* 132 (2013): 749–67 (755–67); cf. Milgrom, *Leviticus 1–16*, 392.
[11] Eliade, *The Sacred and the Profane*, 20.

It is possible, however, that sacred space is not determined by the substantive divine presence in a particular place. Instead, as Smith argues, societies are the primary force in creating sacred spaces and ascribing them with religious significance.[12] Smith explores ancient Jewish and Christian understandings of sacred space and discusses the human initiative in mapping out holy sites according to social hierarchies. Using the example of Ezekiel's vision of the new temple, Smith contends that the organization of the temple from the Holy of Holies to the outer court of the gentiles represents the order of social classes from the priests who occupy interior holy spaces to the average Israelite and gentile who are separated from those spaces.[13] Smith's conclusion is that sacred spaces are holy only insofar as they are made holy by human beings. There is no substantive divine presence in any particular place except that which is constructed and established by society.

Though Smith makes important points regarding the social role in creating sacred spaces, he minimizes too significantly the real phenomena of human encounters with the divine and religious experience. In the ancient Near East, sacred spaces were not merely physical structures with social agendas. In some instances, they took natural forms (like stones, trees, or mountains) outside of social space. These places carried religious significance because of human encounters with the holy or because they were associated with gifts from the divine such as food.[14] Though some sacred spaces may have been created to uphold social structures,

---

[12] Jonathan Z. Smith, *To Take Place: Toward Theory in Ritual* (Chicago: University of Chicago Press, 1987), 76–95, 115–16.
[13] Smith, *To Take Place*, 56–60.
[14] Harold W. Turner, *From Temple to Meeting House: The Phenomenology and Theology of Places of Worship* (New York: Mouton, 1979), 13–18.

Smith is too reductive in his analysis by diminishing the experiential aspects of divine revelation and encounters with the numinous presence of God that are critical to the theology of Leviticus. Part of Smith's argument stems from what Max Weber calls "the disenchantment of the world," which he argues is a phenomenon that occurred in the West from the sixteenth century onward.[15] In his discussions on the Protestant response to medieval Catholic sacramentality, Weber speaks of the "rationalization of the world" and the movement of theology toward desacralization. Worship is then reduced to a function of instrumentality rather than a mystical experience of the divine. Brown argues that this comes from a particular model of rationality that suggests that once something is explained there is no further need to address religious questions.[16] Instead, Brown contends that what is needed is a resacralizaiton of the world and an enchantment of space that recognizes the validity of religious experience through encounters with the divine both in the natural world and in human constructed spaces.[17]

For the priestly authors of Leviticus, both the substantive divine presence and the role of human construction are necessary for creating the tabernacle. Yhwh's divine presence in the sanctuary is not periodic or occasional for Leviticus. It is, rather, a movement in the life of a covenant people that represents the permanence of God dwelling in their midst. Though God had visited the

---

[15] Max Weber, *The Protestant Ethic and the Spirit of Capitalism* (London: Unwin, 1984), 104–5, 116–17.

[16] David Brown, *God and Enchantment of Space: Reclaiming Human Experience* (Oxford: Oxford University Press, 2004), 17–23.

[17] Brown, *God and Enchantment of Space*, 31–37. For the disenchantment of Scripture, see Walter Moberly, *The Bible in a Disenchanted Age* (Grand Rapids, MI: Baker Academic, 2018).

patriarchs in various ways in the past, Leviticus regards God's divine descent into the tabernacle as a categorically different manifestation of his abiding presence on earth and the dawning of a new era.

God's willingness to dwell amidst his people does not come without its dangers. The tabernacle not only houses the divine presence, but it also contains God's glory, which could destroy Israel if not treated properly. Douglas accurately describes this when she argues, "The danger is two-edged: the people might break through or the Lord might break out, and in either case, people will die. This is the effect of holiness. The holy thing that is not correctly guarded and fenced will break out and kill, and the impure person not correctly prepared for contact with the holy will be killed."[18] The potential peril associated with drawing near to God's presence is not associated with wrath or punishment but, rather, it is the numinous dread and fear of the created before the Creator. Kawashima comments that the tabernacle is an "intrusion of transcendence into the empirical, it is dangerous and volatile, a toxic and hazardous substance, as it were, requiring proper containment."[19] The radiance and luminosity of holiness was not only beautiful to the authors of Leviticus, but it also presented a real and dangerous threat to an unholy people.

Danger is an important concept of holiness in Leviticus but can be difficult for the modern reader to grasp. To contemporary Western rationalism this may seem like nothing more than primitive superstition, but that type of judgment dismisses the

---

[18] Douglas, *Leviticus as Literature*, 146.
[19] Robert Kawashima, "The Priestly Tent of Meeting and the Problem of Divine Transcendence: An Archaeology of the Sacred," *JR* 86 (2006): 226–57 (257); Hundley, *Keeping Heaven*, 182.

rhetorical weight given to the divine presence in Leviticus that was real for the priestly authors. To grasp a theology of Leviticus one must understand Israel's core belief that Yhwh's presence can be deadly if not approached in strict obedience to his commands.

Along with danger, the divine presence is also about power. Within the Holy of Holies, the terrifying power of the almighty God resides and it is only those with authority who may approach in an appropriate manner. Proximity to God is given to the priesthood established by Moses, who is the only non-priestly figure[20] granted the most unrestricted access to the divine. Kilde argues that power is expressed through three different categories in sacred space: (1) divine power; (2) social power, particularly among priestly hierarchies; and (3) personal power, or the spiritual empowerment that people experience in worship.[21] In the priestly theology of Leviticus, each element of power is critical to the functioning order of the tabernacle and the life of Israel.

INHABITING SACRED SPACE: THE ORDINATION OF PRIESTS

The priestly theology of sacred space stresses the importance of holiness for all Israelites but in particular for those priests who will serve in the tabernacle. The lengthy narrative of Leviticus 8 and the ordination of Aaron and his sons is linked to the previous instructions that Moses received in Exodus 29. This is emphasized in the text through the constant refrain of Moses

---

[20] Even though Moses is a descendant of Levi, he is not described as a priest (Exod 2:1–2). Ps 99:6 does, however, consider Moses and Aaron as priests.

[21] Jeanne H. Kilde, *Sacred Power, Sacred Space: An Introduction to Christian Architecture and Worship* (Oxford: Oxford University Press, 2008), 4.

doing everything "as the LORD commanded" (Lev 8:4, 9, 13, 17, 21, 29, 36). In Exodus, Yhwh tells Moses, "I will consecrate the tent of meeting and the altar; Aaron also and his sons I will consecrate, to serve me as priests. I will dwell among the Israelites, and I will be their God" (Exod 29:44-45). If God is to dwell at the heart of his people, then those chosen to serve in the sanctuary must be consecrated. Though there is debate around whether Exodus 29 is earlier or later than Leviticus 8,[22] the clear link between the commandments at Sinai and the inaugural ordination of Aaron and his sons demonstrates the sanctioned method by which priests are set apart for ministry within the tabernacle.

The English term "ordination" renders the Hebrew phrase "filling [the hand]" (*millū'îm*) (Lev 8:33). There is much debate on the meaning of the phrase, but it may pertain to the objects that were used by the priests in their service.[23] The term is only used in the Old Testament for those conferred with priestly duties so it is likely that the ritual of ordination at one time included placing something in the hand of the priest that represented their role and function within the cult. This may reflect what is seen later in the ceremony when Moses places the elements of the sacrifice into the palms of Aaron and his sons to raise as an elevation offering (Lev 8:26-27).[24]

Others relate the ordination rite to the fidelity of the Levites in the golden calf episode when Moses declares that they have "filled their hands" for the service of the LORD after killing those

---

[22] Noth, *Leviticus*, 68-69; Baruch A. Levine, "The Descriptive Tabernacle Texts of the Pentateuch," *JAOS* 85 (1965): 307-18 (310-14).
[23] Martin Noth, *Exodus*, OTL (London: SCM Press, 1962), 230-31.
[24] Levine, *Leviticus*, 54; cf. Milgrom, *Leviticus 1-16*, 539.

unfaithful to Yhwh (Exod 32:29).[25] The Exodus narrative, however, serves as a story of origins for the connection between the Levites and the priesthood. Their cleansing of the impure from the community likely serves as a sign of their future role within the sanctuary. The narrative might also express their release from all family ties in order to serve in the tabernacle.[26]

The ordination of the priests in Leviticus 8 highlights the enactment of a new world order that is initiated by Moses. Just as Moses represents the divine ordering of the cosmos in his completion of the tabernacle, so too does he consecrate and bring into order the ongoing work of the priests within the tabernacle. The ritual of ordination serves to identify the consecration of holy space with the consecration of holy servants. The two are intimately bound together and necessary for the cult to exist. Gorman argues that "Leviticus 8 is a ritual of founding in which there is a convergence of the consecration of sacred space and the institutionalization of the status of the priesthood in such a way that the meaning of sacred space and the meaning of priesthood are interrelated."[27] The priests are bound to the holiness of the sacred site and the altar as they are initiated into its service.

It is important to recognize that the ordination of priests is a communal act in Leviticus. All of Israel is called to be holy and not just those who serve in the tabernacle. The whole Israelite people gather at the entrance to the tabernacle alongside the future priests (Lev 8:3–4) and bear witness to the ritual that sets a select few apart to serve and intercede on their behalf. Theologically, the participation of the whole community is critical

---

[25] Aelred Cody, *A History of Old Testament Priesthood*, AnBib 35 (Rome: Pontifical Institute, 1969), 154.
[26] Noth, *Exodus*, 250–51.
[27] Gorman, *The Ideology of Ritual*, 104.

to the ordination of priests because they are symbolically taking on the burden of Israel's worship in order to offer sacrifices for the Lord on the altar. The recognition and affirmation of the whole community is essential in the ordination rite since all of Israel participates in the cult and all are linked spiritually and sacramentally to the altar for cleansing, forgiveness, and thanksgiving. Leviticus rejects any sort of mysterious exclusivity of priests but, rather, it offers a vision of their intimate connection to the people through the altar. As Feldman rightly argues, "the narrator's choice to allow the reader-Israelite to hear and see the internal workings of the cult challenges the hegemony of the priesthood and centers the ordinary Israelite in the life of the cult."[28] The result is not an equality between priest and layperson but, rather, a division and order for participation in the worship of Yhwh. All Israelites are called to be holy (Lev 19:2), but some are called to the altar to serve the covenant community as intercessors and servants.

Though the entire book of Leviticus is set within the narrative framework of Mt. Sinai, chapter 8 is the first instance of descriptive story telling. The importance of the ordination of priests was worth narrating to express the legitimacy of the Aaronide priesthood as it was established under Mosaic authority. The event is foundational for the inauguration of the cult in the wilderness and though every detail was not likely meant to be repeated, the ritual act of anointing priests is paradigmatic for future generations.

The elaborate ritual begins with a washing as it does for the high priest on the Day of Atonement (Lev 16:4, 24) as he prepares to offer sacrifices in the most holy place. Clothing plays a

---

[28] Feldman, *The Story of Sacrifice*, 198.

significant role in the ordination ritual both in terms of the transformation that the priest experiences as well the representation of different grades of holiness within the tabernacle.[29] The instructions regarding the garments are found in Exod 28:5-39 and the actual making of them is described in Exod 39:1-31. Four of the garments described are only to be worn by the high priest and four are to be worn by all priests. Only the high priest can wear the ephod, the breastplate, the robe of the ephod, and the golden head band. These correspond with the ministry that takes place in the inner zones of the sanctuary such as the daily offering of incense (Exod 30:7-8), the regular tending of the lamps (Exod 27:20; Lev 24:2), and the arrangement of the bread on the table (Lev 24:5-9). The other clothing to be worn by all priests are the plain tunic, the sash, the turban, and the linen undergarments. The clothes are outward signs of the priest's connection to the holiness of the sanctuary and their role within the sanctuary.

The hem of the high priest's ephod was also adorned with alternating pomegranates and bells. This was worn as he ministered in the holy place and presumably offered an audible warning to Yhwh of his presence "so that he might not die" (Exod 28:35). This further precaution, symbolized in the material of his clothing, demonstrates the underlying purpose of the detail and specificity given to the garments of the priests – every command must be meticulously followed for fear of death. The same sentiment is summed up at the end of the ordination process when Moses commands Aaron to follow his orders, "So that you do not die" (Lev 8:35). Milgrom notes that bells in ancient Near Eastern cultures were used to ward off evil spirits but rightly argues that

---

[29] Cf. Haran, *Temples*, 165-74.

this would have been foreign to a priestly theology of the holiness and the sanctity of the most holy places in the tabernacle.[30]

The ordination of the priests is also concerned with the use of sacred space. Throughout the narrative, we are told that the ritual must be enacted at the door of the tent of meeting (Lev 8:3, 4, 31, 33, 35). This is where Aaron and his sons remain throughout the ordination while Moses crosses back and forth between the altar and the priests. Moses somehow transcends the normal priestly regulations as the priest-maker and the inaugurator of the cult.[31]

The length of time (seven days) is a symbolic period of preparation. In the ordination rite, seven days are needed for purgation and purification. The priests must be completely separated from the profane world and any contamination before they enter the sanctuary. A similar time frame is used in Ezekiel 43 when a week of offerings are made to purge and purify the altar. This follows the pattern set in Exod 29:35-37 where a sin offering was to be given on each of the seven days and the altar was to be anointed for seven days. Leviticus only stipulates that ordination was to last for seven days (Lev 8:33).

In terms of the narrative link between Exodus and Leviticus and the timing of the ordination, we recall that Moses erected the tabernacle on the first day of the first month (New Year's Day), which suggests the beginning of a new creation.[32] The following seven days represent the ordering of the cosmos and establishing the first garden dwellers to perform their "priestly work" in Eden. With similar symbolism, Aaron and his sons prepare themselves

---

[30] Milgrom, *Leviticus 1-16*, 504-5.
[31] Anthony Giambrone, *The Bible and the Priesthood: Priestly Participation in the One Sacrifice for Sins* (Grand Rapids, MI: Baker Academic, 2022), 43-53.
[32] On the timings of the ordination and the inauguration of the tabernacle, see Anderson, *That I May Dwell among Them*, 19-48.

for seven days before entering the new Eden of the tabernacle. Set apart for God's service, Aaron will enter from the east on the eighth day to restore humanity's place in the garden.

After sprinkling oil on the altar seven times, Moses pours some of the oil on Aaron's head and anoints him, "to consecrate him" (v. 12). Only the high priest receives this anointing that sets him apart with a particular relationship to the altar. Aaron is connected to the space of the tabernacle in a way that no other person can be. Only he (and not Moses) will be able to enter the most holy space to offer sacrifices annually. He is the most critical link between the Israelites, the Holy of Holies, and the maintenance of God's abode. The anointing of Aaron demonstrates Leviticus' theology of priesthood and its rhetorical defense of a particular line of ancestry that is allowed to enter God's presence in the sanctuary.[33]

In the ordination ritual, both Aaron and his sons lay their hands on the bull and there is some question about whether this represents the transference of sin for atonement. Laying hands on various types of sacrifices is common throughout Leviticus, but this particular offering bears close similarities to the purification offering (*ḥaṭṭā't*) described in Lev 4:3–12, 13–21 for the unintentional sins of the high priest or of the whole people. The laying on of hands in this instance, however, does not suggest the transference of sin. In Num 8:10, the Israelites lay their hands on the Levites so that they may handle the holy materials of the tabernacle. In this instance, they are given authority by the community to handle sacred objects. Later in Lev 24:10–16, the community lays hands on a person convicted of blasphemy, seemingly as a sign of judgment or identification of the guilty party.

---

[33] Cf. Watts, *Ritual and Rhetoric*, 143–51.

Other ancient Near Eastern cultures had similar hand laying rites containing different symbolism. In the ancient Hittite Ritual of Tunnawi, a female laid her hands on the horn of a cow in hopes of transferring its fertility to herself.[34] In ancient Israel, the gesture of laying hands on a sacrificial animal had various possible meanings. At some point, the act may have been associated with legal procedures but only later came to have cultic significance.[35]

When the sacrifice is complete and the blood poured out at the foot of the altar, we are told that it was "consecrated" and "atoned for" (Lev 8:15). No mention is made of cleansing the altar of incense in the inner sanctuary, which is left for Aaron to complete. The emphasis on the cleansing of the material of the tabernacle suggests that the primary symbolism of the sacrifice was to consecrate the sacred space. Though nothing had yet occurred to cause anything to be defiled, the material of the tabernacle remained in its profane state until it was cleansed and set aside by blood. The priests too are consecrated but the narrative emphasizes the link between the sacrifice and the purification of the altar at this point.

A similar act follows with a ram, but this represents the burnt offering (*ōlâ*) detailed in Leviticus 1. It was given in hopes of receiving good favor from God and to attract his attention as the animal was transferred from the material world and transmuted into something that could reach the presence of the divine.[36] The climax of the ceremony comes in the sacrifice of the "ordination ram" (v. 22) or literally "the ram of filling." Here again we find the Hebrew term "filling" (*millūîm*) as described above in the phrase "filling of the

---

[34] David P. Wright, "The Gesture of Hand Placement in the Hebrew Bible and in Hittite Literature," *JAOS* 106 (1986): 433–46.
[35] Milgrom, *Numbers*, 62.
[36] Wenham, *Leviticus*, 56.

hand." This second ram is sacrificed and its blood is used for the symbolic act that confers priestly status. Moses places it on the right ear lobe, the right thumb, and the right big toe of the priests. The ritual is a sign of purgation for the priests as it is for the altar,[37] but the symbolism has further layers. The same ritual occurs only in the cleansing of the leper, which is described in detail in Leviticus 14.

In the rite of the cleansed leper, the blood of a lamb is placed on the right ear lobe, the right thumb, and the right big toe (Lev 14:8–14). This happens after seven days when a leper provisionally crosses the boundary into the camp but remains outside their tent. On the eighth day, the cleansing process is complete when they are anointed with blood and then with oil on the same body parts (Lev 14:15–18). The ritual depicts a movement from the realms of exclusion and death outside the covenant community to full restoration.[38] The blood and oil symbolize the purification and blessing on the person literally from head to toe.

The final act of the ordination is Moses sprinkling a mixture of oil and blood on the vestments of the priests. Aaron and his sons are then commanded to wait at the entrance to the tent for seven days. Moses declares that he has done all that the Lord commanded to "make atonement" for Aaron (Lev 8:34). The inaugural ordination ceremony is one of purgation, ordering, and consecrating the sacred space of the tabernacle as well as consecrating those who will serve in it. The priests are ordained to maintain the order and holiness of God's dwelling. Their lives are forever bound to the altar as they worship in the new Eden on earth where the divine presence dwells. Their duty to serve in the tabernacle is to mediate on behalf of the people; to keep forever at

---

[37] Cf. Ezek 43:20–27.
[38] See von Rad, *OTT*, 1:274–75.

bay the chaos, impurity, and contamination of death; and to maintain order, purity, and life for Israel. As Gorman writes, "The priesthood is established to stand at the intersection of chaos and order, pollution and purity, the holy and the profane."[39]

THE CONSECRATION OF THE ALTAR

The inaugural act of Israel's cult is depicted in Leviticus with high drama. Though there is much repetition from previous instructions concerning offerings, we note the ongoing refrain in the text that everything was done exactly as commanded (Lev 8:5, 6, 7, 21). The scene offers one of the most significant transfers of authority in the Old Testament. As Moses beckons Aaron to "draw near" and "make atonement for yourself and for the people" (Lev 9:7), he passes on a critical role of leadership within Israel. The Mosaic transfer of authority to the office of priesthood establishes its legitimacy in the theology of Leviticus but it also highlights the divine imperative concerning the *need* for priestly service. Israel is an unclean people in need of purification and atonement if Yhwh is to reside in their midst. Moses delivers a covenant people out of Egypt, but he cannot provide for their ongoing cleansing and sanctification. Only the order of priests can stand in the breach for the sake of Israel and ultimately for all of humanity.

Aaron and his sons, having been anointed and prepared for seven days, may now cross the threshold of the tent to offer an atoning sacrifice for themselves and for the people (Lev 9:7–21). The sons help administer the blood and offerings (vv. 9, 12–13, 18–20) as Aaron goes about slaughtering two calves, a goat, a

---

[39] Gorman, *The Ideology of Ritual*, 139. Cf. Balentine, *Leviticus*, 79.

lamb, an ox, and a ram (vv. 2–4). Even for the most skilled butcher, the carving up of animals would have taken some time and the entire ritual was an extended act of worship that included anointing, washing, and burning. Outside the tent, the Israelites would have waited in anticipation with the smells of freshly cooked meat wafting through the air.

After Aaron fulfills Moses' commands, and the commands of the LORD, he assumes his role as priestly intercessor for Israel and cultic mediator. We are told that he blessed the people and then "came down" (v. 22). This means that he may have pronounced the blessing while elevated near the altar, but it seems more likely that he was at the entrance of the tent or just outside it to be more visible. Some rabbis translate the verb as a pluperfect ("having come down"), but others contend that Aaron was standing on some sort of platform near the altar.[40] In either case, Aaron likely pronounced the words of the priestly blessing found in Num 6:24–27.

> The LORD bless you and keep you;
> the LORD make his face to shine upon you and be gracious to you;
> the LORD lift up his countenance upon you and give you peace.
> So shall they put my name upon the people of Israel, and I will bless them.

The blessing is a sign that Aaron's priestly authority has been established.[41] In the inauguration of the cult, Leviticus offers what might be perceived as the idealized vision of priesthood as it was established by Moses. The authority and power conferred upon the high priest is to be used for the life, forgiveness, and

---

[40] Milgrom, *Leviticus 1–16*, 587–88.
[41] See Stephen B. Chapman, *The Lord Bless You: Numbers 6 for the Life of the Church*, Touchstone Texts (Grand Rapids, MI: Baker Academic, 2025).

blessing of God's people. For a brief moment in Israel's history, the purity of the cult offers an untainted, unhindered flow of divine power from heaven to earth through the sacred space of the tabernacle, the altar, and through the priests to the people. The perfection of the tabernacle and priesthood allows for the blessing of Yhwh's protection, grace, and peace upon Israel. Just as the name *qōdeš layhwh* ("Holy to Yhwh") is inscribed on the high priest's diadem, so too is this honor and status conferred on the Israelites as God puts his name upon them through his anointed.

After Aaron blesses the people he returns to the tent with Moses. No explanation is given for why they return but it is likely to pray for the acceptance of the offering. When they emerged, they both bless the people once more and a "fire came out from the LORD" and consumed the offering on the altar (Lev 9:24). The dramatic theophany is summed up in the people's response as "they shouted and fell on their faces." The inauguration of the cult and the priesthood is complete. As Milgrom argues, the symbol of the fire "renders the Tabernacle the equivalent of Mount Sinai. God's presence was made manifest at both places."[42] This is not, as Milgrom contends, a priestly elevation of the tabernacle over Mt. Sinai but, rather, it is the continuation of God's revelation of his presence. From the fire of the burning bush to the fire of Mt. Sinai, God's final resting place for Leviticus rightfully concludes in the tabernacle.

Sacred spaces can have social or political motivations behind their construction, but they can also be founded because of encounters with the divine presence. In the priestly theology of Leviticus, we find that both aspects of creating sacred space are

---

[42] Milgrom, *Leviticus 1–16*, 574.

true. Israel constructs everything according to the commandments of Yhwh and Moses. The tabernacle space allows the priestly class limited access to the tabernacle for the sake of maintaining its holiness. The ritual procedures are obeyed by Moses, Aaron, and his sons and the result is the revelation of God's acceptance through divine fire. At the end of Exodus, the tabernacle Moses constructs is consecrated when the "glory" (*kābôd*) of the Lord descends upon it and no one can enter (Exod 40:34-35). Though God's glory is present, the sacred space is not complete. It still needed to be purged and sanctified for the work of the priests. The two events of Exodus 40 and Leviticus 9 cannot be separated. They may be seen as two stages that complete the divine descent of Yhwh to dwell in the midst of his people (Exod 25:8), or they also might represent the one event of the altar being consecrated.[43] However the narrative is read, in the final form of Leviticus the divine fire upon the altar represents the inauguration of the cult and the beginning of Israel's new covenant relationship with their God.

DEFILING SACRED SPACE

The issue of defiling or contaminating sacred space is at the forefront of the theology of Leviticus. The possibility of desecrating God's holy abode always looms largely behind strict regulations and rituals. The theological motivations for such caution and precision stem from the deep reverence and fear of divine holiness and the desire to secure the ongoing presence of God in his tabernacle. For the priestly authors of Leviticus, the glory of God represents both the power to destroy and the power

---

[43] Anderson, *That I May Dwell among Them*, 36-48.

to bring life. It is only through exact obedience to his command that they can ensure their own safety and protection from God's potential judgment.

Immediately following the climax of the altar being consecrated by divine fire, that very same fire brings death upon Aaron's sons. A similar example of faithfulness followed by flagrant disobedience is seen in the golden calf narrative of Exodus 32. Balentine sees this as the distinct pattern of "God's *creation*, Israel's *uncreation*, and God's *re-creation*."[44] Just when the narrative entices us into a place of peace and harmony between God and his people, the reader is jolted abruptly as the intrusion of human arrogance invites God's judgment and destruction.

The laconic Hebrew sums up the desecration of God's altar and holy space in a mere three verses. It begins with Nadab and Abihu taking up their censors to perform their priestly duties. But rather than a fragrant aroma, they offer up "strange fire" (*'ēš zārâ*). The adjective *zārâ* might be translated "alien," "profane" (NKJV), "unholy" (NRSV), or, more likely, "unauthorized" (CEB, ESV) in this instance since we are told immediately after that their actions were not as the Lord had commanded (Lev 10:1). There has been extensive debate on the meaning of "alien fire" since the term does not occur elsewhere in the Bible and there is no other explanation given for the divine punishment of Aaron's sons.[45]

---

[44] Balentine, *Leviticus*, 83.
[45] Exod 30:9 prohibits the use of "strange incense" (*qəṭōret zārâ*) on the altar, which likely refers to anything apart from the prescribed daily incense offerings. Aaron's sons may have entered the tent at an improper time with an unprescribed offering and so suffered death. It is also possible that they were challenging Aaron's authority as high priest. See Levine, *Leviticus*, 60; Rolf Rendtorff, "Nadab and Abihu," in *Reading from Right to Left: Essays on the Hebrew Bible in Honour of David J. A. Clines*, ed. J. Cheryl Exum and H. G. M. Williamson, JSOTSS 373 (New York: T&T Clark, 2003), 359–63.

The "alien fire" may have been tied to their unauthorized entrance into the holy place where the altar of incense stood and where the coals from their censors were to be filled (cf. Lev 16:1–2). It may also have been the wrong mixture or was associated with incense offerings to other gods. Whatever the case, the narrative is unambiguous about why the two perished – they acted "such as he had not commanded them" (Lev 10:1; cf. Numbers 16).[46]

The fire that consumes the sons came out "from the presence of the LORD" (Lev 10:2; cf. Num 16:35), which offers the exact language previously expressed in Lev 9:24 of God's acceptance of Aaron's sacrifice. The priests are consumed by the fire but unlike the previous offering they are not wholly burned. Their bodies are carried out of the camp by Aaron's cousins (Lev 10:4–5). This leaves the nature of their death ambiguous, but Moses' response to Aaron offers some insight. The cryptic phrase, "Through those who are near me I will show myself holy" (Lev 10:3), expresses the danger associated with drawing near to Yhwh's holiness.[47] Moses met with God "face-to-face" (Exod 33:11) and bore the radiance of glory in his own countenance (Exod 34:29) because of his obedience. But for those who approach God's holiness with presumption or disobedience in his sanctuary, the result is immediate death.[48]

---

[46] Gary Anderson, "'Through Those Who Draw Near to Me, I Will Show Myself Holy': Nadab and Abihu and Apophatic Theology," *CBQ* 77 (2015): 1–19.

[47] Liane M. Feldman, "Ritual Sequence and Narrative Constraints in Leviticus 9:1–10:3," *Journal of Hebrew Scriptures* 17 (2017), 32, translates "I will be sanctified by those near to me, but before all of the people I will be present." This highlights the necessity of holiness in the priests who come into contact with God's holy altar.

[48] Nihan, *Priestly Torah*, 588, argues for a double meaning that expresses the positive aspect of being glorified by priests who obey and also the negative

We noted above the rhetorical force of Moses doing everything "as the LORD had commanded" in chapter 8, which continued in chapter 9 (vv. 6, 7, 10, 21). The successive repetitions stress complete obedience and highlight the disobedience of Aaron's sons and the consequence of treating Yhwh's commands with contempt. The emphasis of the story is not on the specifics of "alien fire" but, rather, the focus is on the disregard of Aaron's sons to preserve the holiness of God's sacred space according to his command. Levine is right to argue that the story is didactic in teaching the priests and the Israelites that the balance of life and death hang on complete obedience to God's command.[49] Whether the command is how to offer incense on the altar or how to treat one's neighbor with love and righteousness, to honor Yhwh's name as holy is to live according to his word.

The final phrase of v. 3 sums up the human response to God's judgment, "And Aaron was silent." This brief scene has incorporated the smells of incense, the dramatic visual of divine fire, two dead bodies lying on the ground, and dejected silence in the presence of God's holiness. Aaron's stillness marks the grief of his loss and acknowledgment of God's judgment. Moses commands him and his remaining sons not to mourn but to let the community mourn on their behalf (Lev 10:6). In normal circumstances, only the high priest is not allowed to show outward signs of mourning for the dead (Lev 21:10–12), but Aaron's other sons must remain with him inside the tent to preserve their state of holiness. Despite tragedy, the purity of the sanctuary and

---

where God's glory is revealed through their disobedience and death. Though not an exact parallel, the New Testament deaths of Ananias and Sapphira in Acts 5 offer a similar didactic narrative concerning disobedience in the presence of the Holy Spirit for the newly formed Christian church.

[49] Levine, *Leviticus*, 58.

the priests must be preserved to prevent the outbreak of God's holiness on the whole congregation (Lev 10:6).

The silence of Aaron and his sons and the mourning of Israel are a reminder of the priestly calling to holiness and their intimate connection to the people. The high priest is set apart for holiness in such a way that even the death of his family cannot distract him from his duty or potentially make him unclean. He must be utterly committed to service in the sanctuary to preserve its holiness so that God may be glorified among the people.

In this brief episode, we discover another layer in the theology of Leviticus. The high priest is meant to be the greatest human representation of God's holiness in Israel, but he does not stand alone. The community must bear the weight of his suffering so that he might continue to maintain the sanctuary. Israel's priesthood is designed around mutual, interdependent relationships within the covenant people that sustain both the holiness of the cult and the holiness of the people. If there is a breakdown on either side, the results could be catastrophic.

Aaron's silence is broken by the voice of Yhwh. This is the only time God speaks directly to Aaron in Leviticus and he gives him a new commandment for priests while serving in the sanctuary – they should not consume wine or strong drink (Lev 10:8–9). The prohibition against alcohol may seem unwarranted, but it may allude to the fact that Nadab and Abihu were intoxicated at the time of their transgression.[50] There seems no other plausible explanation for why this particular law would be instated for the

---

[50] Milgrom, *Leviticus 1–16*, 634; Watts, *Ritual and Rhetoric*, 113; Nihan, *Priestly Torah*, 591. Feldman, *The Story of Sacrifice*, 104–7, 113, fails to mention the prohibition of alcohol but contends that Nadab and Abihu were punished for seeking personal gain through their priestly role.

priests as a statue "forever throughout your generations" at this point in the narrative.

Leviticus 10 presents a visual and didactic illustration for what can happen when God's holy sanctuary is profaned by disobedience. When human presumption trivializes the power and presence of God, it leads to the profanation of the tabernacle and strips the cult of its power to offer sacrifices to Yhwh. The actions of Nadab and Abihu disregarded the mystery of ministering in the presence of God's holiness and reduced worship to human technique. The rhetorical thrust to readers of Leviticus is that every act of worship must be in strict obedience to God's command and performed with awe and reverence. Watts, however, argues that the rhetorical force is on the sole authority of the Aaronide priesthood.[51] Though this is emphasized in the narrative, the more important message is that lineage means nothing if a priest does not perform their duties according to Yhwh's command. The holy God of Israel demands holiness in his priests and people, not as a divine tyrant but as the divine King whose glory can bless or potentially destroy.

We find a parallel to the Nadab and Abihu narrative in another text concerning the profanation of God's tabernacle and his holy name (Lev 24:10–23). It is significant that these are the only two narratives in Leviticus because they both deal with honoring God's holiness and the death penalty. The first case concludes with God's punishment on Aaron's sons, but in the second case Moses takes the role of judge and the Israelites act as executor against the one who blasphemes God's name.

Though the second narrative takes place outside the sanctuary and is concerned with a layperson, the tabernacle and the holiness

---

[51] Watts, *Ritual and Rhetoric*, 111–18.

of God's presence in the Israelite camp are at stake. The perpetrator is half Israelite and half Egyptian, which raises the question of whether the full weight of the law applies. In the midst of a fight with another Israelite, the man curses God's name and is brought before Moses (Lev 24:11–12). God provides his judgment and Moses instructs the Israelites who witnessed the event to lay hands on the guilty party. Then he is taken outside the camp and stoned to death.

The cursing of God's name in the camp offers a second didactic narrative that mirrors what happened with Aaron's sons inside the tabernacle. Though the main concern of the story is how the law is applied to resident aliens or those who are not full Israelites, it also is concerned with profaning holy space and the divine name. From the chosen lineage of Aaron to a half-Egyptian, to defile sacred space by profaning God's name results in the death penalty. The *ritual actions* of Nadab and Abihu offering alien fire are commensurate with the *spoken word* used to curse God's name. Both are treated as an affront to God's glory and holiness because they disrespect the power associated with his name and his home.

What some scholars perceive as an "intrusion" in the narrative actually provides a critical link between the sacred space of the tabernacle and the Israelite camp. Douglas argues that these two narratives are key to the ring structure of the whole book because they guide the reader around the holy space of the tabernacle.[52] In the first instance, the priests defile the outer court through their unacceptable offerings. In the second, the cursing of God's name by a non-Israelite in the camp is comparable to defiling the inner sanctum of God's dwelling. Both ritual acts at the altar and spoken

---

[52] Douglas, *Leviticus as Literature*, 194–217.

words within the camp have the potential to desecrate God's holy dwelling.[53]

Whether one agrees with Douglas' ring structure or not, what is clear is that Leviticus promotes a theology of holy space that extends beyond the tabernacle and into the Israelite camp. If the priests can defile the tabernacle through unauthorized rituals, then the Israelites (or foreigners) have the power to do the same through unauthorized words or actions. Once again, we find that Leviticus' theology of holiness is deeply rooted in the connection between God's home and Israel's home.

Holy space within the tabernacle relies on the faithful service and purity of the priests, but holy space must also be preserved by the whole community of Israel. Though there are different grades of holiness extending outward from the Holy of Holies, Leviticus envisages the entire land and its inhabitants as participants in the movement of God's divine presence and sanctification. Whether in matters of moral or cultic purity, all of Israel is called to discern between the sacred and the profane (Lev 10:10) because each tribe, clan, family, and person is responsible, in some way, for upholding the divisions that God established in the primordial acts of separating and classifying all creation (cf. Gen 1:4, 6, 7, 18). Israel's participation in maintaining distinctions between the sacred and profane point to their symbolic role as a "priestly kingdom" (Exod 19:6) restoring divine order to God's good creation.

HOLINESS AND THE LAND

The concentric rings of holiness in the theology of Leviticus move from the innermost parts of the sanctuary to the outer courts and

---

[53] Milgrom, *Leviticus 23–27*, 2141; Balentine, *Leviticus*, 191–93.

then beyond into the realms of life within the desert camp and finally to the holy land. From the earliest history, the land is seen as an integral participant in the covenant between Yhwh and his people.[54] From Eden to the exodus, God promises the patriarchs and their offspring that they will be a "landed" people[55] who will flourish in a home of peace, safety, and fruitfulness where Yhwh will abide in their midst.

Like the tabernacle, the land too must be holy if it is to be a place of abundance and life. From the innermost sanctum, God's holiness flows outward and, to lesser degrees, it resides with Israelites throughout the land.[56] The Israelites must take extreme care to live according to the commandments so that they do not pollute the land. This is emphasized in Leviticus and later in Num 35:34, "You shall not defile the land in which you live, in which I also dwell; for I the LORD dwell among the Israelites." The land is thus a shared place, a communal home between Yhwh and his people who are restoring his creation to the fullness of its beauty and life by living according to his commands.

The spatial and physical aspect of holiness is important to grasp in the theology of Leviticus. Holiness is not merely an inward state of purity through one's personal devotion or faith. There are real, physical and spatial aspects to holiness that filter through the material world. This comes as a result of Yhwh's real presence dwelling in the midst of the people in the tabernacle. This state of holiness is not only preserved through appropriate sacrifices in

---

[54] Walter Brueggemann, *The Land: Place as Gift, Promise, and Challenge in Biblical Faith*, 2nd ed. (Augsburg: Fortress Press, 2002), 15–26.
[55] Brueggemann, *The Land*, 8–13.
[56] Jacob Milgrom, *Leviticus 23–27: A New Translation with Introduction and Commentary*, AB 3B (New Haven: Yale University Press, 2001), 2301.

the tabernacle, but it comes through righteous living, justice, mercy, and the love of one's neighbor. When this type of covenant obedience is made manifest, the land will be filled with holiness and will respond in fruitfulness as it was created to do (Pss 72:16–17; 85:10–12; 147). Consequently, if Israel does not walk in the commandments, the land will wither and suffer (Lev 26:19–20; cf. Hos 4:1–3; Jer 3:1–9, 12:4). The rituals performed at the altar and the ethical behavior of Israel demonstrate a connection between the people and the land that runs deeply throughout the theology of Leviticus and, indeed, much of the Old Testament. As Heibert argues,

> These rituals recognize the integral link between divine activity and the soil's fertility. They express thanksgiving to God as the source of nature's bounty. They also enact and sacralize the connection between people and soil. Made by God from arable soil and commissioned by God to farm it, the worshipper offers the soil's produce as service to God, as an act, one might almost say, of self-definition. The point of orientation behind all of this ritual, and the understanding of the human and the divine that they entail, is the recognition of the dependence of human survival on productive soil.[57]

The rich connections between the land and the people offer a wholistic ecology in the theology of Leviticus that understands the consecration of the divine presence as something that has an impact in both the physical and spiritual realms. As Brown contends, "The biblical tradents remind us that the moral world, the ethos of the cosmos, is quite real. Yet it is not purely a matter of empirical observation .... In the ancient cosmologies, moral

---

[57] Theodore Hiebert, *The Yahwist's Landscape: Nature and Religion in Early Israel* (Oxford: Oxford University Press, 1996), 143.

imagination constituted a generative nexus between mythos and ethos, between sense perception and faith."[58]

In the theology of Leviticus, Israel can never own or claim the land in perpetuity (Lev 25:23). They are tenants on Yhwh's property, called to cultivate a community of holiness that blesses the land and in return receives blessing from the land. What is remarkable about this theological construction in Leviticus is that Israel's relationship to the land is always one that recognizes divine ownership, which alludes to the fact that they are bound by the laws and commands of the Lord of the land, Yhwh. Though God has delivered them from slavery to freedom and will plant them in the land, this does not constitute an unbridled use of the land. Instead, their status as resident aliens and tenants on the land leads to the ethical implication that no Israelite should be landless or bound in slavery forever. Nor should any Israelite work the land without giving it its Sabbath rest (Lev 25:2–4). They must care for the land, and its inhabitants, with justice and righteousness, which also means periodically restoring the land to others at the Jubilee (Lev 25:8–55).

The temptation for Israel was always to revert to treating the land as their possession and not as a gift. Private ownership is not condemned in Leviticus, but it is always framed within Yhwh's desire for freedom from slavery, the canceling of debt, and sabbath rest for his people, the land, and all its inhabitants. The lure of economic prosperity, of forgetting their story of salvation from Egypt, and flourishing at the expense of the poor were always dangers for God's people in the land. As Brueggemann argues,

---

[58] William P. Brown, *The Ethos of the Cosmos: The Genesis of Moral Imagination in the Bible* (Grand Rapids, MI; Cambridge: Eerdmans, 1999), 22–23.

"Landed people are tempted to create a *sabbathless* society in which land is never rested, debts are never cancelled, slaves are never released, nothing is changed from the way it is now and has always been."[59] Self-sufficiency and arrogance were always the dangers of being settled and secure in the land. As Moses warned the Israelites before entering Canaan, "Do not say to yourself, 'My power and the might of my own hand have gotten me this wealth'" (Deut 8:17). The pride of possession and neglect of Yhwh's ownership of the land would ultimately lead to the landlessness of exile and the hope of restoration.

The priestly theology of Leviticus also emphasizes the holiness of the land through its personification.[60] The land is often referred to as a living, breathing entity as if exerting its own will in relationship to the people and to Yhwh. We read that the land vomited out its prior inhabitants who defiled it by their sin (Lev 18:24–25; cf. 20:23) even though the conquest had not yet taken place.[61] The judgment of Yhwh and the land against the Canaanites serves as a warning to the Israelites and a reminder

---

[59] Brueggemann, *The Land*, 60.
[60] Milgrom, *Leviticus 23–27*, 2185, contends that the Holiness Code resists calling the land holy because, "It would not be a far remove from the theology of the pagan world, which hypostatized nature as representing, even embodying, various deities, who were members of the divine assembly, or independent and even malevolent forces." Leviticus does not divinize nature, but it does depict the land as a real and active participant in the covenant. Its use of anthropomorphic language reveals an agent within God's creation that acts in accordance with his divine will (cf. Lev 18:24–28). For further discussion, see Mari Joerstad, *The Hebrew Bible and Environmental Ethics: Humans, Nonhumans, and the Living Landscape* (Cambridge: Cambridge University Press, 2019), 72–80.
[61] Cf. Brent A. Strawn, "On Vomiting: Leviticus, Jonah, and Ea(a)rth," *CBQ* 74 (2012): 445–64; Jonathan Morgan, "Transgressing, Puking, Covenanting: The Character of Land in Leviticus," *Theology* 112 (2009): 172–80.

that the land is not theirs to do with as they please. If defiled by sin, the land will cast out the guilty inhabitants and purge itself of anyone who rebels against Yhwh's rule.

This type of personification of the land need not have emerged only from a postexilic perspective.[62] The natural connection between the people and the gift of the land is seen throughout the Pentateuch. In the patriarchal period, the language is nuanced toward the land as a grant or gift, which differs slightly from the emphasis in Leviticus. Von Rad argues that we should divide the land into its "historical" reference, which was marked by the land granted to the patriarchs, and its "cultic" conceptions as seen in the priestly writings where Yhwh is the owner of the land.[63] There is no need, however, to make such a bifurcation but, rather, we might see the historical and cultic views as two sides of the same coin.[64] Both visions of the land offer a wholistic picture concerning that which has been divinely given as a gift and that which belongs to the king. Land grants in the ancient Near East shared similar notions of both gift and respect for the land as it remained under the king's dominion.[65] Yhwh is both the giver of the land and the one who dwells in it with his people, which encompasses both historic and cultic traditions.

One of the most significant theological developments in Leviticus is the link between sabbath rest and the land.

---

[62] Contra Gerstenberger, *Leviticus*, 256–57; cf. Milgrom, *Leviticus 17–22*, 1582.

[63] Gerhard von Rad, "The Promised Land and Yahweh's Land in the Hexateuch," in *The Problem of the Hexateuch and Other Essays* (London: SCM, 1966; repr. 1984), 79–93. For a more detailed discussion, see Christopher J. H. Wright, *God's People in God's Land: Family, Land and Property in the Old Testament* (Grand Rapids, MI: Eerdmans, 1990), 5–43.

[64] Wright, *God's People*, 10.

[65] See Ronald E. Clements, *God and Temple* (Oxford: Blackwell, 1965), 51–55, on divine ownership of the land in Ugaritic literature and Canaanite myth.

In Leviticus, the land deserves sabbath rest as much as the people. Just as humanity is given the gift of rest to be refreshed, so too the covenant command takes into consideration the revitalization of the soil and emphasizes the trust that Israel must place in Yhwh for their provision. Israel is later condemned for their failure to offer the land sabbath rest. It is only after their exile that the land is said to be given time to rest, which alludes to the fact that Israel's abuse of the land led to the destruction of Jerusalem (Lev 26:35; cf. 2 Chron 36:21; Jer 17:21–27). The motif of the land's holiness in the priestly theology in Leviticus raises the level of the land's sanctity and its relationship to the command of Yhwh and his divine presence.

The command of Lev 25:2 is that "the land shall observe a sabbath for the LORD." Though Israel is given the sabbath commandment in the decalogue, in this instance, it is the land itself that shall observe sabbath rest. Unlike the provisions for the sabbath year in Deuteronomy 15, which focus on debt release, Leviticus is concerned with the actual soil on which the Israelites dwell. The cessation of agricultural activity takes precedence in the sabbath year and though debt release is part of the sabbath command (Lev 25:10), the greater concern seems to be with the health and care of the land.[66]

Weekly sabbath rest is mandatory but upon entering the land the Israelites are to sow and harvest for six years. Even so, "in the seventh year there shall be a sabbath of complete rest for the land, a sabbath for the LORD" (Lev 25:4). A similar prescription is found in Exod 23:10–11; but in Leviticus, the seventh year is

---

[66] For agricultural practices in ancient Israel, see Oded Borowski, *Agriculture in Iron Age Israel* (Boston: ASOR, 2002) and Oded Borowski, *Daily Life in Biblical Times*, ABS 5 (Atlanta: SBL Press, 2003).

specifically referred to as a sabbath year. The use of the superlative "absolute sabbath" (*šabbat šabbātôn*) highlights the significance of the event. The land is to lie fallow and be completely undisturbed for an entire year. Yet the command is also followed by the modifier, "a sabbath *to/for* the LORD" where the prepositional *lāmed* (*la-yhwh*) indicates ownership. The sabbath is a gift that belongs to, and is given by, Yhwh.

For the priestly authors, the sabbath is not merely a time of ceasing. Any nation can stop their agricultural work for designated periods to refresh the soil. Indeed, the practical effect of allowing the land to lie fallow or utilizing crop rotation prevents contamination from alkaline deposits that could occur through heavy irrigation.[67] The sabbath, however, is the priestly vision of Yhwh's gift of holy time for his people and for the land. It is a time for refreshment and restoration and to be sanctified in Yhwh's rest (Exod 31:13, 17). The vital connection between the health of the soil and the health of the community is significant in Leviticus' theology. Israel is to participate in the wider ecosystem that exists between fertility, health of the soil, family, and community if they are to live as God's holy people.[68]

The extraordinary emphasis placed on the sabbath in connection with the land conveys the power of the sacralized world in Leviticus. Such a belief sees the entire land as holy space inhabited by the divine. It was not uncommon in other ancient cultures to identify gods with particular lands;[69] but in Leviticus, there is a

---

[67] For other ancient Near Eastern irrigation practices, see Thorkild Jacobsen, *Salinity and Irrigation Agriculture in Antiquity* (Malibu: Undena, 1982).
[68] Wendell Berry, *The Gift of Good Land* (San Francisco: North Point, 1981), 138, 276, 278–79.
[69] Michael Hundley, *Gods in Dwellings: Temples and Divine Presence in the Ancient Near East* (Atlanta: SBL Press, 2013), 1–15, 34.

dynamic relationship between tenancy, time, and obedience. To truly flourish as tenants on Yhwh's land, Israel must remain obedient to the commands that are given to establish justice, mercy, and righteousness. To be holy as God is holy, to love one's neighbor as oneself, and to treat the land as a fellow participant in Yhwh's salvation is to fully enter into the promised rest of the sabbath for Israel and for all creation.

Leviticus 26 completes the discourse on the land with the blessings that will come through Israel's obedience and the curses that will result from disobedience. The first two verses on idolatry and keeping the sabbaths (i.e., the sabbath and the Jubilee) (Lev 26:1–2) sum up the essence of the holiness commandments that began in chapter 19. If these two commandments are transgressed, Israel faces the curse of being stripped from a holy land that will be devastated by Yhwh with plague, pestilence, and war. The terrifying picture painted in Lev 26:14–33 is a sobering reminder for the people that Yhwh's presence and holiness in the land is not inviolable. If his people stubbornly spurn his commands and live in the impurity of their sin, he will not allow his blessing to be upon them. Instead, the holy land that was meant to produce in abundance and be filled with peace and security will become a place of desolation where even Israel's enemies who seize the land will be appalled by its state (Lev 26:32). With Israel in exile, however, the land will finally enjoy the sabbath rest God had promised it (Lev 26:34, 43). The land as an autonomous participant in Yhwh's holiness and salvation might be striking to the modern reader but because the land was central to every aspect of Israelite life, it is not surprising that Leviticus treats the land as its own character in the story of redemption.

The final chapter of Leviticus has often been considered a supplement to the core material of chapters 17–26. It begins with the typical introductory statement, "The LORD spoke to Moses, saying . . .," which denotes a new section of instructions or commandments. The content returns to making vows, but now includes the addition of how one can monetize the value of a human being (Lev 27:3-8), which is likely based on their capacity for manual labor rather than their social status. The monetization of an animal for a vow is found in vv. 9-13, and vv. 14-25 deals with vows that pertain to houses and land. The last section (vv. 26-34) offers various regulations relating to the previously mentioned vows. In sum, these final commands echo the initial sacrificial material of chapters 1-7 but introduce the monetary value ascribed to particular items, whether human beings, homes, or gifts from the land, that are associated with offerings to Yhwh. The chapter ends with a repetition of 26:46 and that all these commandments were those that God gave to Moses for the people of Israel.

THE JUBILEE

The commandments concerning Jubilee express the demand for justice in Yhwh's land and the desire to prevent generational bondage occurring among the Israelites. The deliverance from Egypt was a sign that God's people should never return to the burden of perpetual slavery. The Israelites have gone from being Pharaoh's slaves to slaves of Yhwh as the climax of the Jubilee laws indicate. "For to me the people of Israel are servants [slaves]; they are my servants [slaves] whom I brought out from the land of Egypt: I am the LORD your God" (Lev 25:55).[70] Though slavery

---

[70] The Hebrew noun 'ebed can having the meaning "servant," but it is also often used as "slave" in different contexts.

and indentured servitude were a part of agrarian life in ancient Israel, they were never to be permanent among God's people.[71] Generational bondage and injustice in the land could not be found among a people called to holiness.

At the core of life in the land was the family unit or the "house of the father" (*bêt 'āb*), which was much larger than the modern idea of a household consisting mainly of one's immediate relations.[72] The household in the ancient world consisted of generations of men and women living together alongside servants, slaves, or resident aliens.[73] The household was connected to the kin group or clan, which represented one's kinship and larger extension of family that lived together in a protective, supportive association.[74] Beyond this was one's tribe or wider affiliation with a particular blood line. In relationship to the land, the kin group was the most important in terms of inheritance and land tenure.[75]

---

[71] On debt slavery, see Gregory Chirichigno, *Debt Slavery in Israel and the Ancient Near East*, JSOTSS 141 (Sheffield: JSOT Press, 1993); Kristine H. Garroway, *Children in the Ancient Near Eastern Household* (Winona Lake, IN: Eisenbrauns, 2014).

[72] J. David Schloen, *The House of the Father as Fact and Symbol: Patrimonialism in Ugarit and the Ancient Near East* (Winona Lake, IN: Eisenbrauns, 2001), 49–62; Norman K. Gottwald, *The Tribes of Yahweh: A Sociology of the Religion of Liberated Israel, 1350–1050 B.C.E* (New York: Orbis, 1979), 292.

[73] For female roles critical to the function of the household, see Carol Meyers, *Households and Holiness: The Religious Culture of Israelite Women* (Minneapolis, MN: Fortress Press, 2005); Carol Meyers, "Was Ancient Israel a Patriarchal Society?," *JBL* 133 (2014): 8–27.

[74] Joseph Blenkinsopp, "The Family in First Temple Israel," in *Families in Ancient Israel*, ed. Leo Purdue et al. (Louisville: Westminster John Knox, 1997), 48–103 (50–52); Gottwald, *The Tribes of Yahweh*, 257–84.

[75] See Wright, *God's People*, 48–58. The power of patrimonial memory in connection with land and kin is also demonstrated in modern tribal people as seen in Andrew Shryock, *Nationalism and the Genealogical Imagination:*

This connection was critical in the pre-monarchic period as it formed the economic model that protected extended families in the land and preserved their rights to redeem land to ensure the ongoing viability of their ancestry.[76]

The laws of Lev 25:23-28 begin with the declaration that the land is Yhwh's and that the Israelites are "aliens" (*gērîm*) and "tenants" (*tôšābîm*) within it meaning that they are subject to the rule of the Lord. The emphasis on Yhwh's ownership, and that no one has inalienable rights to the land, stands as the theological foundation for the following requirements. The laws also bind kinship ties and responsibilities to one's tenure within Yhwh's land. One does not dwell in the land independently but, rather, there is a critical social web of relationships that dictate how one lives in the land according to Yhwh's rules.

The possible reasons for an Israelite's land-loss are not given in detail but are merely summed up by the general phrase describing a relative who "falls into difficulty" (Lev 25:25, 35, 39, 47), a rendering of the Hebrew root *m-w-k* ("become impoverished"). The verb conveys the sense of sinking low or experiencing hardship, which could come from any number of circumstances. The idea is that a person/family becomes financially insolvent and they are forced to sell part or all of their land or even themselves and their families.[77] The priestly authors of Leviticus recognized the

---

Oral History and Textual Authority in Tribal Jordan (Berkeley: University of California Press, 1997).

[76] The corresponding laws of "release" (*šĕmiṭṭâ*) in Deut 15:1-2 presuppose the existence of a fallow year for the land and were likely influenced by the sabbatical year described in Leviticus.

[77] Laura Culbertson, "A Life-course Approach to Household Slaves in the Late Third Millennium B.C.," in *Slaves and Households in the Near East*, ed. Laura Culbertson (Chicago: University of Chicago Press, 2011), 36-40.

uncertainties of agrarian life and attempted to mitigate the perpetual impoverishment of families and broader clansmen. The redemption of the land by a kinsman redeemer provided a means for one who had fallen on hard times not to be bound in debt or slavery in perpetuity. The book of Ruth illustrates the role of the kinsman redeemer through Boaz who is related to Naomi (Ruth 3:1–2). Ruth asks Boaz to redeem Naomi's land inheritance but he must defer to another next-of-kin who is closer in relation. When that person declines, Boaz is able to purchase the land and secure the safety and future of both Naomi and Ruth along with their future generations (Ruth 4:1–13).[78]

The laws of Jubilee represent a socioeconomic system that recognized the need for land redistribution over time to protect the Israelite households and the larger clan. The redemption of land, as Wright argues, "was *not* provided that an Israelite who, for whatever reason, failed to maintain his property should automatically and immediately have it restored to him, but that a person's descendants should not have to suffer in perpetuity the consequence of the economic collapse of his generation."[79] This was critical in ensuring that the Israelites would not fall back into generational slavery. Leviticus envisions a society where economic and social justice in relationship to the land is critical in preserving the dignity and life of God's people. The laws also sought to preserve the family unit (*bēt 'āb*) living on the land because the land was their only means for sustaining life and maintaining the

---

[78] The oldest laws of land release and cycles of agricultural rest are found in the covenant code (Exod 23:11). These were likely influenced by the seven-year cycles found in ancient Canaanite myths and practices documented in texts from Ugarit. See C. H. Gordon, "Sabbatical Cycle or Seasonal Pattern," *Orientalia* 22 (1953): 79–81.

[79] Wright, *God's People*, 124.

stability of the household.⁸⁰ Laws regarding city dwellings are secondary in the text (Lev 25:29–30) because they do not have agricultural land as the primary means of income. It is the arable land, and the people of the land (*'am hā 'āreṣ*), not the city, that is of primary importance for Leviticus.

There is much debate regarding when sabbath and Jubilee laws were composed and if they were ever enforced. Levine contends that Leviticus 25 finds a close parallel in the context of Nehemiah 5 and a postexilic Persian period when the Judeans were returning to the land.⁸¹ He argues that Nehemiah, in effect, proclaims a time of "release" for the people and that the commands of Leviticus 25 should be seen as later additions to the commands of Deuteronomy 15 and the redemption of indentured servants on the seventh year.⁸² Though there are similarities, the historical setting for Nehemiah's proclamation of release is significantly different from that envisaged in Leviticus 25.⁸³ The radically new situation that the exiles found themselves in when returning to the land does not correspond well with the legislation found in Leviticus. Instead, it is more likely that sabbath and Jubilee laws reflect a monarchic (or pre-monarchic) agrarian society that aimed to establish a socioeconomic system of land distribution and debt release that was equitable among households, clans, and

---

[80] Borowski, *Daily Life*, 25–29.
[81] Levine, *Leviticus*, 273–74. For land tenure in the Persian period, see Yochanan Muffs, *Studies in the Aramaic Legal Papyri from Elephantine* (Leiden: Brill, 1969), 16–29.
[82] Levine, *Leviticus*, 274–75. Cf. Baruch A. Levine, "Late Language in the Priestly Source: Some Literary and Historical Observations," in *Proceedings of the Eighth World Congress of Jewish Studies* (Jerusalem: World Union of Jewish Studies, 1983), 69–82.
[83] See Milgom, *Leviticus 23–27*, 2257–69.

tribes.⁸⁴ Though the legislation may have evolved over time during, or after, the monarchy, the system reflects an agrarian tribal/clan social setting concerned with preserving localized household ownership of the land.⁸⁵

Land tenancy and the Jubilee are concluded in Leviticus 26 with a list of blessings and curses. This summative section draws together the whole of the law, both ritual and ethical, by calling Israel to obedience. The first and second commandments of the Decalogue are repeated (Lev 26:1) as a mandate against idolatry and the worship of God alone. This is followed by a further emphasis on obedience to the sabbath, which is elevated to the same level of holiness as the tabernacle (Lev 26:2). Milgrom contends that these are the additions of a postexilic priestly redactor who assumed that Israel's idolatry and failure to keep the sabbath resulted in the Babylonian exile.⁸⁶ Whether they were original or an addition, *they express a theology that underscores the sanctity of time and space within the land.* Holiness can only be achieved by being set apart from the idolatry and practices of Israel's neighbors so that they might worship God alone. To do so they must maintain a reverence for God's sanctuary (*miqdāš*) and keep (*šāmar*) the sabbath, which preserves the family (*bēt 'āb*), the alien, and the land. The sabbath preserves the life and health of the community and offers a pattern for sabbath years, rest for the land, and the release of the Jubilee. By beginning with these commands at the outset of chapter 26, the priestly authors highlight the theological principles expressed throughout the whole

---

⁸⁴ Wright, *God's People*, 125–28. Leviticus also makes no mention of a monarch in the role of land redistribution.

⁸⁵ For biblical witnesses to the legal standing of household or clan ownership of the land, see 1 Kings 21; Isa 5:8; Jer 34:12–16; Micah 2:1–2; 2 Chron 36:21.

⁸⁶ Milgrom, *Leviticus 23–27*, 2275–79.

book: worship Yhwh alone and keep his home – and every Israelite home – holy.

The list of blessings and curses are set up in a parallel structure demonstrating rewards for obedience and punishment for disobedience.[87] They begin with blessing, fertility, and peace in the land against the enemy (Lev 26:3–10) with the promise of God's abiding presence (vv. 11–13). The result of disobedience will be famine, defeat, and lack of harvests (vv. 14–22) followed by war, pestilence, famine, and God's abandonment of his people to exile (vv. 23–39). We note the emphasis on the land (*'ereṣ*), which occurs twenty-three times in chapter 26 and seventeen times in vv. 3–39. Balentine contends that the rhetorical emphasis draws the reader back to the fact that, "Neither Israel nor the land can survive the neglect of the sabbatical rest that allows them to replenish their energies, renew their capacities, and fulfill their God-given destinies."[88] The focus of the blessings/curses is on the whole of Israel and the people dwelling in the land. There is no distinction made between priest and layperson, but all will suffer the consequences of disobedience, including the land, which will also experience the covenant curses (cf. Gen 3:17–19).

As dire and striking as the curses are that Yhwh will inflict on Israel, a sense of hope is preserved in the possibility of confession and repentance (vv. 40–41) where God will remember his covenant and the land (v. 42). A theology of hope comes to the fore where sin and defilement of the land and tabernacle, no matter how extreme, can be cleansed and healed through humility, repentance, and time. This links back to the sacrificial and purity laws of 1–16 where the commands and rituals allow for Israel to

---

[87] Levine, *Leviticus*, 276.
[88] Balentine, *Leviticus*, 200; cf. Gerstenberger, *Leviticus*, 406–9.

approach God's holiness to maintain their covenant relationship. Leviticus is clear about the terrifying prospect of God's judgment for disobedience, but it does so with the future hope of forgiveness, restoration, and atonement made for the people and the land.

Leviticus presents a theology of holy space that encompasses the sanctuary, the land, and sacred time. The source of holiness that must be contained and mediated by the priests in the tabernacle extends to every Israelite home and to the land that sustains them. The covenant bond between Yhwh, Israel, and the land shapes the laws and prescriptions around the sabbath, sanctified time, and the Jubilee. Holiness requires rest for the people and rest for the land. It also requires justice and freedom for all those who work the land. Leviticus offers a vision of a Yhwh as a benevolent king who has gifted his people with tenancy to serve in his kingdom. Yet this king is also just and will not tolerate the abuse of his creation. The land will be given its proper rest (Lev 26:43) even at the expense of an exiled people. Yet even in the midst of exile, there is hope for future redemption and deliverance.

CHAPTER 5

Love Your Neighbor (Leviticus 17–22)

THE HOLINESS CODE

Scholarship since the time of Julius Wellhausen (1844–1918) has tended to view the distinctive linguistic and thematic material of Leviticus 17–27 as a sign of different authorship with a different agenda than the P material. Wellhausen's unfortunate stereotypes of priests as largely consumed only with cultic matters contributed to his argument that the ethical material in Leviticus derived mainly from the prophetic tradition.[1] Later, August Klostermann labeled Leviticus 17–26 as the "holiness code" to distinguish it from the Priestly material of chapters 1–16.[2] The division between the Priestly materials and the Holiness Code (H or HC) has been assumed in Old Testament scholarship ever since, though debates continue on its dating and redaction.

In the twentieth century, some new perspectives on the Holiness Code emerged. Karl Elliger argued that H must be considered in relation to the priestly material as redactional

---

[1] Wellhausen, *Prolegomena*, 376–80.
[2] August Klostermann, *Der Pentateuch: Beiträge zu einem Verständis und seiner Enstehungsgeschichte* (Leipzig: A. Deichert [Georg Böhme], 1893), 368–418.

additions that were made over time.³ Since then, the two most significant proposals have come from Israel Knohl and Jacob Milgrom who have argued for a "holiness school" (HS) that was active in priestly circles around the eighth century BCE.⁴ Both Milgrom and Knohl, with their own nuances, contend that the theological movement toward social justice and ethical holiness began with the eighth-century prophets (especially Isaiah and Micah). The dramatic sociopolitical events from ca. 740–701 BCE brought about a priestly reform that rebalanced a prior emphasis on cultic sacrifice. The theological shift to justice and righteousness as key aspects of holiness took shape within the Jerusalem priesthood around the time of Hezekiah and influenced Ezekiel and the exilic/postexilic priestly circles responsible for the formation of Torah. Knohl and Milgrom's preexilic dating of H marks a departure from most Old Testament scholars.

Not all are convinced by historical-critical arguments and have, instead, sought to find consistency and harmony throughout the entire text of Leviticus. Wilfred Warning, in a detailed study of the linguistic features of Leviticus, concludes that "the relation of P and H outside Leviticus ought to be reconsidered, because Leviticus reveals a text where a distinction between P and H is seemingly irrelevant, or even nonexistent."⁵ His textual survey points to the fact that there are linguistic and thematic similarities that exist throughout Leviticus. Rolf Rendtorff agrees and sides with Mary Douglas' ring theory, which proposes that Leviticus should be read as a single composition that cannot be artificially

---

³ Karl Elliger, *Leviticus* (Tübingen: Mohr Siebeck, 1966), 176.
⁴ Knohl, *Sanctuary of Silence*, 212–16; Milgrom, *Leviticus 17–22*, 1332–64.
⁵ Wilfred Warning, *Literary Artistry in Leviticus* (Leiden: Brill, 1999), 180.

broken into two separate documents.⁶ Other scholars such as James Watts have focused on the rhetorical nature of the text. Watts contends that Leviticus offers a defense of the Aaronide priesthood with a particular priestly rhetoric that supported the power of the priestly institution in Second Temple Judaism.⁷

One point that is often neglected in scholarly arguments about H is the theological connections between ritual and ethical behavior. Balentine contends that "the rituals of holy worship are not only inextricably wedded to the ethics of holy living; they are also fundamentally *generative* of the community's motivation to obedience."⁸ The transformational nature of ritual, and the knowledge gained from it, inspire Israel's obedience to the ethical call of holiness. In this sense, ritual is generative of ethical living because the physical repetition of making offerings, adhering to food and purity regulations, or participating in annual festivals engenders a knowledge of the holiness of God, which in turn influences the way one treats their neighbor. As Balentine argues, ritual and ethics are "inextricably wedded" because they both emerge from a distinctive theology of who Yhwh is and how he commands his people to live in holiness.

Ritual acts performed at the altar and ethical treatment of one's neighbor are inseparable. Thus, we can see that the rituals of sacrifice, food laws, or purity commands also give rise to an ethical mandate for holiness within the family and community. As we hear at the end of the dietary laws in chapter 11, "For I am the LORD your God; sanctify yourselves therefore, and be holy, for

---

⁶ Rolf Rendtorff, "Is It Possible to Read Leviticus as a Separate Book?" in *Reading Leviticus: A Conversation with Mary Douglas*, ed. John F. A. Sawyer, JSOTSS 227 (Sheffield: Sheffield Academic Press, 1996), 22–35.
⁷ Watts, *Ritual and Rhetoric*, 142–72.
⁸ Balentine, *Leviticus*, 142.

I am holy" (Lev 11:44). Though this verse is often attributed to an H (HS) redactor, the echo of Lev 19:2 is not accidental.[9] The call to holiness and the *imitatio Dei* is as critical to Leviticus 1–16 as it is to 17–26.

A BRIDGE FROM GOD'S HOME TO ISRAEL'S HOME

Scholars have long noted that Leviticus 17 acts as a bridge between the ritual commands concerning the tabernacle and the ethical commands of the following chapters. It has been described as a bridge because it connects the sacrificial and ritual material of chapters 1–16 with the rest of the book.[10] As noted above, the division between chapters 1–16 and 17–26 need not be thought of as reflecting completely different schools of authors. Instead, we can begin to see the theological flow in Leviticus from ritual to ethical behavior that takes place at this juncture of the book in a special way.

Different scholars have offered theories as to how chapter 17 acts as a link in the whole book. In her ring theory, Mary Douglas proposes that chapter 17 is the clasp that connects the inner circle (1–16) to the outer circle (18–27). She bases her argument on the ring structures found in Greek poetry from the eighth century BCE and contends that Leviticus neatly divides into chapters 1–16, which form the first part of the ring, which is then

---

[9] Cf. Baruch Levine, "The Language of Holiness: Perceptions of the Sacred in the Hebrew Bible," in *Backgrounds for the Bible*, ed. M. P. O'Conner and D. N. Freedman (Winona Lake, IN: Eisenbrauns, 1987), 241–55.

[10] For linguistic parallels between Leviticus 16 and 17, see Erich Zenger, "Das Buch Levitikus als Teiltext der Tora/des Pentateuch. Eine synchrone Lektüre mit diachroner Perspektive," in *Levitikus als Buch*, ed. Heinz-Josef Fabry and Hans-Winfried Jüngling, BBB 119 (Berlin: Philo, 1999), 65–67, 71–73.

Love Your Neighbor (Leviticus 17–22) 161

linked by chapter 17 to the second half of 18–27.[11] Milgrom agrees with Douglas on the ring structure but argues that a Holiness redactor was responsible for selecting priestly material for chapters 1–16 and then creating the bridge of chapter 17 as it relates to the framework of chapters 18 and 20 around the beginning of H in chapter 19.[12] Milgrom maintains his argument for the distinctive characteristics between P and H despite agreeing to the unity of Leviticus' final structure. Whereas Milgrom and others find textual divisions in Leviticus' composition and redaction, a synchronic reading reveals a theological unity and consistency within the text.

Though there is general agreement among scholars that chapter 17 forms a structural link or bridge to the remaining chapters, there has not emerged a fuller theological explanation for the connection being made between cultic regulations and the ethical commands that follow. Wenham contends that the shift moves from ritual regulations governing "public life and worship" to those concerned with "personal and private affairs of individuals."[13] Though this provides a general overview of the differences, there may be finer nuances that help illuminate the text's theological meaning.

To use the illustration of the home that has been discussed thus far, we find a natural transition in chapter 17 from concern for holiness in relation to God's home (the tabernacle) to life in relation to Israel's home (the family). This is not so much a division between public and private life but, rather, the concern is with *the movement of holiness from the tent of Yhwh to the tents of Israel*. In chapters 1–16, the concern with appropriate priestly

---

[11] Douglas, *Leviticus as Literature*, 41–53, 192–94, 222–27.
[12] Milgrom, *Leviticus 17–22*, 1364–67.
[13] Wenham, *Leviticus*, 241.

sacrifice and maintaining the purity and sanctity of Yhwh's dwelling place offers a movement that guides the reader toward the tabernacle. This is most explicit in chapters 1–7 in the descriptions of sacrifices that take place at the altar within the tent. Chapters 8–10 usher us inside the holy place through the narration of events that took place at the inauguration of the cultic site and the consecration of the altar. The shift to the purity laws of 11–15 move us back to everyday Israelite life, but they do so only insofar as the commands relate to maintaining the purity of the tabernacle (cf. Lev 15:31). The purity laws consistently focus on the holiness of the tabernacle by regulating who can draw near to Yhwh's home. Finally, chapter 16 allows the reader entrance into the Holy of Holies, the inner most sanctum of God's dwelling, and reveals the duties of the high priest on the Day of Atonement. This climactic moment in the Israelite cultic calendar serves as the culmination of all sacrifice and the complete purification of God's home.

In chapter 17, we transition from moving inward toward God's dwelling place to life outside the sanctuary – from God's home to Israel's home. Since the commands of chapter 17 focus on the nature and consumption of blood, they create a link at the altar between blood that is shed on Yhwh's table and the portion of the sacrifice brought into Israel's home to be eaten at the family table. We also note a shift in language in chapters 17 and 22 where the more common term *bənê yiśrā'ēl* ("the Israelites") is substituted with the more focused, *bêt yiśrā'ēl* ("the household of Israel").

There are five laws around the prohibition of consuming blood in relation to the home in chapter 17. The first two commands prohibit domestic animals being killed outside the tabernacle (vv. 3–7) and that there can be no sacrifices offered apart from Yhwh's altar (vv. 8–9). The commands around blood in vv. 10–12 form the crux of the chapter, which give the rationale for the previous commands and provide a basis for those following concerning the eating of game (v. 13) or touching a dead carcass (vv. 15–16).[14] Though we are dealing with the physical material of sacrifice (animals and blood), we note that the mention of priests only occurs in the introduction where Moses is commanded to "speak to Aaron and to his sons and to all the Israelites" (v. 2) and in reference to the priest making the well-being offering (v. 6). The commands are directed primarily at the average Israelite but because sacrificial blood is involved, the priests must necessarily be involved as well.

The prohibition against secular slaughter is not compared with sacrifice at an alternate shrine but with something that is done "in the open field" (Lev 17:5). The comparison between the tent of meeting and the open field delineates between sacred and secular space. To shed blood on the "face of the field" (ʿal-pənê haśśādeh) is to offer incorrectly the most sacred substance of life given by God in the profane world. There may be an allusion here to the innocent blood of Abel who was murdered by Cain. Cain invited Abel out into the field (śādeh) where he killed him and left the blood of his brother to be received by the open mouth of the earth where it cried out for justice (Gen 4:8–11; cf. 1 En. 22:7; Heb 12:24). Because shedding blood apart from the altar is tantamount to murder (Lev 17:3–4), the actions of Cain against his brother serve as a reminder of the crime and punishment for shedding blood.

Milgrom contends that the "open field" could refer to chthonic worship rituals that involved digging a circular trench in the earth and then pouring sacrificial blood into the center.[15] Other ancient

---

[14] Wenham, *Leviticus*, 240; Milgrom, *Leviticus 23–27*, 1448–49.
[15] Milgrom, *Leviticus 17–22*, 1460, 1490–93.

Near Eastern cultures had traditions of offering blood to the gods of the underworld and we may find a similar example in Saul's hasty sacrifice after his battle with the Philistines (1 Sam 14:31–35). Though speculative, this may also account for Leviticus' prohibition of offering to "goat-demons" (Lev 17:7), which may be a reference to the satyrs or the chthonic goat-demons of the underworld. Milgrom points out that goats were also identified with the Ugaritic god of the underworld, Mot, who may be associated with the demon Azazel in the *Yom Kippur* rite.[16]

Whether the offerings Israel made in the open field were connected to biblical stories of fratricide, chthonic worship, or something performed in profane space, the injunction of Leviticus is to consider the life-blood of any animal (or human) as the sole property of Yhwh. The formally profane acts committed in the open field must undergo a conversion of purpose and intent so that they might become well-being offerings (šəlāmîm) given at the opening of the tent of meeting. This is so that any blood and fat offerings may be a "pleasing aroma" to Yhwh rather than a crime against him and the order of his creation. The theological concern of Leviticus here is not for the centralization of worship at a single sanctuary. Instead, what is at stake is the distinction between sacred and profane space when dealing with the most precious substance of blood. All sacrifice of domestic animals must take place at an authorized shrine because the blood of all animals is imbued with the life of the divine creator. Lifeblood that is shed for the table of the Israelites is directly linked to the table of Yhwh – the altar.

There has been, however, a long-standing debate dating back to the early rabbis about whether this command contradicts the

---

[16] Milgrom, *Leviticus 17–22*, 1462.

permission of secular slaughter in Deut 12:15–16.[17] The key interpretive verb is *šāḥaṭ* ("slaughter"), which can refer to both non-sacrificial and sacrificial killing. To harmonize the restrictions of Leviticus with Deuteronomy, commentators have argued that *šāḥaṭ* is limited to the ox, lamb, and goat. This restricted view of the verb would allow for slaughtering other animals outside of the central sanctuary as long as the blood was drained from the animal. Milgrom, however, contends that the ban on all non-sacrificial slaughter is the "radical innovation of H," which likely implies a current or previous time in Israel's history when non-sacrificial slaughter was practiced and approved, possibly according to the altar laws of Exod 20:24–25 (cf. 1 Sam 14:31–35).[18]

If *šāḥaṭ* is taken in its broadest sense and Leviticus prohibits any form of non-sacrificial slaughter of domestic animals, then the laws suggest some sort of reform of previous practices of sacrificing "in the open fields" or to other demons. For this type of prohibition to exist, there would need to be local shrines where the Israelites could offer their animals. Douglas makes an important point as she highlights that ancient farmers had to maintain the male to female balance of their flocks in order to preserve the surrounding grazing lands. To do so, flocks would have to be thinned through the killing of animals or by the castration of males. Since blemished animals (i.e., castrated) could not be offered at the altar, there would be no way for the Israelite to kill the animal. If they were abiding by the Levitical laws, the frequent sacrifices of animals at a local shrine would be one of the only ways to achieve, "an economically viable ratio of males to females ... In that case it would be impossible and even

---

[17] Hartley, *Leviticus*, 269–71.
[18] Milgrom, *Leviticus 17–22*, 1452–53.

ridiculous to require livestock farmers to do every killing at a central place."[19] This very important, practical point seems to be exactly what Deuteronomy addresses in its more pragmatic allowance for profane slaughter to take place outside of a centralized sanctuary (Deut 12:15-16). If the Levitical prohibitions regarding sacrifice are taken in their broadest sense, then a decentralized system of regional sanctuaries must have been assumed.

Whether H was being innovative or not,[20] the prohibitions around meat and blood point to a reform from previous practices where Israelites offered sacrifices wherever they chose, possibly to other gods/demons. The rhetorical imperative of Leviticus, however, is that all blood can only be handled by authorized personnel within the authorized space of Yhwh's sanctuary. Such strict limitations necessarily required practical access to shrines for farmers throughout the tribal territories. Unless Leviticus is proposing some impossible utopian practice, which seems unlikely considering the very practical instructions of the sacrificial and purity laws, there must have been decentralized shrines where authorized sacrifices could take place.

The reason for such strict adherence to all slaughter being offered at the sanctuary by authorized priests is given in the crux of the chapter (vv. 10-12). The penalty for ingesting the blood of an animal is that the offender will be "cut off" (*kārat*) from the covenant community (vv. 4, 9, 10, 14 ,16). Only v. 10 specifically states that the agent of the punishment is Yhwh himself (cf. Gen

---

[19] Douglas, *Leviticus as Literature*, 95-96.
[20] Baruch Schwartz, "'Profane' Slaughter and the Integrity of the Priestly Code," *HUCA* 67 (1996): 15-42; Baruch Schwartz, *The Holiness Legislation: Studies in the Priestly Code* (Jerusalem: Magnes, 1999), 97-101 (Hebrew).

Love Your Neighbor (Leviticus 17-22) 167

4:11–16).²¹ So sacrosanct is the shedding of blood that the retribution for unlawful slaughter is exacted by the divine. The precise meaning of being "cut off" has been debated but some possibilities are childlessness, premature death, punishment on descendants, excommunication, death by another person, or exclusion from the afterlife.²² Such drastic consequences for shedding blood are explained in v. 4 where the person who has "shed blood" (*dām šāpak*) is liable for the "guilt of bloodshed" (*dām yêḥāšēb*). The principle of *lex talionis* is invoked here through the repetition of *dām* and offers echoes of the Noachide instructions given after the flood that humans should "not eat flesh with its life, that is, its blood" (Gen 9:4). This is followed by the parallel command that shedding the blood (both animal and human) will require a reckoning from God (Gen 9:6). The underlying principle is that shedding the blood of an animal unlawfully is the equivalent to murder.

Lev 17:11 states, "For the life of the flesh is in the blood; and I have given it to you for making atonement for your lives on the altar; for, as life, it is the blood that makes atonement." Though v. 11 points to blood as given "for atonement" (*ləkappēr*), we recall that this chapter is moving us from God's home to Israel's home by linking altar to table. The subject matter of the offering in chapter 17 is the *šəlāmîm* (v. 5) or the more general burnt offering (*'ōla*) (v. 8) and not specifically the *ḥaṭṭā't*, which is associated with expiation. Some scholars contend that Lev 17:11 addresses all sacrifices, but this misses the distinctiveness of the *šəlāmîm*, which is an offering consumed by the laity in the home. The regulations around bloodshed offer overarching principles

---

²¹ For the active verb with God as subject see Lev 20:3-6; Ezek 14:8.
²² Milgrom, *Leviticus 1-16*, 457-60.

regarding sacrifice but more specifically relate to the killing of animals for the sake of food for the Israelite household. In this bridge between God's home and Israel's home, Leviticus offers a universal principle for blood that relates to the cult (v. 11) but, more importantly, it links the sanctity of blood to the economy (*oikonomia*) of the household.

Milgrom contends that v. 11 is an innovation by H, which has created an expiatory function for the *šəlāmîm*. In this instance, the sacrifice provides atonement or expiation for the offerer for the sin of murder committed when slaughtering an animal.[23] However, it seems unnecessary to separate between P and H when chapter 17 is merely addressing two concepts that have to do with blood. The first is the universal principle of blood as it pertains to life found in v. 11 and the second is how that life is connected both to God and, by necessity, his altar for atonement. There is no need to designate the *šəlāmîm* as expiatory to atone for the murder of an animal. Instead, the general principles of atonement, blood, and sacrifice are extended, by analogy, to blood that is spilled for the consumption of meat, which must be done according to God's commandments or else it will be synonymous with murder.

Leviticus offers a theology of the material world and how it stands in relation to God's table and to the table of the Israelites. Blood is the chief substance of all creation in relation to the altar because it bears the God-given life of a creature and thus can be used for atonement or as a ransom for human sin. This, however, is only achieved when Israel brings blood to an authorized altar through the official priests. The latent power of blood can only be fully harnessed through the power of the altar to expiate, cleanse,

---

[23] Milgrom, *Leviticus 17-22*, 1474-78.

and bring new life.[24] Chapter 17 teaches the Israelites that the food they eat is imbued with the power of God and that the blood of animals, the preeminent source of life given for atonement, must never be consumed.

The transition from the altar to table, or from Yhwh's home to Israel's home, is fully achieved in Leviticus 17. This will lead to the second theological movement of Leviticus, which is the call to ethical holiness both within the family and toward one's neighbor. Israel is to be holy as Yhwh is holy, which means that everything from the innermost familial relationships to the treatment of the foreigner and even ethical care for the land must reflect God's holiness.

SEXUAL ETHICS AND THE HEALTH OF THE FAMILY

We have noted that the theological imperative of Leviticus is the call for Israel to be holy in both cultic and ethical matters. If chapter 17 acts as a bridge from cultic holiness in relation to God's home to ethical holiness in Israel's home, then chapters 18 and 20 take us one step further into the most intimate of household spaces – the bedroom. The summative call to holiness and the *imitatio Dei* of Lev 19:2 sit between the pillars of chapters 18 and 20, both of which highlight the critical mandate for sexual purity within the family. How Israel loves their neighbor begins first with how they love and respect those closest to them in the home.

Chapters 18 and 20 share similar content but contain an inverse structure. Chapter 18 begins with the injunction to obey the statutes and commandments of Yhwh (vv. 1–5), which is

---

[24] Milgrom, *Leviticus 17–22*, 1479.

followed by a set of sexual prohibitions (vv. 6–20, 22–23) and a command against offering child sacrifices to Molech (v. 21). It concludes with a warning against sexual defilement that will pollute the land and, consequently, vomit out its inhabitants, which happened to its previous inhabitants (vv. 24–30).

Chapter 20 repeats similar themes but contains slightly different structural and linguistic features. The opening verses offer strict commands against Molech worship or the use of mediums and the punishment for such behavior (vv. 1–6). This is followed by the call to obey the statutes and commandments (vv. 7–8) and a list of sexual prohibitions (vv. 9–21) that include various punishments including death, childlessness, and being cut off from the people. The concluding exhortation to obedience again warns of being vomited out for abhorrent sexual practices with further commands to distinguish between clean and unclean things so that Israel might live in holiness and enjoy the blessings of the land (vv. 22–27).

The list of sexual restrictions in Leviticus 18 may appear scandalous to the modern reader. Were the Canaanites (and the Israelites) really having intercourse with mothers, step-mothers, cousins, nieces, neighbor's wives, or even animals? Some of the prohibitions listed may have had to do with Canaanite fertility cults or chthonic rites.[25] In most of the commands, however, the person being addressed is the paterfamilias or possibly the eldest son. The father's house (*bēt 'āb*) could be composed of three to five generations living in close proximity. The firstborn son would

---

[25] Milgrom, *Leviticus 17–22*, 1570, notes that in the Hittite laws bestiality was permitted with a horse or a mule but was prohibited with an ox, a sheep, or a dog. See Ephraim Neufeld, *The Hittite Laws* (London: Luzac, 1951), § 200A, §§ 187–88.

assume the head of household when the father became too elderly and other brothers may have created their own homes next to the father's house or nearby but they would still remain under the authority of the paterfamilias.[26] Leviticus assumes the role of the household father in maintaining appropriate sexual divisions within the family and protecting the roles and identities of each member. We recall the priestly notion of division and order within creation and how crossing forbidden boundaries or mixing forbidden things leads to chaos or destruction. In a similar manner, Leviticus applies this worldview analogically to sexual relations within the family. In this case, crossing these boundaries leads not only to the breakdown of the family but to the defilement of the land.

In chapter 18, there are fifteen commands against incest (Lev 18:6–18) that use the phrase "uncover the nakedness" as a euphemism for sexual intercourse. The underlying presupposition in these commands is that sexual relations within the household are critical to the life of holiness. Though not explicitly stated, the assumption is that intercourse is appropriate within the bond of marriage between a husband and wife and must take place at the proper time (i.e., not during menstruation) to procreate and thus fulfill God's commandment to be fruitful and multiply (Gen 1:28). Anything outside of this results in the unnatural mixing of divinely appointed categories that defile familial relationships and pollute the land (Lev 19:24–25).

One theological theme that emerges from these commands is the use of power within the family and the role of the paterfamilias in maintaining proper sexual distinctions between

---

[26] Norman Gottwald, *The Tribes of Israel* (Mary Knoll, NY: Orbis Books, 1979), 285–92.

family members. Just as the sabbath command requires the father to ensure that the entire household rests on the seventh day, so too do the commands regarding sexual behavior come under his authority. The abuse of power results in the breakdown of relationships and experiences of betrayal instead of mutual trust. If the father (or possibly another male in the family) chooses to have intercourse with anyone in the household beyond their wife, it could lead to the misogynistic treatment of women who were vulnerable to male power and demands. The story of Amnon and the rape of Tamar (2 Samuel 13) offers an illustration of uncontrolled lust that results in incestuous abuse of an innocent sister and the complete disintegration of the family. Leviticus is concerned with the appropriate use of power within the household in order to preserve the trust and safety of its members. This is to ensure that the most vulnerable are protected and given the safety and space to grow in their roles and identities within the home to contribute to its health, flourishing, and purity.

In the food laws, we saw how physical appetites were restricted for the sake of purity and holiness in relation to the tabernacle. In a similar manner, Leviticus 18 and 20 impose limits on sexual appetites for the sake of preserving the wholeness and holiness of the family. In both instances, Leviticus creates a link between holiness and restricting natural human appetites. This was not a type of asceticism but, rather, it demonstrates Leviticus' belief that living in holiness also requires the sanctity of sexual relations within the marriage bond for the benefit of the whole family and the wider covenant community. Physical and sexual appetites are not condemned in Leviticus, but they are firmly located within the boundaries that God establishes for mutually flourishing human relationships. For Israel to be a holy people and dwell within the land, they must be distinct from the nations that surround them especially in regard to sexual relations within the family.

Leviticus offers various punishments for sexual transgressions, but the most dramatic is the pollution of the earth. The idea that the land suffers as a result of human sin is rooted in the creation narrative. The disobedience of the first garden dwellers results in the ground being cursed (Gen 3:17).[27] From this point in Genesis, the contamination of the land by human sin becomes a consistent motif throughout the biblical text (cf. Gen 4:12; 6:1–6; Num 35:33–34; Deut 24:4; Isa 24:5–6; Jer 3:2; Ezek 36:18) but, as Milgrom contends, Leviticus is the only place where sexual sin is directly linked to the punishment of being vomited out of the land.[28] He argues that, "Ritual impurity always allows for purification through atonement. But the sexual abominations of Lev 18 (and 20) are not expiable through ritual."[29] This is a significant theological point in Leviticus because the buildup of sexual sin among the Israelites is likened to a consistent poisoning of the land that will result in exile and the vomiting out of its inhabitants. We recall that Leviticus speaks of the land enjoying the sabbath rest it was denied by Israel when they were sent into exile (Lev 26:34–35), but there is no remedy given for the land when it is polluted by sexual sin. So serious are sexual transgressions against family members and others that they are punishable by death (Lev 20:10–14), or being cut off (Lev 20:18), or for the entire covenant community to be expelled from land (Lev 18:28; 20:22).

---

[27] See Mark Scarlata, *Wine, Soil, and Salvation in the Hebrew Bible and New Testament* (Cambridge: Cambridge University Press, 2024), 23–38.
[28] Milgrom, *Leviticus 17–22*, 1572–84.
[29] Milgrom, *Leviticus 17–22*, 1573.

The prohibitions concerning sexual purity are also linked to the pagan god Molech (Lev 18:21; 20:1–5). There are different theories regarding the origins of this name derived from the root *m-l-k*, but in Leviticus it is most likely associated with the Ugaritic god of the underworld, Mot, who was worshiped in the Canaanite ancestral cult.[30] It may seem puzzling to move from inappropriate sexual activity within the family to sacrificing a child, but the command may be linked to Canaanite cultic practice. Weinfeld follows the rabbis in arguing that the context of forbidden sexual relations in chapters 18 and 20 allude to the fact that Molech worship was characterized not by child sacrifice but by illicit sexual intercourse. He proposes that the phrase "to pass through fire" referred to the giving of offspring to Molech as a dedication to the deity and not the actual killing of the child.[31] The biblical evidence, however, may point to the fact that child sacrifice was, indeed, practiced by the Israelites. The Deuteronomistic Historian's summary of the fall of the Northern Kingdom (2 Kgs 17:17) and condemnation of both Ahaz (2 Kgs 16:3) and Manasseh (2 Kgs 21:6) offer explicit references to the Israelites making their children "pass through fire" (cf. Isa 57:5–6). Only Josiah is credited with having defiled the Topheth, an apparent shrine or altar to Molech, so that, "no one would make a son

---

[30] George C. Heider, *The Cult of Molek: A Reassessment*, JSOTSS 43 (Sheffield: Continuum International, 1985), 113–49.

[31] Moshe Weinfeld, "The Worship of Molech and of the Queen of Heaven and Its Background," *Ugarit-Forschungen* 4 (1972): 133–54. Cf. John Day, *Molech: A God of Human Sacrifice in the Old Testament* (Cambridge: Cambridge University Press, 1989); Calum M. Carmichael, *Law, Legend, and Incest in the Bible: Leviticus 18–20* (Ithaca, NY: Cornell University Press, 1997), 14–44; Heath D. Dewrell, "Whoring after the Molek in Leviticus 20,5. A Text-Critical Examination," *ZAW* 127 (2015): 628–35.

or a daughter to pass through fire as an offering to Molech" (2 Kgs 23:10). Milgrom raises an important cultural point about the pervasive forms of ancestral worship throughout the biblical world and how these were tied to Israel's own practices of necromancy or Molech worship.[32] Necromancy, which is linked to Molech worship in Lev 20:2, 27, sought to lure spirits up from the dead through various blood rites and chthonic worship. The clearest biblical example of this is Saul's engagement with the medium of Endor (1 Sam 28:4–25). Saul seeks out the counsel of Samuel who appears like a "divine being" (*'elōhîm*) in anthropomorphic form and speaks to the king. Necromancy and ancestral worship was common among Israel's neighbors and from the biblical text it seems that the practice of worshipping the dead was engrained in popular Israelite religion.[33] Leviticus, however, seeks to ban these unauthorized cultic practices in chapters 18 and 20 by equating the perversion of sexual sins with the practices of worshipping Molech and necromancy.

In addition to incest and other chthonic practices, Leviticus also condemns same-sex acts committed by men. "You shall not lie with a male as with a woman; it is an abomination" (Lev 18:22; 20:13).[34] This is followed by a command not to have sexual relations with animals (Lev 18:23; 20:15–16). From the analysis

---

[32] Milgrom, *Leviticus 17–22*, 1768–85.
[33] Karel van der Toorn, *Family Religion in Babylonia, Syria and Israel* (Leiden: Brill, 1996); Karel van der Toorn, *God in Context: Selected Essays on Society and Religion in the Early Middle East*, FAT 123 (Tübingen: Mohr Siebeck, 2018), 323–33.
[34] The translation "abomination" suggests something that is abhorrent in the sense of violating a social/religious boundary. See Saul M. Olyan, "'And with a Male You Shall Not Lie the Lying down of a Woman': On the Meaning and Significance of Leviticus 18:22 and 20:13," *Journal of the History of*

above, an initial interpretation of these prohibitions is that they could somehow relate to chthonic rituals or possibly Canaanite fertility rites. Same-sex activities were not uncommon in the biblical world. These may have occurred alongside the work of male/female prostitutes, though the idea of cultic prostitution has come under question in recent scholarship.[35] Israelite sons or daughters were prohibited from the work of temple prostitution (Deut 23:18–19), and Leviticus prohibits same-sex acts within the household that could threaten its stability and purity.[36] Once again, the intended recipient of the command is the paterfamilias exerting their power through possible sexual abuse of others within the family. In this case, Leviticus prohibits same-sex acts within a household as a possible abuse of power that leads to the destruction of the family and the defilement of the land.

Same-sex acts are labeled an "abomination" (Lev 18:22; 20:13). This word is repeated four times in Lev 18:26–30 specifically in relation to the ways of the Canaanites and the defilement of the land. The emphasis on sexual prohibitions, whether incestuous, same-sex, or with animals, all relate back to Israel being distinct from the ways of the Canaanites. The concern of Leviticus at this point is that Israelite families refrain from sexual activities that

---

Sexuality 5 (1994): 179–206; Jerome T. Walsh, "Leviticus 18:22 and 20:13: Who Is Doing What to Whom?" *JBL* 120 (2001): 201–9.

[35] Stephanie Lynn Budin, *The Myth of Sacred Prostitution in Antiquity* (Cambridge: Cambridge University Press, 2009), 14–47, argues against the commonly held belief that there were sacred prostitutes associated with the Canaanite cult. Cf. Edward Lipiński, "Cult Prostitution and Passage Rites in the Biblical World," *The Biblical Annals* 3, 60 (2013): 9–27; Phyllis A. Bird, *Missing Persons and Mistaken Identities Women and Gender in Ancient Israel* (Minneapolis, MN: Fortress Press, 1997), 40–41, 199–202; Phyllis A. Bird, *Harlot or Holy Woman?: A Study of Hebrew Qedešah* (University Park: Penn State University Press, 2019).

[36] Cf. Feder, *Purity and Pollution*, 175–206.

may have been part of Canaanite cultic rituals, or other practices, so that they might remain holy.

The condemnation of same-sex relations in Leviticus is listed alongside other sexual sins and its punishment of death echoes the same punishments for adultery or cursing one's father or mother (Lev 20:9–10). The sexual prohibitions seem to be concerned with male power and how it is wielded within the household. Thus, sexual activity between males or females, with animals, or incestuously is condemned because Leviticus perceives it as the crossing of a social and religious boundary that disrupts the natural order of God's creation, the order of the family, and the act of procreation that is reserved for the marriage covenant between a husband and wife.

Milgrom argues that the ban on same-sex relations should be read in relation to God's command in Genesis 1 to be fruitful and multiply.[37] The birthrate among ancient Israelites was a constant concern not only for sustaining one's lineage but also for populating a land in which the Canaanites were also reproducing. Same-sex activity results in male copulation without the potential for reproduction. This may have been seen as a misuse of the life intended for reproduction and a betrayal of the covenantal promises of a people that would vastly multiply throughout their generations (Gen 17:2–7).

Another point in relation to creational motifs is the notion of maintaining proper divisions within God's natural order. We noted that the priestly account of order in Genesis 1 provides the framework for divisions between what is pure and impure. If the same symbols are applied to sexual unions, then the approved bond between male and female within marriage (Gen

---

[37] Milgrom, *Leviticus 17–22*, 1565–70, 1786–90.

2:21–24) stands as representative of the social vehicle that enables appropriate procreation.[38] If this classification is transgressed, order breaks down and Leviticus sees this as a path leading to chaos.

The theology around the commands for sexual purity within the household seem to be working on two levels. The first is to protect the natural divisions that God has established in creation to fulfill the mandate of reproduction between a husband and wife. To achieve this blessing of the original created order and to fulfill the Abrahamic covenant, the roles and identity of each family member within the household must be preserved so that illicit sexual relations do not lead to the breakdown of mutual trust and love. The roles of father/mother, son/daughter, brother/sister are given sexual boundaries and limitations so that each one might grow and fulfill their responsibility to the other and to the household. The additional commands prohibiting sexual relations between men (or with animals) are also situated within the goal of protecting the purity and blessing of the family.

The second layer of meaning is tied to Israel's call to holiness in relation to their Canaanite neighbors (Lev 18:24–25). Israel is to be distinct from the Canaanite practices of sexual immorality, child sacrifice, or chthonic rites that may have been associated with Molech. Such practices led to the defilement of the land and to the vomiting out of the inhabitants. Instead, Israel is to pursue holiness through sexual purity in the household, which will result in the stability and life of the family and its ability to produce

---

[38] Walsh, "Leviticus 18:22 and 20:13," 201–9, contends that the concern of Leviticus is maintaining proper order in sexual relations where the female is the receptor and the male the penetrator. For a male to be penetrated would be a sign of shame and defies that natural order seen in creation.

offspring. By protecting the most intimate sexual relationships within the family, Israel will maintain its purity of their households and the land to bring about blessing and fertility.

The commands around sexual relations in Leviticus 18 and 20 establish ethical behaviors that are fundamentally concerned with purity and protecting the family. The ethical purity of God's people in Leviticus begins in the most intimate spheres of the Israelite home. Leviticus is concerned with what it perceives as the natural order and boundaries that shape sexual relationships. The underlying assumption is that sexual activity is shared between a husband and wife for the sake of procreation and the population of the land. The necessity of having children was critical to ensure future generations and the continuing life of Israel. To preserve the sanctity and holiness of sexual relationships within the household is yet another area where Leviticus applies its theology of order and division for the sake of holiness.

THE *IMITATIO DEI*

The ethical call to sexual purity within the home in chapters 18 and 20 act like support structures to the preeminent call to holiness found in Leviticus 19. The grounding pillars of relational harmony in the interior life of the family lay the foundation for how Israel is to engage with the external world. The love, fidelity, and respect displayed among family members is now to extend to one's neighbor and to the alien. For a biblical book that is often characterized by the particulars of cultic and ritual matters, the heart of Leviticus reveals the covenant love and grace of Yhwh toward Israel and his desire for them to imitate and reflect that love to one another and to the world.

Milgrom argues that Leviticus 19 is not only the center of the book but the fulcrum of the entire Torah.[39] His assessment is justified since the entire raison d'être of Israel's life in the land is to be a "kingdom of priests and a holy nation" (Exod 19:6). For Leviticus, this is summed up under the theological rationale of the *imitatio Dei*, "You shall be holy, for the I the LORD your God am holy" (Lev 19:2). To imitate Yhwh's holiness is to be obedient to his command. Thus, chapter 19 sets out a series of instructions on how holiness is reflected from the home out to the wider community through one's love for God, neighbor, and the alien in the land.

The structure of the chapter is shaped around the formulation "I am Yhwh (your God)," which occurs like a musical refrain guiding the reader to the next series of commands and offers the motivation for obedience. The opening verse echoes Exod 20:2 and the beginning of the Decalogue, which is again heard in the final verses referring to the God "who brought you out of the land of Egypt" (Lev 19:36). The intentional resonance with the Sinaitic delivery of the Decalogue in Leviticus 19 can be heard through either direct repetition of the commandments or allusions to them. The first two commandments of the Decalogue are suggested in 19:4. The third commandment is repeated in 19:12 and both the fourth and fifth are recited in 19:3. Commandments six and seven are alluded to in 19:16 and 19:29, while the eighth and ninth are repeated in 19:11. The tenth commandment against coveting may be implied in 19:35–36, which prohibits cheating with unjust measurements.

Other echoes of Exodus might also be heard when God commands Moses to "speak to all the congregation of the people of

---

[39] Milgrom, *Leviticus 17–22*, 1768.

Israel" (Lev 19:2a). The identical phrase occurs with Moses as the subject in Exodus just prior to the construction of the tabernacle (Exod 35:4). He speaks to "all the congregation of the people of Israel" and invites them to bring their offerings for the construction of the tabernacle. The inclusion of "all the congregation" in Lev 19:2a as a preface to the following commands is a poignant reminder to Israel that each person's contribution to holiness is vital to maintaining Yhwh's presence among them. The construction of the tabernacle required gifts from the whole congregation to make a suitable home for Yhwh's divine presence and now it requires the ethical obedience of the whole congregation to ensure that Yhwh remains among them. The connection between the building of the tabernacle and the corporate call to ethical living form another bond between ritual and moral obedience.

Chapter 19 contains a mixture of both apodictic ("you shall ...") and casuistic ("if/when ...") commands, which begin in the home. It is not without reason that the initial call to be holy (v. 2b) is followed by the command to honor one's parents and keep the sabbath (v. 3). The fourth and fifth commandments act as a bridge in the Decalogue between how one worships God and how one treats their neighbor. We have argued that the movement of holiness in Leviticus from 1–16 to 17–26 is one that shifts from Yhwh's home to Israel's home, which was seen in chapters 18 and 20. The structure of chapter 19 continues this pattern by stressing first the honoring of the patriarch and matriarch of the family who reflect the authority of God to their children. This is followed by the sabbath command and the prohibition against making idols (Lev 19:3–4). Both practices are tied to worship within the Israelite home and are enforced by the paterfamilias.

A similar injunction regarding the sabbath is repeated in v. 30 but this time the sabbath rest of the household is elevated to equal status with Yhwh's home. "You shall keep my sabbaths and reverence my sanctuary: I am the LORD." The theological significance of this statement cannot be overestimated. Leviticus considers the Israelite home and its inhabitants as a veritable mirror image of Yhwh's sanctuary and the priests who serve there. The consecration of holy time on the sabbath is identified with the rituals and sacrifices connected to the altar. At the outset of Leviticus 19 we find that the three commandments from the Decalogue set the tone for the entire chapter – holiness that reflects God's tabernacle begins in the life and worship of the home, which then extends outward to rest of the community.

The next section on the well-being offerings (vv. 5–8) seems to draw us back to the altar of the tabernacle but the commands are, in fact, directed toward the home. Commentators have struggled to see the connection between eating an offering and the preceding weightier commands of the Decalogue. The concern of the command, however, is consuming what has been sacrificed on the altar in a timely manner by the family. This is the only instance in Leviticus where the holiness of the altar is literally connected to the Israelite table since the animal has been taken from the sacred shrine and brought into the family home. Milgrom rightly argues, "the family must treat every act of eating a meat meal as a sacred rite" and that this connection possibly contributed to the later rabbinic doctrine of the home replacing the nonexistent Temple.[40] What has been sacrificed on the altar must be eaten before the third day or else the worshipper will profane what has been offered as holy to the Lord and will be cut off (Lev 19:7–8). The seemingly severe penalty (cf. Lev 7:16–18) highlights what has already been made clear in the food laws of Leviticus 11 – the

---

[40] Milgrom, *Leviticus 17–22*, 1616.

holiness of God's table is connected to the holiness of Israel's table. To eat food offered to Yhwh that shows signs of becoming putrefied is to profane the value of the offering and the holiness of God's name (cf. Lev 22:32).

The life of holiness then moves from table to field and care for those outside of the household in vv. 9-10. The rules for leaving a remainder of the harvest or fallen grapes in the vineyards for the poor and the alien shift the focus to how the Israelite family responds to those in need or how they share their table with others.[41] The command, however, is not simply to offer charity out of one's wealth to the poor but, rather, the Israelites were to sacrifice their own sustenance for the sake of others.

Most ancient Israelite farms were small, dynamic ecosystems that relied on the work of each family member and animal to sustain its production of food or other products. In subsistence farming, there can be no waste since the margins of gain were slim or in some seasons nonexistent. With the chance of limited rainfall or the inability to purchase seed, many Israelite families would experience "hungry seasons" where there was very little to eat. Archaeologist Baruch Rosen calculates that the average Israelite subsistence farmer would experience a shortfall of about fifteen million calories per year.[42] This meant that the average family would experience food shortages for approximately sixty days a year.[43]

---

[41] The rabbis later stipulated that a sixtieth part of a harvest was the minimum requirement to fulfill this law (*Pe'ah* 1:1-2).

[42] Baruch Rosen, "Subsistence Economy in Iron Age I," in *From Nomadism to Monarchy: Archaeological and Historical Aspects of Early Israel*, ed. Israel Finkelstein and Nadav Na'aman (Jerusalem: Israel Exploration Society, 1994) 339-51 (348-49).

[43] Carol Meyers, *Rediscovering Eve: Ancient Israelite Women in Context* (Oxford: Oxford University Press, 2013) 54-58.

Unlike other parts of the world, Israel was reliant mainly on the summer and winter rains. These fell between late October and late April. There were no vast systems of irrigation for their crops like in Egypt or parts of Mesopotamia. Much of the land in Israel is rocky and hilly, which led the Israelites to create terraced fields like their gentile neighbors. This allowed them to be self-sufficient and to produce enough for their own needs but little, if any, for trade in the marketplace.[44] Thus, the command to leave part of one's harvest for the poor was not a gift out of one's abundance but, rather, it was sacrificing one's essential food supply to those in need. The holiness of God is made manifest through the generosity of his people when they provide food that sustains the life of those who are hungry. Like the manna in the wilderness, Israel is to trust in Yhwh's provision for their needs so that they can provide for the needs of others.

The following section (vv. 11–18) offers a list of ethical commands concerning how one relates to others in thought, word, and deed. These commands were discussed extensively by the rabbis and influenced early Christian behavior especially as they were expressed in the epistle of James.[45] The principle of loving your neighbor as yourself sits as the cornerstone for all ethical commands. To love one's neighbor is the summation of moral obedience to Yhwh and defines holiness as something that cannot be achieved by cultic means alone. The purity of God's home can only be sustained through the purity of relationships in the Israelite's home. To be holy as Yhwh is holy is to discover the

---

[44] Meyers, *Rediscovering Eve*, 45–47.
[45] For further detail and discussion, see Luke T. Johnson, "The Use of Leviticus 19 in the Letter of James," *JBL* 101 (1982): 391–401, cited in Hartley, *Leviticus*, 325.

divine image in the other and to share in communion with them. Leviticus expresses a theology whereby holiness can *only* be achieved when one actively engages in relationships that are characterized by justice, charity, and love.[46]

The first set of commands (vv. 11–13) deals with the question of theft and property. This refers to the intentional deception of another in word or deed. Whether one actively seizes another person's possessions or whether they act deceptively to achieve the same ends, God will punish both. This is highlighted by the final command not to withhold the wages due to a worker (cf. Deut 24:14–15; Jer 22:13). Though referring to a practice in subsistence agrarian life, the command is paradigmatic for acting justly in economic transactions and not deceitfully for one's personal gain or at the expense of those in need. Israel is to be a people who do not "deal falsely" with others whether they are within or outside of the covenant community.

It is one thing to steal or lie to one's peers, but Leviticus also offers a theology of justice and charity in relation to those with disabilities (Lev 19:14). Deuteronomy often refers to the "orphan and the widow" as a category for those who are the poorest and most vulnerable to abuse in society. Leviticus never employs this language but, instead, specifically names those with physical disabilities. The deaf and the blind here represent a category of people who have some sort of disability and are reliant upon the charity of others for their survival. To diminish the value of a vulnerable human being by dealing with them unjustly, disrespectfully, or spitefully is an affront

---

[46] For an overview of interpretations, see Kengo Akiyama, *The Love of Neighbour in Ancient Judaism: The Reception of Leviticus 19:18 in the Hebrew Bible, the Septuagint, the Book of Jubilees, the Dead Sea Scrolls, and the New Testament*, AGJU 105 (Leiden: Brill, 2018).

to God. Though no specific punishment is given, the verse ends with the command "you shall fear your God: I am the LORD," which assumes divine retribution for such behavior and the potential for being cursed by Yhwh (cf. Deut 27:18).

The legislation against demeaning or ridiculing those with physical disabilities, however, is not merely concerned with the general precepts of caring for the "poor." The explicit mention of cursing the deaf or causing the blind to stumble are intentional acts of cruelty. To be holy, Israel is to demonstrate kindness and care to those who have some type of physical impediment because they are no less part of the community.[47]

The theology of Leviticus cuts sharply into contemporary Western ideology where the concept of personhood is often linked to the human capacity for rational thought, independence, and self-advocacy. This presumes that to be an authentic, useful human being one must be able to articulate their ideas, defend their positions, and engage with other rational human beings. Stanley Hauerwas challenges this notion and argues that disability is not to be seen as less than human but characterizes a critical aspect of what it means to be human. "We are creatures. Dependency, not autonomy, is one of the ontological characteristics of our lives. That we are creatures, moreover, is but a reminder that we are created for and with one another. We are not just accidentally communal, but we are such by necessity."[48]

---

[47] See Stanley Hauerwas, *Suffering Presence: Theological Reflections on Medicine, the Mentally Handicapped, and the Church* (Edinburgh: T&T Clark, 1988); John Swinton, *Critical Reflections on Stanley Hauerwas' Theology of Disability: Disabling Society, Enabling Theology* (Oxford: Taylor & Francis Group, 2005).

[48] Stanley Hauerwas, *Sanctify Them in the Truth: Holiness Exemplified* (Nashville: Abingdon Press, 1999), 147–48. Cf. John Swinton, *Becoming*

Mutual interdependence and care for those with physical disabilities are critical to the Levitical concept of holiness and anticipate the following commands that climax with the call to love one's neighbor as oneself.

The commands concerning justice and slander (vv. 15–16) highlight legal judgments within the community. The focus here is on the "courtroom" where cases of slander, unjust profit, or impartial preference are at stake. These more outer workings of the law, however, are paralleled by the inner judgments or hatred of the heart that cannot be tried in any court. The remarkable inclusion of v. 17 and the command not to hate kinfolk in one's heart (*lēbāb*) is a testimony to Leviticus' sensitivity to the human condition.[49] External obedience to the commandments does not ensure holiness in God's people. The authors of the text understood the critical link between the inner intentions of the heart and outward actions. To hate your neighbor or to harbor a grudge is to plant a seed that might grow into full-blown vengeance. Instead, Israel is to love their neighbor as themselves.

The command to "love" (*'āhab*) in the Pentateuch can be misinterpreted merely as a personal emotion one feels for someone else. William Moran has demonstrated that the term "love" was often used in international diplomacy and covenant agreements in other ancient Near Eastern cultures.[50] In these cases, love conveyed the sense of "fidelity, loyalty, obedience" of the lesser party (vassal) to the lord or king (suzerain). Moran

---

Friends of Time: Disability, Timefullness, and Gentle Discipleship (Waco, TX: Baylor University Press, 2016), 87–114.

[49] James L. Kugel, "On Hidden Hatred and Open Reproach: Early Exegesis of Leviticus 19:17," *HTR* 80 (1987): 43–61.

[50] William Moran, "The Ancient Near Eastern Background of the Love of God in Deuteronomy," *CBQ* 25 (1963): 77–87.

contends that this use is apparent in the covenantal language of Deuteronomy, but it is likely that a similar meaning is conveyed in Leviticus in relation to obedience to Yhwh's command.

The act of "love" is demonstrated by obedience to the covenant but in Leviticus 19 it is specifically concerned with how you treat your neighbor (*rēʿ*) or those around you.[51] Love begins with reverence and fidelity to one's parents/family (v. 3) and then extends outward to the community of Israelites and even to the alien in the land (Lev 19:34). Leviticus defines love as treating others with justice and impartiality while also showing compassion and kindness to the poor and the most vulnerable in society.[52] A similar theology of love is expressed in the prophet Micah who commends the Israelites "to do justice, and to love kindness, and to walk humbly with your God" (Mic 6:8). "Love" in Leviticus is both an emotion or feeling one has for another person as well as demonstrating fidelity and obedience to Yhwh's covenant through acts of justice, mercy, and compassion.

According to rabbinic tradition, rabbi Hillel was once asked to teach the entire Torah to a gentile who said he would convert if Hillel could do it while he stood on one foot. Hillel responded: "What is hateful to you, do not to your neighbor: that is the whole Torah, while the rest is commentary thereof; go and learn it" (*b. Šabb.* 31a). Jesus restates the Levitical command in the positive, "Do to others as you would have them do to you" (Luke 6:31; Matt 7:2). The natural question arises from the lips of the lawyer in St. Luke's gospel, "Who is my neighbor?" (Luke 10:29). In the

---

[51] Jon D. Levenson, *The Love of God: Divine Gift, Human Gratitude, and Mutual Faithfulness in Judaism* (Princeton, NJ: Princeton University Press, 2016), 1–58.

[52] See Jacqueline E. Lapsley, "Feeling Our Way: Love for God in Deuteronomy," *CBQ* 65 (2003): 350–69.

context of Leviticus 19, one's neighbor (rēʻ) primarily refers to those within the covenant community.[53] The commands preceding v. 19 are concerned with "your people," "your brother," and "the sons of your own people" (vv. 16–18), all of which relate to fellow Israelites. The spheres of relationships, however, were not limited to one's immediate family but expand outward to any who dwelled within the covenant community. The Israelites were to provide food for the poor and sojourner (vv. 9–10) and they were required to treat hired workers with justice (v. 13) and love the alien as themselves (v. 34). Though the primary focus of the command refers to fellow Israelites, the love of one's neighbor extends beyond kin relationships.

The more difficult interpretation comes in the question of *how* to love one's neighbor. The translation of the phrase "as yourself" (*kāmôkā*) is most often taken as reflexive with the sense of doing to others as you would do to yourself.[54] The other possible, but less frequent, translation is adjectival, which could be paraphrased, "love your neighbor, the one who is like you," once again possibly intending love to be shown only to fellow Israelites. This sense is less likely, however, due to the second half of the chapter, which addresses how you treat the alien (*gēr*) who sojourns in the land (vv. 33–34).[55] The Israelites are not to oppress the alien but to "love him as yourself (*kāmôkā*)" (v. 34). The basis for this love finds its roots in historic experience through a shared sense of oppression, humiliation, vulnerability, and suffering. The love for

---

[53] Richard Elliott Friedman, "Love Your Neighbor – Only Israelites or Everyone?" *BAR* 40 (2014): 48–52.

[54] Abraham Malamat, "'Love Your Neighbor as Yourself': What It Really Means," *BAR* 16 (1990): 50–51.

[55] Rolf Rendtorff, "The *Ger* in the Priestly Laws of the Pentateuch," in *Ethnicity and the Bible*, ed. Mark G. Brett (Leiden: Brill, 1996), 77–87.

aliens is mandated because "you were aliens in the land of Egypt" (v. 34). Israel's love should stem from empathy with those who suffer the same fate that they (and their ancestors) once knew in Egypt.

The rationale for loving your neighbor and the alien as yourself comes from knowing what it means to be human and what it means to suffer under the oppression of the institutions of power in the world. For Israel, this meant identifying with their historic experience of slavery in Egypt as a means of identifying with the suffering and needs of others. This would help them nurture a sense of empathy toward others and identify with them as fellow human beings. Rowan Williams writes, "Empathy, that is, the imaginative identification with a perspective that is not my own, is not just an optional extra in our human identity and our human repertoire, it's something without which we cannot know ourselves. Without identification with the other, I don't know myself."[56] To identify with one's neighbor is the beginning of love. Israel is commanded to love their neighbor as themselves because love is at the heart of what it means to be human.

The final section of the chapter (vv. 19–37) deals with other issues that relate to the Israelite home. Rather than addressing each individually, we shall focus on those that have to do with Israel's relationship to the land. The first set of prohibitions refers to breeding animals of different kinds, sowing different types of seeds, or mixing fabrics (v. 19). Gerstenberger attributes these commands to ancient demonic beliefs and that improper mixing could violate boundaries and cause conflict between spiritual

---

[56] Rowan Williams, *Being Human: Bodies, Minds, Persons* (London: SPCK, 2018), 58.

entities. This might bring disaster on the community.[57] There is little evidence, however, that the demonic is of main concern in this verse. Others contend that the prohibitions are symbolic of intermarriage or assimilation with other cultures, or that the unlawful mixtures transgress the natural order and division of God's creation.[58] Milgrom rightly notes that certain mixtures in Leviticus can only take place in the divine realm or in the direct presence of God. This is seen in the cherubim (a mixed divine creature) on top of the ark (cf. Ezek 1:5–11) and fabrics made of linen and wool that were found in the curtains of the tabernacle and the clothing of the priests.[59] This is one instance where the mirroring of Israel's home does not find correspondence with Yhwh's home. There are certain things between the divine and human realms that should not be transgressed.

In Chapter 3, we discussed the nature of purity and impurity in relation to the tabernacle. We witnessed symbolic divisions based on social and religious orders that reflected the hierarchy and symmetry of God's design in the cosmos. This same principle is now applied to the life of the farmer in relation to the land. Just as the priest was to "distinguish between the holy and the profane, and between the unclean and the clean" (Lev 10:10) so too is the average Israelite to maintain distinctions of holiness and purity in how they treat the land.

The analogy between farmer, priest, and the land is not accidental. God's command to till and keep the land (Gen 2:15) is treated as a sacred act in Leviticus and one that ensures that the land will remain holy. A similar sentiment is found in the prophet

---

[57] Gerstenberger, *Leviticus*, 273.
[58] Wenham, *Leviticus*, 269–70; Douglas, *Purity and Danger*, 54–56.
[59] Milgrom, *Leviticus 17–22*, 1656–65.

Isaiah who commends the wisdom of the Lord that is reflected in the farmer's orderly sowing and reaping from the earth (Isa 28:23–29). The mixing of different animals, seed, or fabrics all represent human attempts to step beyond what Leviticus perceives as the ordained role of humanity in relation to God's creation. In this sense, the farmer is treated like the priests in his relationship to the land. He is to maintain its purity and distinction without presumption or hubris in attempts to manipulate what God has created as good.

Leviticus' vision of the farmer's relationship to the land is far from modern industrialized farming techniques that often rely on monocultures, genetic modifications, and chemical inputs. This has diminished the traditional notion of husbandry. Wendell Berry contends that the farmer as "husband" is critical to understanding the relationship between humanity and the land. "Husbandry pertains first to the household; it connects the farm to the household ... To husband is to use with care, to keep, to save, to make last, to conserve ... Husbandry is the name of all the practices that sustain life by connecting us conservingly to our places and our world; it is the art of keeping tied all the strands in the living network that sustains us."[60] This type of care for the land is what Leviticus expresses through its commands both in chapter 19 and elsewhere. Israel is to work and tend to the land that they have been given by maintaining its order and allowing it to produce in abundance as Yhwh had intended.[61]

---

[60] Wendell Berry, "Renewing Husbandry," in *Wendell Berry: Essays 1993–2017*, ed. Jack Shoemaker (New York: Library of America, 2019), Epub edition, "Renewing Husbandry." Cf. Davis, "Identity and Eating," 3–14.

[61] See Davis, *Scripture, Culture, and Agriculture*, 80–100.

Further connections between holiness and the land are found in vv. 23–25, which prohibit eating fruit from the trees of the land. When the Israelites plant fruit-bearing trees, they cannot eat from them until the fifth year. The Hebrew of v. 23 is difficult because of the unusual phrase *waʿăraltem ʾet ʿorlātô*, which literally means "You shall keep its foreskin uncircumcised." Some translations offer the more figurative rendering, "you shall regard their fruit as forbidden" (NRSV, ESV, JPS), but this loses the significance of the metaphor of young trees as "uncircumcised." Uncircumcision in the Old Testament can refer to the lips (Exod 6:12), the heart (Deut 10:16; Ezek 44:9), or the ears (Jer 6:10) and contains the negative connotation of something that does not function properly. For farmers to leave the tree "uncircumcised" means that they are to remove the bud of the fruit from the tree when it blossoms.[62] In this sense, the tree or vine is not fulfilling its natural potential to bear fruit until the fourth year when it is allowed to blossom and produce. The metaphor of uncircumcision is used to remind the Israelite farmer that fertility and the land first belong to Yhwh (cf. Lev 25:23). Foregoing three years of fruit and then setting aside the first fruits to Yhwh in the fourth year are a sign of restraint and dedication of what is holy from the land to the God's altar. Israel is again reminded that they are tenants on the land as their first fruits are given to the Lord of the land as a sign of honor and thanksgiving.

Finally, the Israelites are forbidden from giving their daughters over to prostitution (v. 29) because to do so would cause the land to be prostituted and defiled. This may have referred to cultic prostitution associated with a temple/shrine or other prostitution. In either case, the action of the daughter is linked to the father

---

[62] Cf. Milgrom, *Leviticus 17–22*, 1677–80.

who is responsible for maintaining the holiness and purity of the household and the land. A parallel is drawn in Lev 21:9 when the daughter of a priest engages in prostitution and defiles her father but with the sentence of being burned to death. Both examples convey the notion that impurity can be passed from daughter to father and then on to the land or potentially the tabernacle. The analogy between farmer and priest is critical to Leviticus' theology of holiness. The interdependence of the family is connected to the holiness of the tabernacle and the land. Both Israelite males, whether priest or farmer, are instrumental in maintaining the purity and order of God's sacred tabernacle and land.

A culture that allows for the prostitution of its children is one that bears a sickness and profanity that will ultimately fill the land with "depravity" (*zimmâ*) (Lev 19:29). Ellen Davis raises the important issue of modern sex trafficking and argues that often poorer farmers might sell or prostitute their children as a last resort. She writes, "A depraved economy such as the one that now holds the whole globe in thrall is dangerous equally to land and to daughters, to farm families altogether, for all have become commodities, interchangeable goods, valued only for their fleeting contribution to the profits or pleasure of the relative few who have prospered."[63] Such an economy is the opposite of what Leviticus envisages for a holy people. Instead, Leviticus presents of vision of Israel as a society that rejects the commoditization of the land and the devaluation of human beings. Life in the land was not meant to be an economy of building excessive profit, hoarding resources, and exploiting others for personal gain. Instead, Israel was called to an economy of neighborliness. They were to sustain social and economic relationships within the

---

[63] Davis, *Scripture, Culture and Agriculture*, 92.

community (which included the alien) and in relation to the broader land community of soils, water, and animals for the mutual benefit of the whole.

The call to be holy as Yhwh is holy is a summons to the Israelite household and their ethical relationships with their neighbors, the alien, and the land. The purity of the family begins with holiness in the most intimate sexual relationships (chapters 18 and 20) and then moves beyond the inner chambers of the home to agricultural life on the farm. To be holy is to live ethically in all social and economic dealings and in how one treats their livestock and the land. This wholistic call to holiness offers a natural transition from purity in the sanctuary to purity in the home. For Leviticus, the call to be holy as God is holy is not some abstract command reserved only for the spiritual or the illuminati. *Becoming holy is to commit one's ways in acts of love and charity toward other human beings and toward the land community.* The commands of Leviticus 19 demonstrate that actions regarding how we treat our family and neighbor are ways in which the follower of Yhwh can become holy as he is holy. Though this is taken within the whole scope of the cult, the point of the command is to offer guidelines for how one becomes like God by what they do and how they treat other human beings and the wider land community.

FROM LAY HOUSEHOLD TO PRIESTLY HOUSEHOLD

The return to priestly concerns in chapters 21 and 22 shift from the lay population to regulations around the holiness of those who serve within the tabernacle. The move, however, continues the themes described above about holiness within the home. These commandments are not a part of chapters 1–16 because they are concerned with priestly purity as it relates to the *management of their own households*. A priest who is defiled by their unethical treatment of family or neighbor is unfit to serve within the sanctuary. In a more direct manner, we find that the priest's home, and its purity, is connected to Yhwh's home.

The commandments to the priests reflect the previous instructions to the lay people, but we find that restrictions on family life are elevated along with the standards for holiness. On two occasions, God's commandments are specifically addressed to Aaron and his sons and to all the people of Israel (Lev 21:24; 22:18). Laypeople are charged with holding the priests accountable to a higher state of holiness as the Lord commands, "you shall treat them as holy, since they offer the food of your God; they shall be holy to you, for I the LORD, I who sanctify you, am holy" (Lev 21:8). The increased restrictions are to ensure that the household of the priest does not become defiled so that the priest does not inadvertently contaminate God's holy place. Communal responsibility for holiness is a central theme running through chapters 17–26. The priests of Leviticus are not an elite social group above other Israelites but, rather, their integration into the larger community is integral to their own calling to holiness.

The initial instructions are given to all priests concerning death and marriage (vv. 1–9), which then turns to the stricter restrictions given to the high priest on the same topics (vv. 10–15). The next section introduces the topic of blemishes or physical deformation concerning priests who can serve in Yhwh's sanctuary (vv. 16–24). Chapter 21 turns to the eating of sacrificial food in the priest's home (Lev 21:1–9) and to the eating of his extended household (vv. 10–16). The final section contains instructions on blemished animals and what may be offered at Yhwh's altar (vv. 17–33) and concludes with the summary reminder that it is

Yhwh alone who sanctifies and who has set Israel apart to be holy having brought them out of the land of Egypt (vv. 31-33).

The stricter restrictions around the priestly home are to be expected considering their role in the sanctuary and proximity to God's holiness. They cannot be defiled by coming into contact with dead things such as corpses so certain limitations are made on when they can mourn and become defiled. Only in the death of the nearest kin (i.e., mother, father, son, daughter, brother, or sister) is the priest allowed mourn, but they may not shave their heads or beards or disfigure their body. These physical rituals were pagan practices related to ancestral worship or mourning the dead.[64] A similar command is given to the high priest but he is completely restricted from coming into contact with a dead body, even if it is his own father or mother (Lev 21:10-12). The command seems unfair, but it demonstrates the significance Leviticus places on the purity of the only person who comes in closest contact with Yhwh in the Holy of Holies. Therefore, the home of the high priest is to conform to the strictest requirements of purity even when that means giving up some of the most important family obligations.

The wife of the priest, likewise, is held to a higher standard of purity. She must not be a prostitute or a woman who has been defiled or divorced (Lev 21:7). The high priest may only marry a virgin of his own kin to protect the purity of his offspring who will potentially serve in the Holy of Holies (Lev 21:13-15). Though we do not find repeated warnings on sexual relationships within the

---

[64] The shaving of the head or beard as a sign of mourning was common among Israel's neighbors such as the Moabites (Isa 15:2) and the Philistines (Jer 47:5). Milgrom, *Leviticus 17-22*, 1801-2, notes that cutting hair as a sign of mourning was also known among the Greeks (Homer, *Odyssey*, 4.197), the Persians (Herod. 9.24) and in Babylonia (*ANET*, 339-40).

family, the purity of those relationships is presumably based on the commands of chapters 18 and 20.

The final section of chapter 21 may seem callous or unjust to the contemporary reader. Any priest with blemishes or physical deformities are excluded from serving in the tabernacle. Within the religious and cultural framework of Leviticus, however, these restrictions can be easily understood. The physical symbol for holiness is the wholeness, completeness, and purity of a human, animal, or object. Any blemish or imperfection (like skin disease) was an outward sign of impurity and the forces of death that could not come into contact with God's holy sanctuary.[65] Yet as was the case with the leper, restrictions on priests with some sort of physical "imperfection" was not a sign that Yhwh cared for them any less or that they were somehow a lesser member of the covenant community. The issue had to do with purity and proximity to the tabernacle space. Whether an offering, the offerer, or the priest serving at the altar, all that is presented before Yhwh must be without blemish (cf. Lev 22:22–24).

Though these restrictions exclude those of priestly descent from serving in the sanctuary, they are permitted to eat the offerings that are "of the most holy as well as of the holy" (Lev 21:22). This is not an insignificant thing as in Lev 22:10–16 explicit instructions are given to lay people never to consume the priestly portion lest they incur guilt for doing so. The laws excluding priests with any type of physical blemish were not instituted for the sake of discriminating against those with physical disabilities. Instead, they are connected to the broader systems of belief around purity

---

[65] See Jeremy Schipper and Jeffrey Stackert, "Blemishes, Camouflage, and Sanctuary Service: The Priestly Deity and His Attendants," *Hebrew Bible and Ancient Israel* 2 (2013): 458–78.

and holiness in reference to who and what can come into the presence of God.

The challenge is that the commands do discriminate and prevent people with disability from worshipping Yhwh at his altar. The prophet Isaiah understood these laws to be for a specific time in Israel's history, but they were not permanent. He foresees a day when eunuchs (those who are physically blemished) and foreigners who were once restricted from approaching will be brought into Yhwh's house: "These I will bring to my holy mountain, and make them joyful in my house of prayer; their burnt offerings and their sacrifices will be accepted on my altar; for my house shall be called a house of prayer for all peoples" (Isa 56:7).

The following commands in Lev 22:1-16 focus on the sacred offerings that come from Yhwh's table to the priest's table. Qualifications are made concerning lay people eating what is offered on the altar or concerning those who are ritually unclean. The priest's home requires a higher standard of holiness because of their duties within the tabernacle and because they bring portions of God's food to their families. The underlying theology is that animals and offerings consecrated to Yhwh remain holy even if they are taken from his holy dwelling. If that which is holy is profaned in the priest's home, it will cause them to "bear guilt" (*wəhiśśî'û 'ōtām 'ăwōn*) and profane God's name (Lev 22:16). Unlike the layperson's home, the priests are charged with stricter standards of purity because sanctified offerings from the altar are their portion and sustenance.

The end of chapter 22 recapitulates the theme and language of blemishes from Lev 21:18-20. The subject matter, however, is not the priests but the animals that are brought for voluntary sacrifices. The burnt offering (*'ōlâ*) could be brought for different reasons including the votive offering (*nēder*) or the freewill offering (*nədābāh*). The emphasis is on the wholeness of the animal that is given for sacrifice. Anything that has a visible blemish or defect is an affront to Yhwh. Disrespecting the altar by bringing unsuitable animals is an act that profanes God's holy name (Lev 22:2).

Final instructions are given regarding when an animal can be slaughtered and the stipulation not to kill a newborn with its mother on the same day (vv. 27-28). Gerstenberger compares the prohibition with to the command not to boil a kid in its mother's milk (Exod 23:19; Deut 14:21) and argues that both have to do with magical associations or taboos around mixing things.[66] A plain sense of the text, however, may read the command as an ethical approach to how one treats animals. Though Milgrom argues that the text does not offer a humanitarian rationale for not sacrificing a newborn and its mother on the same day, he recognizes this reading in the rabbinic tradition.[67] Targum Pseudo-Jonathan's translation of Lev 22:28 contains the addition, "My people, children of Israel, just as I am merciful in heaven, so you shall be merciful on the earth. You shall not slaughter a cow or a ewe, it and its offspring, on the same day." The commands of chapter 22 are summed up with the statement "You shall not profane my holy name, that I may be sanctified among the people of Israel: I am the LORD; I sanctify you, I who brought you out of the land of Egypt to be your God: I am the LORD" (Lev 22:32-33). The emphasis on Yhwh's name being sanctified among the people and Israel being sanctified by Yhwh are a reminder of the historical setting of Egypt and that the transition from the death of slavery is not complete until the people have been sanctified to God.

---

[66] Gerstenberger, *Leviticus*, 331.
[67] Milgrom, *Levitiucs 17-22*, 1884-85.

CONCLUSION

Gerstenberger argues that the Holiness Code offers a "bewildering variety" of commands that may reflect a comprehensive attempt to offer Jews a catechism for religious life.[68] Yet what may seem bewildering to modern readers was likely understood by ancient readers as the natural flow of holiness from Yhwh's home to Israel's home. The *imitatio Dei* of Lev 19:2 demonstrates that the love of God in the theology of Leviticus offers no distinction between how one acts toward the sanctuary and how one acts toward their neighbor. The covenant response of love and holiness is mandated for every aspect of life whether cultic or ethical. Leviticus understands holiness as something that is both tied to the sacred world of blood, sacrifice, and Yhwh's altar, but it also presents holiness as something to be performed in one's daily behavior. To become like Yhwh is to love one's neighbor, to love the alien, to love the land, and to demonstrate this through daily acts that lead toward holiness. The ethical mandates in the Holiness Code reveal a theology that is concerned with justice, righteousness, and mercy within the relationships of Israel. Sacrifice, worship, atonement, purity, and ritual holiness are critical to forming and generating an ethic for how one lives in holiness in relation to the whole community. In his discussion on the philosophy of Judaism, Abraham Heschel writes, "In exposing ourselves to God we discover the divine in ourselves and its correspondence to the divine beyond ourselves. That perception of correspondence, our discovering how acts of human goodness are allied with transcendent holiness, the sense of the sacred context of our candid compassion – is our most precious

---

[68] Gerstenberger, *Leviticus*, 261–65.

insight."[69] Heschel's words echo the sentiments of Leviticus – to demonstrate acts of human goodness is to be aligned with the holiness of God and to experience the sacredness of his world and his holiness within oneself.

---

[69] Abraham Joshua Heschel, *Moral Grandeur and Spiritual Audacity*, ed. Susannah Heschel (New York: Farrar, Straus and Giroux, 1996), Epub edition, ch. 1, "To Be a Jew: What Is It?"

CHAPTER 6

Living in Sacred Time (Leviticus 23)

HOLY TIMES AND SEASONS

Another important aspect in the theology of Leviticus and its emphasis on the connection between Yhwh's home and Israel's home is the nature of time and the celebration of "sacred occasions" or "holy convocations" (*miqrā'ê qōdeš*). These "fixed times" (*mô'ădîm*) established a ritual pattern throughout the year that drew Israelite communities together to recall the story of God's salvation, to celebrate his provision, and to be reminded of their calling to live as a kingdom of priests and a holy nation.

Sacred festivals bring order to the year and act as pedagogical moments in the home and within the wider community to teach about the God of Israel and his acts of salvation. They set apart particular times to re-actualize historic events of the past, to give thanks in the present, and to anticipate God's future blessing. The ordering of sacred occasions in Leviticus provides Israel with a standardized calendar that serves as a liturgical scaffolding for worship throughout the year. The rituals and memories expressed through communal acts draw the people back to their core identity, their relationship to God, and their relationship to one another.

Ritual calendars are well attested throughout the ancient Near East. Many of these calendars followed the lunar cycle and occurred around times of harvest. Most festivals were connected to agricultural themes while others were devoted to ancestral worship or to the maintenance of the local temple and deity.[1] Others were often governed by political motivations where the primary actors were the priests (or high priest) and the King.[2] One of the shared similarities across ancient Near Eastern cultures is that festivals were celebrated on the first month and/or the seventh month of the year around the vernal or autumnal equinox. These times were associated with new year rites and linked to agricultural festivals. The first month in spring celebrated the harvest and first fruits while the seventh month represented the end of the autumn harvest and preparation for the winter rains.[3] These festivals could last anywhere from one to seven days and were common among Babylonian and Mesopotamian calendars. The six-month festival cycle, along with similar rites and ritual observances, demonstrate shared practice among Western Semitic cultures in their celebration of harvest and other religious observances.[4]

---

[1] See Mark E. Cohen, *The Cultic Calendars of the Ancient Near East* (Bethesda, MD: CDL Press, 1993).

[2] See Jan Wagenaar, *Origin and Transformation of the Ancient Israelite Festival Calendar* (Wiesbaden: Harrassowitz Verlag, 2005), 123, and his comparison of Leviticus 23 with the first millennium Babylonian Akītu Festival where the king is ceremonially humbled so that he might be subsequently renewed and supported by the deity.

[3] Bryan C. Babcock, *Sacred Ritual: A Study of the West Semitic Ritual Calendars in Leviticus 23 and the Akkadian Text Emar 446* (Winona Lake, IN: Eisenbrauns 2014), 21–24.

[4] Babcock, *Sacred Ritual*, 25–28; cf. Moshe Weinfeld, "Social and Cultic Institutions in the Priestly Source against Their Ancient Near Eastern Background," in *Proceedings of the Eighth World Congress of Jewish Studies, Panel Sessions: Bible Studies and Hebrew Language* (Jerusalem: World Union of Jewish Studies, 1983), 95–129.

One of the oldest "calendars" is the inscription found in the ancient Canaanite city of Gezer (about twenty miles west of Jerusalem) that details the yearly cycles of harvest. Thought to be from around the tenth century BCE and written in Paleo-Hebrew (or possibly Phoenician), the text relates the different agricultural seasons:[5]

> Two months gathering
> Two months sowing
> Two months late planting
> One month cutting flax
> One month barley reaping
> One month end of reaping
> Two months pruning/ One month summer fruit.

This may have been a folk song or an exercise for writing practice. Whatever its function, the text reveals the rhythm of ancient Israel around the yearly cycles of harvest and preparation.

Scholars have noted both similarities and differences between Leviticus 23 and other ancient Near Eastern calendars.[6] Bryan Babcock contends that the antiquity of the Levitical calendar can be established when compared to the calendar text known as Emar 446, which comes from the ancient city of Emar in northeast Syria. He notes that both texts share a multi-month calendar, which was written to the general population rather than to priests in particular. Both texts are orientated around the vernal and

---

[5] Shemarayahu Talmon, "The Gezer Calendar and the Seasonal Cycle of Ancient Canaan," *JAOS* 83 (1963): 177–87; Mark S. Smith, *The Early History of God: Yahweh and the Other Deities in Ancient Israel*, 2nd ed. (Grand Rapids, MI: Eerdmans, 2002), 20.

[6] Richard S. Hess, "Multiple-Month Ritual Calendars in the West Semitic World: Emar 446 and Leviticus 23," in *The Future of Biblical Archaeology: Reassessing Methodologies and Assumptions*, ed. James K. Hoffmeier and Alan Millard (Grand Rapids, MI: Eerdmans, 2004), 233–53.

autumnal equinoxes with shared seven-day festivals as well as ritual meals on the evenings before a major festival.[7] Babcock demonstrates multiple points of similarity between Emar 446 and Leviticus 23 and gives good reason to see the biblical text influenced by an earlier (second millennium BCE) calendrical form that was utilized by the authors of Leviticus.

Approaching the calendar of Leviticus 23 from biblical and linguistic evidence, Knohl argues that the festival legislation found in the earliest priestly text was later reworked by the Holiness School and was updated to include popular religious rituals common among ordinary Israelites.[8] He traces the differences between the older priestly legislation found in Numbers 28–29 and Leviticus 23 and argues that these represent different redactions of the Priestly Torah. Knohl contends that there are two streams of thought in the festival legislation. The first is that of Priestly Torah, which has no concern for popular practices but is focused solely on sacrifice. Following Kaufmann, he argues that priestly temple service is only concerned with the offerings and not the practices associated with popular Israelite religion or those celebrations that involved the whole community outside the temple.[9] It was only later with the redactions of the Holiness School that practices connected to agricultural festivals were blended with priestly elements.

Knohl's strict division between priestly and popular religion, however, is unwarranted. Even if the calendar prescriptions in Numbers 28–29 are concerned with specific sacrifices, this does not necessitate that the temple priests operated in isolation or had

---

[7] Babcock, *Sacred Ritual*, 214–39.
[8] Knohl, *The Sanctuary of Silence*, 11, 42.
[9] Knohl, *The Sanctuary of Silence*, 44–45.

little concern for "popular" religious events. The priests, too, were part of local Israelite communities with homes and families that participated in the celebrations of the agricultural year. Their service in the temple or regional shrine was not isolated from the people but was often performed with the people. To argue for their complete disconnection from the normal practices of Israelite life is to create an artificial divide that can potentially distort the theological importance of both cultic and "popular" rituals in the life of Israel.

Jacob Milgrom offers another view of the calendar in Leviticus and argues against Knohl's "priestly-popular" view.[10] He contends that Leviticus 23 was composed by H in the eighth century BCE before undergoing further redaction in Babylonian exile. Unlike Knohl, Milgrom argues that though Leviticus 23 relies on the P text of Numbers 28–29, it is entirely the product of H.[11] His theory furthers the idea that Israel's calendar was shaped over time through various redactions that moved from local to regional celebrations at the temple. Milgrom stresses that though an earlier ancient Israelite festival calendar existed, Leviticus 23 represents a pre-Hezekian tradition focused on the authority and centrality of the Jerusalem temple.

A different approach to the idea of religious practice in ancient Israel is offered by Brett Maiden who argues against the traditional dichotomy between popular and official religion. He contends that, from the standpoint of human cognition, ritual acts that are performed within the official temple precincts and those celebrated in homes, villages, or local shrines share similar

---

[10] Milgrom, *Leviticus 23–27*, 1981–96, 2054–80.
[11] Milgrom, *Leviticus 23–27*, 2056.

structural features.[12] This means that household religious practices in ancient Israel provide a continuity with temple worship rather than a discontinuity. As Maiden contends, "we might reasonably regard family religion as official religion writ small, or if one prefers, official religion as family religion writ large. In either case, the difference between the home and temple, ancestors and the national deity, were not nearly as great as often imagined."[13] Approaching the sacred festivals of Leviticus from a cognitive perspective suggests that ancient Israel did not distinguish between home and tabernacle but, rather, their seasonal celebrations provide a wholistic view that weaves together the life of the land and the people with the work of the priests.

Though it is impossible to determine the exact layers behind the liturgical calendar presented in Leviticus 23, it is apparent that Israelite festivals and practices have been preserved and transformed over time. Agricultural and cultic rites were reshaped into a fixed yearly cycle of festivals, many of which offered etiological explanations for the Exodus events. The priestly authors of Leviticus demonstrate their theological imagination by reforming and redacting a yearly liturgy for worship, ritual, and teaching that draws together the whole community and offers a means by which Israel can preserve its identity. The festival calendar thus became a critical theological structure and rhythm for times and

---

[12] Brett E. Maiden, *Cognitive Science and Ancient Israelite Religion: New Perspectives on Texts, Artefacts, and Culture* (Cambridge: Cambridge University Press, 2020), 29–63.

[13] Maiden, *Cognitive Science and Ancient Israelite Religion*, 63. Cf. Saul M. Olyan, "Family Religion in Israel and the Wider Levant of the First Millennium BCE," in *Household and Family Religion in Antiquity*, eds. John Bodel and Saul M. Olyan (Oxford: Blackwell, 2008), 113–26.

seasons that pointed to Israel's past, recalled their covenant relationship with Yhwh, and maintained their common life together.

A PRIESTLY THEOLOGY OF TIME

In Leviticus, the order of the seasons is dictated by the order of the cosmos brought into being by Yhwh.[14] The one who established the movement of the sun, moon, and stars is the one who has given a pattern for the order of liturgical time. It is within this cyclical movement of the seasons that humanity finds itself as both keeper and sustainer of the world. To do so, however, humanity must be attuned to the rhythms of the creator God who has ordered and classified all things in his wisdom. Life without sacred occasions and sacred interruptions to daily work blurs into monotony, listlessness, and can even lead to the oppression of the poor (cf. Amos 8:4–6). Communal celebration and ongoing recognition of God's divine works and presence are essential to the fullness of life and the flourishing of a holy people.

The tripartite structure of the cosmos is reflected throughout Leviticus' theology of space and time.[15] Heaven above is the realm of God and his angelic beings. This is the place where time is marked by ongoing worship as envisaged by Isaiah when he witnesses the heavenly throne room where the seraphim endlessly fall before the almighty God singing, "Holy, holy, holy" (Isa 6:1–8). Below the throne of God is the earth that is governed according to the cycles of the sun and moon. This is the footstool of the great king (Isa 66:1) and the place where his people live and

---

[14] Cf. Jenson, *Graded Holiness*, 209.
[15] Blenkinsopp, "The Structure of P," 275–92. Cf. Milgrom, *Leviticus 1–16*, 721–26; Jenson, *Graded Holiness*, 216–18.

serve him. The third layer is the waters or under the waters in the deeps, which hint at the forces of chaos that still lurk but remain under Yhwh's authority.[16]

The cosmological order thus becomes the basis for the ordering of times, seasons, the tabernacle, and the community of Israel. The priests are to remind the people of sacred times and seasons. They must draw people into the holy rhythms of practicing sabbath and other festival days to give thanks, to repent, to humble themselves, and to recall continually the mighty works of Yhwh who delivered them from Egypt and planted them in the land.

The need to establish ritualized time is driven by the priestly desire to be in harmony with the order of creation. Gorman argues, "The Priestly writers, faced with the need to hold back chaos and maintain the order of creation, look to ritual as the means to accomplish this. Ritual, thus, becomes a means by which humans participate in the ongoing order of creation. Their existence is made meaningful as they participate in the never-ending drama of creation in ritual."[17] This drama is lived out year after year in the celebration of sacred festivals as reminders that the people of God continue to participate in the ongoing drama of salvation being worked out in the world.

The liturgical year is divided into two halves in Leviticus. The first half of the year begins in the spring, the first month of the Hebrew calendar, with the festivals of Passover and Unleavened Bread (Lev 23:4–8), First Fruits (vv. 9–14), and the Feast of Weeks

---

[16] See Othmar Keel, *Symbolism of the Biblical World: Ancient Near Eastern Iconography and the Book of Psalms* (Winona Lake, IN: Eisenbrauns, 1997) 26–55.
[17] Gorman, *The Ideology of Ritual*, 231.

(Pentecost) (vv. 15–22). The second half of the year is marked by autumnal celebrations in the seventh month with the festival of Trumpets (vv. 15–22), the Day of Atonement (vv. 26–32), and the festival of Booths (vv. 33–36, 39–43). In both halves, we find that key moments of the Exodus are remembered alongside the patterns of seedtime and harvest.

For the authors of Leviticus, the holiness of sabbath time is the foundation stone for the entire liturgical year. In no other biblical calendar does the sabbath receive such prominence as in Leviticus 23. The seventh day of rest offers the numerical pattern that is the key to all holy convocations and the ordering of the year. There are seven annual festivals that were often framed by seven days of rest. The seventh year was the sabbatical year for the land and the forty-ninth year (7 x 7) preceded the Jubilee and the time of release. The importance of the sabbath and the seven-day pattern for work and rest lies at the heart of sacred time for the priestly authors.

Though Leviticus 23 and Numbers 28–29 are the two places where the whole liturgical year is laid out, other texts in the Pentateuch also offer detailed prescriptions concerning specific festivals (Exod 23:12–19; 34:17–26; Deut 16:1–17). It is often presumed that Numbers is the older priestly calendar because its concern is mainly the required sacrifices offered on festival days.[18] Kiuchi contends that the legislation in Numbers is not necessarily the older text but may simply address a different situation or was written for a different purpose.[19] In Leviticus 23, however, we find

---

[18] Milgrom, *Leviticus 23–27*, 2054–56; Knohl, *The Sanctuary of Silence*, 8–14. Cf. Hryhoriy Lozinskyy, *The Feasts of the Calendar in the Book of Numbers Num 28:16–30:1 in the Light of Related Biblical Texts and Some Ancient Sources of 200 BCE–100 CE* (Tübingen: Mohr Siebeck, 2022).

[19] Nobuyoshi Kiuchi, *Leviticus*, AOTC (Downers Grove, IL: IVP, 2007), 419.

a stronger theological emphasis on the nature of the festivals and holy time. Though Numbers may represent an earlier priestly tradition regarding the specific offerings given at each festival, the principal difference between the two is their rhetorical intent. Leviticus is concerned with communal celebrations throughout the year while Numbers records specific offerings associated with certain feasts.

In Deuteronomy, however, greater concern is placed on celebrations at the centralized shrine. Former festivals celebrated among families such as Passover were restricted to a single sanctuary (Deut 16:2–8). Centralization of worship in Jerusalem meant that pilgrimages were costly and difficult for many. Weinfeld contends that Deuteronomy's concern is for the "secular institutions" that govern the nation and though the central sanctuary is critical, he notes the paradox that the law "has almost completely ignored the sacral institutions which the chosen place must necessarily imply and without which the conduct of sacral worship is unimaginable."[20] Though legislation around the festivals varies in the Pentateuch, Leviticus 23 offers a fixed liturgical calendar that is primarily concerned with family and communal celebrations rather than worship at a centralized shrine.

SABBATH

The theological foundation for holiness and sacred time in Leviticus is the sabbath. The sabbath legislation accounts for the weekly rhythm of life in the Israelite home and expands to yearly practices of rest that culminate in the Jubilee. There is no other

---

[20] Moshe Weinfeld, *Deuteronomy and the Deuteronomic School* (Oxford: Clarendon Press, 1972), 183–86.

weekly ritual that sums up Israel's call to holiness than setting aside a day of sacred time and rest each week.

The first three verses of Leviticus 23 have historically been seen as an addition to the festival legislation.[21] It is possible that earlier priestly texts did not see the sabbath as a particular festival throughout the year but that later priests increasingly understood the theological significance of weekly rest and gathering together to study Torah. The Essenes of Qumran considered the sabbath to be a "fixed time" (*mô ʿēd*) and a weekly celebration when trumpets could be blown.[22] Even Josephus describes the proliferation of the sabbath practice in the Second Temple period and writes that, "there is not one city, Greek or barbarian, nor a single nation to which our custom of abstaining from work on the seventh day has not spread, and by which our fasts and lighting up lamps, and many of our prohibitions as to our food, are not observed" (*Con. Ap.* 2:282).[23] This may be an overstatement, but it does indicate the importance that Hellenistic Jews placed on ceasing from work and gathering together weekly.

The prescriptions of Leviticus 23 state that Israel should celebrate a sabbath of complete rest (*šabbat šabbātôn*) or, as Alter translates, an "absolute sabbath."[24] It took place from evening to evening in the traditional Jewish practice, but there may have been a time in Israel's history where the sabbath began at

---

[21] Knohl, *The Sanctuary of Silence*, 14.
[22] CD 12.4; 4Q493; 4Q512. Cf. *Antiq.* 3:294.
[23] For a comparison of later Jewish and Christian calendars, see Daniel Stökl Ben Ezra, "Seasoning the Bible and Biblifying Time through Fixed Liturgical Reading Systems (Lectionaries)," in *The Construction of Time in Antiquity: Ritual, Art and Identity*, ed. Jonathan Ben-Dov and Lutz Doering (Cambridge: Cambridge University Press, 2017), 227–47.
[24] Robert Alter, *The Hebrew Bible: A New Translation with Commentary* (New York: W. W. Norton, 2019).

sunrise.[25] The emphasis on avoiding all daily work associated with one's life in the six-day week is critical to the health of the community and allowed individuals and families the opportunity to be refreshed as God was refreshed on the seventh day of creation (Exod 31:17).[26]

In Num 28:9–10, the sabbath is not referred to as a "sacred occasion" but only the prescriptions for offerings are given. The concern is with what is presented at the altar (two male lambs, a grain and a drink offering) and not with the complete ceasing of work as is made clear in Lev 23:1–3.[27] Knohl argues that the weekly sabbath offerings continued, but in later times they became more closely associated with ceasing from one's labors as was emphasized by the priestly redactors.[28] However, since the fourth commandment in both versions of the Decalogue associates rest with the sabbath day, it is more likely that this was part of its earliest institution in Israel.

As we consider the theology of the sabbath in Leviticus, we find that the priestly authors have placed the sanctification of time (sabbath) in parallel with the sanctification of space (tabernacle)

---

[25] See Lutz Doering, "The Beginning of Sabbath and Festivals in Ancient Jewish Sources," in *The Construction of Time in Antiquity: Ritual, Art and Identity*, ed. Jonathan Ben-Dov and Lutz Doering (Cambridge: Cambridge University Press, 2017), 205–26.

[26] See Mark W. Scarlata, *Sabbath Rest: The Beauty of God's Rhythm for a Digital Age* (London: SCM, 2018); Walter Brueggemann, *Sabbath as Resistance: Saying No to the Culture of Now* (Louisville, KY: Westminster John Knox Press, 2014).

[27] Contra Wagenaar, *Origin and Transformation*, 120, who argues, "the list of festivals in Num 28–29 presents an elaboration of the festival calendar in Lev 23 and the list of festival sacrifices in Ezek 45:17– 46:15. Num 28–29 is the last comprehensive list of ancient Israelite festivals preserved in the Old Testament."

[28] Knohl, *The Sanctuary of Silence*, 18.

through God's command, "You shall keep my sabbaths and reverence my sanctuary: I am the LORD" (Lev 19:30; 26:2). Here we find the language of the Decalogue in Deut 5:12 with the command to "keep" (šāmār) the sabbath rather than "remember" (zākār) as found in Exod 20:8. In Leviticus, however, the sabbath instruction is also linked to one's "fear" or "reverence" of God's tabernacle. Leviticus makes the argument that *the holiness of time is equivalent to the holiness of place.*[29]

To encounter God in the consecration of time by keeping the sabbath is no less awesome than approaching his numinous presence in the holiness of the sanctuary.[30] This theological development is critical for Leviticus because the sanctification of time on the sabbath is primarily an undertaking of the household that does not require proximity to a shrine. This allows communities beyond Jerusalem to participate in holiness through sacred time if they cannot approach God's sacred space. Weekly celebration of the sabbath and the consecration of time provides a rhythm for Israelite households and communities to be reminded of Yhwh's rest and will pave the way for synagogal worship in the Second Temple period and beyond.

It is likely that Leviticus modifies ancient Israelite traditions concerning the sabbath and that its emphasis on sabbath time and obedience stemmed from the tumultuous period of the eighth century BCE or possibly after the Babylonian exile. The seventh day was hallowed because it was a ritual sign of the covenant that sanctified the Israelites (Exod 31:13) and drew them into the

---

[29] See Abraham Joshua Heschel, *The Sabbath: Its Meaning for Modern Man* (New York: Farrar, Straus and Giroux, 1951), 13–24.
[30] In later biblical texts, the sabbath is often paralleled with the sanctuary in the context of its desecration (Ezek 22:8, 26; 23:38; 1 Macc 1:39, 45).

holiness of God's time (Gen 2:2-3) while allowing them to rest together as families and communities (Exodus 16). If God had consecrated time from the beginning of creation (Gen 2:3) according to the priestly theology, then we can see the natural evolution of how the holiness of sabbath emerges in relation to the holiness of the sanctuary.

Though Leviticus is often associated with detailed prescriptions for sacrifice, there is another layer to the life of holiness that is maintained by the consecration of time and rest. Sabbath is critical for the life of the home, the community, and the nation. Later in history, it will become essential for preserving a landless and dispersed people as a means through which all Jews might weekly consecrate holy time to worship together. Abraham Heschel reflects on the history of the sabbath in Jewish practice. "Judaism is a *religion of time* aiming at the *sanctification of time* ... Judaism teaches us to be attached to the *holiness in time*, to be attached to sacred events, to learn how to consecrate sanctuaries that emerge from the magnificent stream of the year. The Sabbaths are our great cathedrals."[31] Sacred time in Jewish tradition becomes the experience of sacred space as the sabbath and festivals become great monuments of worship.

The sanctification of time offers the opportunity to find anchor points in the endless stream of seasons and years. Keeping the sabbath and consecrating time is a way of re-creating the tabernacle in the presence of the community of faith. To gather together without the burden or anxiety of work is a way in which Israel could turn their hearts towards worship, praise, and refreshment. In Leviticus, the sabbath is the cornerstone of Israel's experience of time throughout the liturgical year. Festivals emerge

---

[31] Heschel, *The Sabbath*, 8.

from the pattern of the seventh day of holy ceasing, consecrating, and entering into the promise of God's rest.

THE FESTIVALS

The Passover and Unleavened Bread (Lev 23:4–8; Num 28:16–25): The Passover sacrifice and the feast of Unleavened Bread were likely two ancient festivals in Israel that were joined together to mark the liberation from Egypt and the birth of Israel as a nation. The Passover command to place blood on doorposts contains similarities to a springtime rite performed by nomadic shepherds as an apotropaic sign to ward off evil spirits and to protect the fertility of the flocks.[32] It is possible that this symbol of protection was transferred to the Passover narrative as the Israelite firstborn were unharmed by Yhwh as he passed through Egypt.[33]

The Feast of Unleavened Bread finds parallels in the ancient Canaanite practice of cleansing the home of the previous year's leaven to begin afresh in the new year.[34] Spring marked the barley harvest in Israel as the first crop of their calendar year, which also would have been the time to start anew with fresh leaven. The departure from Egypt symbolized a time of purification and new life at the beginning of a new year and so the agricultural festival of purging leaven from the home was adapted to mark Yhwh's cleansing of his people and leading them out of death and slavery.

---

[32] Noth, *Exodus*, 91; cf. Roland De Vaux, *Ancient Israel: Its Life and Institutions*, trans. John McHugh (London: Darton, Longman and Todd 1961), 484–90.
[33] Scarlata, *Abiding Presence*, 93–101.
[34] De Vaux, *Ancient Israel*, 490–93.

The Unleavened Bread celebration is also called a "feast" (*ḥag*), which is a term that often denotes a pilgrimage.[35] This designation is a sign that the festival was not meant to be celebrated in one's home. In early Israel, it was likely a trip to the regional shrine (1 Sam 7:16) but following the legislation of Deuteronomy and a central cultic site, some Israelites would have had a more significant journey to Jerusalem. The offerings for the Passover were to be made "by fire" (Lev 23:8) but they are not specified in Leviticus (cf. Num 28:3).

These two ancient practices were brought together to form one festival representing the rites that encompassed Yhwh's judgment, protection, and the deliverance of his people from Egypt.[36] The yearly celebration of Passover and Unleavened Bread, like all the events surrounding the Exodus, were not merely recollections of God's actions at a particular point in time. Instead, they were celebrated as an ever-present reality for each generation of Israelites who identified themselves with their ancestors anticipating God's salvation from their oppressors. Though Passover rites may have taken different forms over time (cf. Ezek 45:21–25), there is one Passover that is commemorated and re-actualized at the beginning of each liturgical year as a sign of rebirth and the anticipation of God's coming redemption.[37]

The two festivals are the first of the liturgical calendar. Before the Passover event, Moses announced to the people, "This month

---

[35] Hans Dieter Betz, *Religion in Geschichte und Gegenwart 1–6*, 3rd ed. (Tübingen: Mohr Siebeck, 1957–65), 2:910.

[36] J. B. Segal, *The Hebrew Passover from the Earliest Times to AD 70* (London: Oxford University Press, 1963), 78–188; Nahum Sarna, *Exploring Exodus: The Heritage of Biblical Israel* (New York: Schocken, 1986), 85–89.

[37] James Plastaras, *The God of Exodus: The Theology of the Exodus Narratives* (Milwaukee, WI: Bruce, 1966), 146–47.

shall mark for you the beginning of months; it shall be the first month of the year for you" (Exod 12:1). It was celebrated on the fourteenth of Nisan, which was the first month after the spring equinox. Every generation of Israelites would celebrate this day as a "memorial" (*zîkkārôn*) of their freedom from bondage and birth as a new nation. For Leviticus, the liturgical year begins with the act of salvation par excellence in the Old Testament that signifies Israel's beginnings as a covenant people. This national identification is a powerful reminder of their former life of slavery and Yhwh's sovereignty over heavenly and earthly powers.

The First Fruits (Lev 23:9–14; Num 28:26–31): The next feast day is framed by the initial refrain, "The LORD spoke to Moses ...," which sets apart the following instructions from the previous though the festivals appear to be placed side by side. The waving of the grain offering is to take place "after the sabbath" (23:11), which follows the final day of the Unleavened Bread. The first sheaths of barley are to be given to the priests to wave as an offering to the Lord. The people must also offer a year-old lamb without blemish and a grain offering mixed with oil and a drink offering of wine. This is the only feast that is prefaced with "when you enter into the land" and looks forward to the wilderness generation settling in Canaan. All other festivals can be celebrated during the wilderness wanderings.

The first fruits was an agricultural festival that recognized the abundant bounty that the Lord provided from the land.[38] Its celebration was not only a matter of thanksgiving for God's provision, but it was also a political and religious declaration that Yhwh is the Lord of the harvest and not the Canaanite god, Baal.

---

[38] See Harold L. Ginsberg, "The Grain Harvest Laws of Lev. 23:9–22 and Num. 28:26–31," *PAAJR* 46–47 (1979–80): 141–53.

In ancient hymns, Baal rode upon the clouds and commanded the thunder, lightning, and rain, which demonstrated his power and gifts of fertility to the land.[39] Baal was depicted as the great warrior who defeated the god of the sea and sat enthroned on Mount Zaphon.[40] Later biblical prophets asserted Yhwh's authority over Mount Zaphon (Isa 14:13–14; Ps 48:1–3) and the festival of first fruits offers a similar, more subtle, polemic against any rival fertility gods.

The offering of the first fruits is presented as a commandment in Lev 23:10 ("You shall bring the sheaf of the first fruits"), but it was not mandated according to Num 28:26. Instead, it is descriptive of what people do in Israel at the beginning of harvest. "On the day of the first fruits, when you offer a grain offering . . . ." The language suggests a practice that was well known at the time and some scholars have argued that this happened during a period before the centralization of the sanctuary in Jerusalem.[41] People could have brought their grain offerings to one of the regional shrines at Bethel, Shiloh, or Gilgal without having to make a specific pilgrimage to Jerusalem.

The act of waving the sheaths was possibly a ritual sign of blessing that mimics the waving of flourishing grain in the fields.[42] The Mishnah describes the ritual as it was performed during the Second Temple period. "How is one to do this? He inserts his two

---

[39] COS 1:241–74; Nick Wyatt, *Religious Texts from Ugarit*, 2nd ed. (Sheffield: Sheffield Academic, 2002), 388–90.

[40] On the relationship between Yhwh and Baal, see Frank M. Cross, *Canaanite Myth and Hebrew Epic: Essays in the History of the Religion of Israel* (Cambridge, MA: Harvard University Press, 1973), 147–94. Cf. John Day. *Yahweh and the Gods and Goddesses of Canaan*, JSOTSSS 265 (Sheffield: Sheffield Academic Press, 2002).

[41] Noth, *Leviticus*, 170.

[42] Knohl, *The Sanctuary of Silence*, 25.

hands underneath the objects being offered and carries them to and fro. He lifts them up and lowers them."[43] The actions of the priest may represent the fullness of the offering with movements side to side as well as the fullness of God's provision in the harvest. The lifting up signifies an offering back to God out of what he had given. The ritual may contain layers of symbolism, but the act of waving the sheaves was a general sign of celebration and gratitude for what God had provided.

The festival of first fruits probably found its roots in ancient agricultural practices of making a thanksgiving offering from the first harvest of the year, but in Leviticus' liturgical calendar, it has been inextricably linked to the Exodus events. The produce of the harvest looks forward to God's provision of land promised to the patriarchs and a life of "landedness," to borrow Brueggemann's phrase that so aptly sums up the fullness of covenant blessing when one is safe and flourishing in the land.[44] Following the great celebration of deliverance and redemption from Egypt, Israel is to remember to give thanks to the God who provides for their sustenance and life in a land of their possession.

The Feast of Weeks or Pentecost (Lev 23:15-22; Num 28:26-31): Following the gift of the first fruits is another agricultural festival celebrating the harvest. The Israelites are to count off seven sabbaths (forty-nine days) following the offering of the sheaves and on the fiftieth day ("Pentecost" from the Greek for "fiftieth") after the final sabbath they are to bring another offering to the Lord. The period of fifty days marks the end of the barley harvest and the beginning of the wheat harvest. During that time, the crops may have been susceptible to natural forces that could have destroyed that years' produce and thus it is possible that

---

[43] M. Menaḥ 5:1.
[44] Brueggemann, *The Land*, xi.

counting seven weeks was also a time of daily prayer for blessing upon the harvest.[45]

The period of seven sabbath weeks is also a foreshadowing of the seven sabbath years of rest for the land that culminate on the fiftieth year of Jubilee. The annual celebration of the feast of Weeks reminded Israel of their place in the land as God's tenants and keepers who were under the stipulations of the covenant. Their gifts back to Yhwh were a continual reminder of their need to care for the land and for the welfare of the people dwelling in the land, especially the poor and those in need. Jubilee was the time for release and restoration in all of Israel (Isa 61:1-4) and Pentecost provided an annual reminder not only of Yhwh's provision, but his desire for justice and liberation in the land.

The prescriptions of what to offer represent the finest new grain in the form of two loaves of bread with leaven. The addition of leaven to an offering for the altar was rare (cf. Lev 2:11; 7:13) but could be given in certain circumstances for the thanksgiving offering of well-being (*tôdat šəlāmîm*). Along with the bread, the offerer was to bring seven lambs, one bull, and two rams as a burnt offering that was consumed fully in flames and ascended to Yhwh as a pleasing aroma.

Additional prescriptions are given for the offering of a male goat for the purification offering (*ḥaṭṭā't*) and two lambs as an offering of well-being (*šəlāmîm*). There is no reason given for why a sin offering must be made at the harvest celebration, but the addition of v. 22 may offer an insight into why this specific sacrifice was necessary. Alongside the joy of the harvest there were always those in need and those who suffered in poverty on the margins of society. These were the people whom Yhwh

---

[45] Milgrom, *Leviticus 23-27*, 1996, 1999-2001.

commanded Israel to provide for by not harvesting the edges of their fields or stripping their vineyards bare (Lev 19:9–10). In celebrating the gifts provided by the Lord at harvest, the people were also to recall how they had treated the poor and the alien among them. It is possible that the purification offering and the well-being offering were to act as a reminder for the Israelites to maintain God's justice in their agricultural practices and to recall the mercy of Yhwh upon his people.

The feast of Weeks marks the end of the three major spring festivals that recall God's redemption of his people from Egypt and his provision for them in the promised land. The yearly cycle of the wheat and barley harvests offered a time to ground Israelite families in the story of Yhwh's salvation and to remember that he is Lord over the land. Leviticus uses ritual celebration and time to draw the people together in remembrance of what God has done. Sacred time and ritual become a form of teaching that incorporates both home and tabernacle in worship.

The Day of Trumpets (Lev 16:23–25; Num 29:1–6): The day of "blasts" or the day of trumpets marks the first day of the seventh month, which later came to be the Jewish new year. This is the first in a series of festivals in the seventh month that marks the end of the hot, dry summer season. It is the beginning of the new agricultural year in Israel when they awaited the winter rains to refresh the soil. Work on the land was at a minimum, which allowed time for mental, physical, and spiritual refreshment as well as anticipating the harvest for the coming year.[46] Like other festival days, work was not permitted and the holy convocation was to be marked by a blasting of the shofar (horn).

---

[46] Wenham, *Leviticus*, 305.

In the ancient world, the horn was used to gather people together, sound an alarm, or prepare the troops for battle. The loud, piercing sound could be heard for great distances and was an important instrument for designating significant moments. The sound might also have been thought to arouse or awaken God to the people's needs as they looked forward to a new year of harvest and prayed for the coming rains.[47] Whatever the effect of the trumpet blast, the reverberation of the shofar through the towns and cities of Israel was an audible interruption that shattered the dull din of the average workday. Sound and music are powerful reminders that wake communities from their routines and enliven memories and emotions associated with particular times or seasons (cf. Num 10:10).[48]

For many Christians, particular Christmas carols offer reminders of the birth of Christ and the Advent season while other hymns evoke memories of Lent, Easter, or Pentecost. Music and sound are interconnected with phenomenological experience. In writing on the bodiliness of sound-experience, Jeremy Begbie contends that, "To speak of the distinctive use of sound in music in which its inherent characteristics are directly implicated in musical meaning...is to speak of musical sound as received through the body, and, as with all sound, this means very much more than through the ears."[49] For ancient Israel, the power of the shofar reverberating through the streets in the seventh month was a clear reminder that the new year had begun.

---

[47] Milgrom, *Leviticus 23–27*, 2018.
[48] Cf. Grimes, *Beginnings in Ritual Studies*, 26.
[49] Jeremy Begbie, *Theology, Music and Time* (Cambridge: Cambridge University Press, 2000), 27.

The Day of Atonement (Lev 16:29–34; 23:26–32; Num 29:7–11): The Day of Atonement, also known as the Day of Purification, or the Day of Purgation (*Yom Kippur*), is more somber in tone as it provides a time to remember individual and communal sins that have defiled Israel and God's holy sanctuary. It is significant that the noun "atonement" is in the plural in Lev 23:27 so that a more literal translation might be "the day of atonements." Milgrom argues that the plural should be understood as a superlative with the sense of "full atonement" or "complete purgation."[50] The day is defined by sacrifice, abstaining from work, and self-denial, which refers to fasting. All of Israel is called to repentance, self-examination, and mourning for the sake of purifying themselves and the sanctuary that has been stained by their sin. Additional detail on the ritual sacrifices of *Yom Kippur* can be found in Chapter 2, but here we shall examine how the day fits within the liturgical year.

The command to cease from work is found in other festival days as well, but on *Yom Kippur* the full weight of such a practice is brought into clear perspective. Anyone who does not fast will be "cut off" from the community (v. 29), which is another way of communicating one's exile and banishment or possibly their exclusion from the afterlife.[51] Anyone who does any work on that day is threatened with punishment that comes directly from the hand of Yhwh (v. 30). This is the only instance in the Levitical laws where God is depicted as the direct agent causing someone to be "destroyed" or to "perish" (cf. Lev 17:10; 23:3–6). Such is the importance of setting aside one day a year as a whole community to recall the ways in which Israel had transgressed the covenant

---

[50] Milgrom, *Leviticus 23–27*, 2022.
[51] Cf. Milgrom, *Leviticus 1–16*, 457–60.

and needed to make restoration through their repentance and sacrifice.

The timing of the festival is of particular import since it is the only place that offers a description of what constitutes the full day of the festival. The ritual of fasting and abstaining from work is to last "from evening to evening." This time frame became the traditional pattern that was applied to sabbath and other festivals though it is nowhere else explicitly stated. It is possible that this designation of evening to evening was originally meant only for *Yom Kippur* and that the traditional "day" constituted the daylight hours from morning till evening following the language of Genesis 1. Later rabbinic teaching established the evening-to-evening pattern, but it is possible that in earlier biblical times sabbaths and festivals began at dawn.[52]

The purification of the people of Israel and the sanctuary on a yearly basis is one of the most significant rituals performed throughout the year. The sacrifices, detailed in Leviticus 16, are reminders that Israel's sins have consequences on the purity of the tabernacle. Whether through sins of commission or sins of omission, the pollution of Israel's transgression throughout the year must be remembered and atoned for to preserve the people and ensure the ongoing presence of God. At the beginning of the year, the call to repentance and cleansing is ritually enacted through fasting and offerings to teach and remind the people of their constant need of forgiveness and purification.

The Festival of Booths (Lev 23:33–44; Num 29:12–34): Five days after repenting of their sins and cleansing the sanctuary, the Israelites are called to celebrate and "to rejoice before the LORD your God for seven days" (Lev 23:40). This is the only festival in

---

[52] Levine, *Leviticus*, 161.

Leviticus where rejoicing is specifically prescribed. The joy comes from a ritual that looks back to the Exodus once again and God's redemption from slavery in Egypt. The first day and the eighth day are to be a "holy convocation" on which no labor is done. This is followed by seven days of offerings "by fire," which are specified in the corresponding passage in Num 29:12–34. The festival is also tied to the land as a celebration of "gathering in" the produce of the harvest (v. 39).

This is one of the major pilgrimage festivals of the year (cf. Deut 16:13) and it is the only festival in which Israel is commanded to build something as a memorial to recall their ancestors' journey through the wilderness. Cohn argues that the desert wanderings remind Israel of its liminal state when they departed from the profane space of Egypt to the sacred space of the promised land.[53] We discussed sacred space in Chapter 3, but the booths provide a different type of shelter that offers a ritual experience of sacred space for all Israelites.

The ritual act of building a booth provides a physical experience for families to create something with their own hands. The physicality of the ritual is critical to the theological message that it conveys. Johnson argues that there is a perceived logical gap between what the Israelites are to know (that their ancestors lived in booths) and how they acquire that knowledge. Leviticus does not offer a series of propositional truths regarding historical facts but, rather, the "logical gap is bridged by ritualized practice that shapes the knower to recognize and subsequently discern what is significant about the historical reality: 'Israel was made to live in booths.'"[54]

---

[53] Cohn, *Shape of Sacred Space*, 13; cf. Scarlata, *The Abiding Presence*, 85.
[54] Johnson, *Knowledge by Ritual*, 153.

The creation of sacred space, and dwelling in that space, during the festival results in a break from normal routine. Families living in booths for seven days upsets life in such a way that it raises questions and provides pedagogical opportunities to reflect on the meaning of why one would do such a thing. The physical act of entering into a newly constructed ritual space is a powerful didactic tool in passing down and maintaining traditions. For Israel, it provides the opportunity to recall their ancestors' wandering through the wilderness, their disobedience, and God's provision for their needs in manna, quail, and water. The wilderness also reminds the people of their propensity to sin, to strive with God, and to test his faithfulness (cf. Psalm 95). Families become actors in the divine drama as they stare up to the sky through their leafy huts to see the stars and remember the God of their ancestors who guided them through the desert.

The "booths" (*sukkôt*) are to be made from "the fruit of majestic trees, branches of palm trees, boughs of leafy trees, and willows of the brook" (v. 40).[55] The term "majestic trees" (*'ēṣ hādār*) is only used here in the Pentateuch and the description inspires images of Eden and the fertile land that God had promised to Abraham and his descendants.[56] This sign of fertility stands in stark opposition to the barren wilderness of the Sinai Peninsula and acts as a reminder of the gift of God's blessing and life.

Dwelling outside in booths for one week might not sound like the most exciting thing to some, but the festival is meant to be one marked by great joy (v. 40). The joy is later explained as one that comes from remembering that the redeemed Hebrew slaves lived

---

[55] Cf. Bell, *Ritual Practice*, 69–93.
[56] See Michael Zohary, *Plants of the Bible* (Cambridge: Cambridge University Press, 1982), 45, 123, 131.

in booths throughout their forty years in the wilderness (v. 43). "All that are citizens in Israel" (v. 42; cf. Deut 16:13) were required to construct their own booths, which would have included those who were aliens and sojourners in the land. The term for "citizen" (*'ezrāḥ*) could have its etymological origins in the botanical description of a tree that was well rooted in the soil (cf. Ps 37:35).[57] To be a citizen of Yhwh's kingdom was to be rooted in his holy land (cf. Exod 15:7; Isa 5:1–6).

The arboreal imagery used throughout the Old Testament expresses the understanding that rootedness is critical for the life of creation and for God's people. Norman Wirzba reflects on agrarian images of trees, vines, and putting down roots and writes, "Rootedness does not restrict life, but is its precondition. Rootedness makes possible the relationships that build fertility, fecundity, and diversity. What is so remarkable about plants is that they *nourish themselves by nurturing the places in which they grow*."[58] The festival of booths was a yearly reminder of a time of rootlessness when the Israelites were guided by Yhwh through the wilderness. It was also a celebration of great joy as they gave thanks to God for remembering his covenant and planting them in the land.

The postexilic celebration of *Sukkot* is recalled in Neh 8:14–18, where every family in Jerusalem constructs a booth on the roof of their house according to the law of Moses. The seven days are spent listening to Ezra read from the book of the Law (Neh 8:18) and all the people rejoiced. This is one of the few windows into postexilic

---

[57] Levine, *Leviticus*, 134.
[58] Norman Wirzba, *This Sacred Life: Humanity's Place in a Wounded World* (Cambridge: Cambridge University Press, 2021), 87; cf. Scarlata, *Wine, Soil, and Salvation*, 65–70.

Jerusalem that reflect a people trying to find their roots once again. Their city had been destroyed, family members killed, and they had been sent into Babylonian exile. Their return to home, their rootedness in the land, takes shape in their practice of an ancient ritual of constructing a booth that ties them to the Exodus and to the promises of God made known to a new generation.

In later Jewish tradition, *Sukkot* included processions around the altar in the Jerusalem temple with palm branches being waved and beaten on the sides of the altar. During each day of the feast, the priests would also collect a golden pitcher of water from the pools of Shiloah, which were poured out to the west and east of the altar.[59] The ritual was a request for God to bless the winds and the rains in the coming season.

For Second Temple Jews, the streams of living waters that flowed from the altar and out of Jerusalem were reminders of Ezekiel's eschatological vision of the temple (Ezekiel 47) and the time of God's full restoration of his people. It was on the seventh, and climactic, day of the festival that Jesus entered the temple, stood up among the crowd of pilgrims, and cried out, "Let anyone who is thirsty come to me, and let the one who believes in me drink. As the scripture has said, 'Out of the believer's heart shall flow rivers of living water'" (John 7:37–38). The gospel author goes on to explain that Jesus said this about the Spirit that was to come as a sign of God's future salvation (John 7:39).

CONCLUSION

Religious calendars throughout the ancient Near East demonstrate humanity's desire to mark sacred times and seasons.

---

[59] M. *Sukkah* 4:6–9.

These gatherings were often based around harvest and the lunar cycles and were occasions to honor the king, pray for the harvest, or to ward off any evil spirits that might bring about famine or tragedy. However they were celebrated, they offered key moments in time that brought communities together to perform ritual acts that reminded them of their identity and their relationship with the divine. As Gorman argues, "Ritual, thus, becomes a means by which humans participate in the ongoing order of creation. Their existence is made meaningful as they participate in the never-ending drama of creation in ritual."[60] Time thus takes on recurrent and stable meaning.[61] The power of ritual and liturgy to shape a community demonstrates the insights of the priestly authors of Leviticus. The formation of a uniform liturgical calendar celebrating the events of the Exodus and harvest created communal bonds and a shared identity for the Israelites. National pilgrimages to Jerusalem became associated with certain festivals but the liturgical year offered local communities the opportunity to celebrate together.

It is likely that the festivals of Leviticus 23 were passed down for generations and date back to some of the earliest Israelite traditions. Over time, some of these festivals were given new meaning in the light of the Exodus events and the story of salvation. The harvest cycles, along with the equinoxes, were reshaped and transformed into ritual practices that continually reminded the people of their covenant identity, their call to holiness, their rootedness in the land, and their allegiance to Yhwh.

---

[60] Gorman, *The Ideology of Ritual*, 231.
[61] Paul Ricoeur, "The History of Religions and the Phenomenology of Time Consciousness," in *The History of Religions: Retrospect and Prospect: A Collection of Original Essays*, ed. Mircea Eliade and Joseph Kitagawa (New York: Macmillan, 1985), 13–30 (21).

The liturgical calendar was one of the most powerful pedagogical tools used by the priestly authors of Leviticus because it applied to every Israelite family. Unlike the focus on specific sacrifices at the tabernacle found in Numbers, the festival calendar in Leviticus is concerned with providing further ties between the home and the altar. Whether celebrating festivals around harvest, repentance, or the cleansing of the sanctuary, Leviticus presents an annual liturgical rhythm for communal participation that includes all the families of Israel and those sojourners dwelling among them. Unlike Deuteronomy, the emphasis in Leviticus is not on worship at a single, central sanctuary. Instead, Leviticus makes provisions so that communities may celebrate at home and make offerings at regional sites.

The celebration of sacred times and seasons shapes religious traditions around the world. Whether Jewish, Christian, Muslim, or other faith groups, the gathering together of people around a common purpose that is connected to worship forms strong communal bonds and identity. The biblical authors of Leviticus understood the power of this practice to shape and root a community of faith in its theological traditions. It is a testimony to their insights that thousands of years later many Jews continue to celebrate the Levitical festivals today and many Christians recall the Jewish calendar as its events were reinterpreted through the life and work of Christ.

Contemporary culture is driven by a rapid acceleration in technology, growth, and production that has changed how we perceive time, which sociologist Hartmut Rosa argues has created a sense of alienation and uprootedness.[62] Continental philosopher

---

[62] See Hartmut Rosa, *Social Acceleration: A New Theory of Modernity*, trans. Jonathan Trejo-Mathys (New York: Columbia University Press, 2017), 285–86.

Byung-Chul Han also comments on the nature of the modern digital world that has lost a sense of sacred time. Society has advanced in the speed of work and communication, which has only increased compulsion and production. He argues that we fail to grow deeper as human beings because of the communicative noise that drowns out the silence and breaks we find in festivals.[63] "We have today entirely lost the capacity for the kind of rest proper to the festival, one that is characterized by both the intensity of life and the intensity of contemplation. Life reaches a true intensity at the very moment the *vita activa* (which in its late modern crisis degenerates into hyperactivity) incorporates the *vita contemplativa*."[64]

On feast days and festivals, human beings experience an intensive form of life as the community gathers together for a united purpose in celebrating the transcendent God. There is a division in time that separates the sacred from the profane, which silences the normal working day to allow participants to enter into celebration. Without this type of exalted time within the cycles of the seasons, life becomes unbearable. "Thus, time that is completely dominated by the compulsion of production, the sort of time we inhabit today, is a time without festival. Life becomes impoverished; it freezes into mere survival."[65] The authors of Leviticus looked beyond life as mere survival and gave Israel a tradition of festivals and celebrations to draw them out of the profane world and into sacred time.

---

[63] Byung-Chul Han, *The Disappearance of Ritual: A Topology of the Present*, trans. Daniel Steuer (Cambridge: Polity Press, 2020), 36–46.
[64] Han, *The Disappearance of Ritual*, 38.
[65] Han, *The Disappearance of Ritual*, 40.

CHAPTER 7

Leviticus in the Old Testament and Beyond

LEVITICUS AND THE OLD TESTAMENT

The theological interpretation of Scripture grows and branches out over time as it is reinterpreted and reimagined in different cultural contexts. In the case of Leviticus, details about purity laws, blood sacrifice, sexual prohibitions, and other commandments that shaped life around the tabernacle/temple became cultic practices that find few similarities with the religions of today. Though some have dismissed Leviticus as irrelevant, throughout history we find its influence in both Jewish and Christian communities who embraced its ritual commands either literally or by finding creative analogies from their principles. In this chapter, we will examine briefly how the book of Leviticus has influenced the Old Testament and how it has shaped both Judaism and Christianity over the centuries.

Leviticus sits at the heart of the Pentateuch and is central to the story of Israel's origins and salvation from Egypt. We have seen that its cosmology parallels the creation narrative of Genesis 1 and the natural divisions decreed by God to bring the universe into order from chaos. Creation theology engenders and fashions liturgical and cultic practice in Leviticus for the maintenance and order of Yhwh's shrine and the life of his people. Leviticus also looks to Genesis to recall the Abrahamic covenant and the promise of numerous descendants and life in the promised land.

The instructions of Leviticus are rooted in the exodus narrative and Israel's liberation from Egypt. Legislation focuses on the promise of divine presence that the God of Israel would not only deliver his people from bondage but that he would come to dwell in their midst (Exod 25:8; 29:43–46). In response to the advent of God's holy presence, the Sinai covenant addresses the need for purity and sacrifice for the ongoing maintenance of the tabernacle. The ritual and cultic commands of Leviticus are ways in which Israel actualizes its theological vision of reality through physical performance both at the altar and within the home.[1] The people are taught how to enact the story of salvation through ritual space, time, sacrifice, and in their relation to the land. Ritual also serves as a critical didactic tool in Leviticus to reveal the character and holiness of Yhwh as well as the sinfulness of the people. Liberation from Egypt through the exodus marked the beginning of Israel's salvation, while the cultic and ethical commands of Leviticus offer a path for the ongoing pursuit of holiness. The "scripturalization" of the cult,[2] or the written transmission of cultic rituals, and Leviticus' formulation of moral laws provide a framework for life and worship that stands apart from other books of the Old Testament.

The revelation of God's commands in Leviticus represents a theology of community that stresses the Pentateuch's larger program of creating a society where all people know their social and religious duties and can hold to account those in roles of power. Even the minutiae of sacrifice and ritual was to be revealed to the

---

[1] Gorman, *The Ideology of Ritual*, 39–60, 229–32.
[2] Anderson, "Sacrifice and Sacrificial Offerings (OT)," *ABD*, 5:874.

whole congregation because every detail of God's word carried significance in the pursuit of holiness. Leviticus makes available both the inner priestly workings of the cult and the commands for purity in the home that shaped the social and religious life of the Israelites.

The relationship between Leviticus and Deuteronomy is one area that has already been touched on throughout this work and has been the subject of much scholarly debate. The theology, tone, and language of both differ in their presentation of the Mosaic laws. The most significant cultic difference between the two books is the centralization of the shrine and profane slaughter that are both commanded in Deuteronomy (Deut 12:15–16).[3] Unlike Leviticus, Deuteronomy assumes the rule of a king and restricts cultic activity to a central shrine presumably under the authority of the monarchy. Leviticus, however, makes no such distinction and we saw that its chief ambition was to preserve the integrity of blood by restricting all sacrifices to an authorized altar. Whereas Leviticus implicitly supports regional shrines under authorized priests, Deuteronomy's focus is on a single site of worship presumably within a monarchical setting.

Levinson argues that the innovations of the Deuteronomic authors reflect the increased desire to dismantle the cultic life of smaller communities in Judah. In an effort to satisfy citizens outside of Jerusalem, the legislation of the central sanctuary tried to ensure "that the loss of the local altars did not entail complete loss of local access to God or, more seriously, that God had

---

[3] The conflict between the two commandments has long been debated by the rabbis. Rabbi Akiva argued that the root š-ḥ-t ("slaughter") applied only to animals designated for sacrifice, whereas Rabbi Ishmael contended that the law applied to any animal that is killed for food or sacrifice. See Milgrom, *Leviticus 1–16*, 28–34; Milgrom, *Leviticus 17–22*, 1453–54.

abandoned the local sphere."⁴ Deuteronomy's reformulation of the altar laws of Exodus, and allowance for profane slaughter, mark a new division between non-religous and religious spheres that constrain cultic activity to a central shrine while also allowing blood to be spilled in a secular context.⁵ Whether Deuteronomy's legislation presupposes Levitical laws or not, its prescriptions around cultic matters restrict worship to a single site while permitting secular slaughter. Leviticus, however, seeks to establish a standardized form for cultic offerings to be performed by any authorized priest in the local shrine.⁶

Despite some discrepancies with other Pentateuchal books, the ritual and ethical commands of Leviticus offer a particular shape to the Sinai covenant delivered by Moses. With an intent to standardize cultic practice, purity regulations, and establish ethical norms, Leviticus offers a theology of holiness that binds Yhwh's home to Israel's home in a way that no other book of the Old Testament does. With holiness as the leitmotif underlying all of Israel's actions, Leviticus helps shape Pentateuchal theology around the real, physical presence of the divine in the tabernacle and the cultic/ethical life that must accompany this new covenant reality.

Looking beyond the Pentateuch, we frequently find the prophetic critique of the Israelite cult and temple practice whether in the North or the South. The prophets castigate the priests for their

---

⁴ Bernard M. Levinson, *Deuteronomy and the Hermeneutics of Legal Innovation* (Oxford: Oxford University Press, 1997), 49–50.

⁵ Whether this constitutes a complete "desacralization" expressed in Deuteronomy is doubtful. See Jacob Milgrom, "The Alleged 'Demythologization' and 'Secularization' in Deuteronomy," *IEJ* 23 (1973): 156–61. See also Bill T. Arnold, "Deuteronomy 12 and the Law of the Central Sanctuary Noch Einmal," *VT* 64 (2014): 236–48.

⁶ Baruch Schwartz, "'Profane' Slaughter and the Integrity of the Priestly Code," *HUCA* 67 (1996): 15–42; Baruch Levine, *In the Presence of the Lord*, 15–52.

failure as shepherds and leaders of God's people who were to discern between the holy and the profane. They were entrusted with Torah but had become as corrupt as those outside the sanctuary walls (Isa 28:7–8; Jer 2:8; 6:13; Ezek 22:6; Hos 4:4–10; Amos 7:16). Critical scholarship has often depicted the prophetic rebuke of priests as an overarching condemnation of the cult, but this oversimplification has resulted in false stereotypes of the prophet's message. Prophetic criticism of corrupt priestly actions stands in agreement with Leviticus. As we have seen, holiness cannot be separated from justice and righteousness in the theology of Leviticus. This aligns with the prophetic critique of a priesthood and nation that has profaned God's name in both social and religious contexts. Prophetic condemnation of priestly action does not reflect a rejection of Levitical laws or the cult but, rather, it upholds Leviticus' call to moral and cultic holiness.[7]

There is not space to examine the whole prophetic corpus, but the prophet Ezekiel is often associated with Leviticus since there are extensive similarities in language between both books.[8] Significant themes in Ezekiel's prophecy are holiness, defilement, and Yhwh's glory (*kābôd*) that is associated with the Jerusalem temple. Ezek 43:1–5 references the movement of the divine presence as it departed from Jerusalem (Ezekiel 8–11), appeared in Babylonian exile (Ezekiel 1–3), and returned to the new temple

---

[7] See Helmer Ringgren, *The Prophetical Conception of Holiness* (Uppsala: A.-B. Lundequist, 1948).

[8] Avi Hurvitz, *A Linguistic Study of the Relationship between the Priestly Source and the Book of Ezekiel: A New Approach to an Old Problem*, Cahiers De La Revue Biblique 20 (Paris: J. Gabalda, 1982); Norbert Lohfink, "The Priestly Narrative and History," in *The Theology of the Pentateuch: Themes of the Priestly Narrative and Deuteronomy* (Edinburgh: T&T Clark, 1994), 136–72 (146–47).

via the east gate (Ezekiel 40–48). The divine presence of God that is central to the theology of Leviticus emerges in the prophet's recollection of exile and restoration.[9]

Also critical to Ezekiel is the building of the new temple by the Zadokite priests. Their participation is crucial in establishing an authentic altar that is appropriate for priestly sacrifices. The detailed description of the temple in chapters 40–48 envisage a reconsecration of the altar based on the pattern found in Leviticus 9. After Yhwh's *kābôd* returns to the temple (Ezek 43:1–5), sacrifices can begin and the altar is consecrated over seven days (Ezek 43:18–26). This culminates on the eighth day, when the altar is cleansed through the atoning sacrifices and Yhwh will once again accept his people's offerings.

The consecration of the altar and the return of the divine presence for Ezekiel also results in the fertility of the land. His vision of living water emerging from the threshold of the temple (Ezek 47:1–12; cf. Joel 3:18) offers an image of blessing pouring out into the wilderness and to the Dead Sea bringing abundant life wherever it goes.[10] Like the covenant blessings of Leviticus 26, Israel will experience the abundance of crops and fertility from the land through their obedience when the sanctuary has been fully cleansed, purified, and atoned for by the appropriate sacrifices made by the authorized priests.[11]

---

[9] See Moshe Greenberg, "The Vision of Jerusalem in Ezekiel 8–11: A Holistic Interpretation," in *The Divine Helmsman: Essays in Honor of Louis Silberman*, ed. James L. Crenshaw and Samuel Sandmel (New York: Ktav, 1980), 143–64.

[10] See Jon D. Levenson, *Theology of the Program of Restoration of Ezekiel 40–48*, HSM 10 (Missoula, MO: Scholars Press, 1976), 7–19.

[11] Cf. Nihan, *Priestly Torah*, 443–45; Nathan MacDonald, *Priestly Rule: Polemic and Biblical Interpretation in Ezekiel 44* (Berlin: Walter de Gruyter, 2015), 19–55.

Ezekiel also makes use of the term *nāśi'* ("prince, chieftain") in relation to the vision of the new temple. The same word is used in Lev 4:22, and what is noticeably absent in both texts is any reference to a "king" who participates in cultic activities. Ezekiel presents the *nāśi'* like a royal patron of the temple who serves as the guardian of Yhwh's shrine and ensures that the priests perform their duties correctly (Ezek 45:17–46:15).[12] The prophet assigns the *nāśi'* a particular role during the new moon and sabbath celebrations, which state that he should position himself in the inner eastern gate and stand to witness the priest make his offering (Ezek 46:1–5). The positioning and role of the leader within the sanctuary to watch the priests highlights his responsibility for overseeing part of the cult.[13] Though similar regulations are not found in Leviticus, we see the prophet expanding on the theology of lay participation in cultic activity. The text of Leviticus opens up the cultic world of the tabernacle for all Israel to witness and Ezekiel takes this one step further by making the *nāśi'* physically present for particular offerings.

In the prophecies of Isaiah, we also discover thematic correspondence with Leviticus particularly through the prophet's emphasis on God's holiness. The title "the Holy One of Israel" occurs across the entire corpus of Isaiah and stands as a commanding motif that is held up against the moral and cultic

---

[12] Paul M. Joyce, "King and Messiah in Ezekiel," in *King and Messiah in Israel and the Ancient Near East: Proceedings of the Oxford Old Testament Seminar*, ed. John Day, JSOTSS 270 (Sheffield: Sheffield Academic, 1998), 323–97; Daniel Bodi, "Le prophète critique la monarchie. Le terme nasi chez Ézechiel," in *Prophetes et rois. Bible et Proche-Orient*, ed. André Lemaire (Paris: Cerf, 2001), 249–57.

[13] Daniel I. Block, *The Book of Ezekiel: Chapters 25–48*, NICOT (Grand Rapids, MI: Eerdmans, 1998), 671–76.

corruption of Israel.[14] The prophet begins his ministry by entering the adytum of the heavenly temple where he required purification from the heavenly altar (Isa 6:5–6). His encounter with the seraphim in the throne room of the Almighty formed his vision of God's power and holiness and influenced his prophecies to Israel.[15] Gammie contends that divine holiness in Isaiah is linked to divine kingship and a divine passion for justice that marks God's salvation for all the earth. "In this affirmation of God as being sovereign in the double sense of being both holy and just, Isaiah shows himself to be very much in the line of the ancient traditions on which he draws."[16] Purity for the prophet is intimately connected to social justice and righteous living. There is an ongoing debate as to whether Leviticus influenced Isaiah, or vice versa, but both texts demonstrate a desire for cultic and ethical purity stemming from a theological conviction of God's holiness.

Another shared characteristic between Isaiah and Leviticus is the association of social justice, purity, and God's judgment. In Leviticus, we argued that the role of the cult was not primarily to appease God's wrath but, rather, its goal was for purification from sin and the purgation of the tabernacle. Yet we also saw that the moral corruption of the people could defile the land and lead to their exile. In Isaiah, the divine judgment for ethical abuses results in punishment (Isa 10:3), but the prophet also employs agricultural images of threshing (Isa 28:27–29), the pruning of vines (Isa 5:1–6), or the burning of chaff (Isa 5:24) to demonstrate that the goal of

---

[14] Isa 1:4; 5:19, 24; 10:20; 12:6; 17:7; 29:19; 30:15; 31:1; 37:23; 41:14, 16, 20; 43:3, 14; 45:11; 47:4; 49:7; 54:5; 55:5; 60:9, 14. Cf. Hos 11:9.
[15] Abraham Joshua Heschel, *The Prophets* (New York: Harper & Row, 1962), 85–90.
[16] Gammie, *Holiness in Israel*, 79.

judgment is also purification.[17] As God does not utterly destroy his people who experience the covenant the curses (Lev 26:40–46), so too does the prophet envisage a time when the people will return to Yhwh and be saved (Isa 30:15).[18] Isaiah's doctrine of God's holiness influenced his prophetic call to purity and helped shaped his vision of future redemption and restoration to the land.

The impact of Leviticus on the rest of the Old Testament is significant in that it presents a theology of God's holiness that is to be mirrored by his covenant people. The patterns for holy living are established through cultic and ethical obedience as they were delivered to Moses at Sinai. Leviticus' presentation of Moses' teaching shaped the social and religious life of Israel and provided a standard of holiness that would later be used by the prophets and reimagined as they looked to future judgment and salvation. Whether in the monarchic period or in postexilic Judea, the tenets of Leviticus formed the life and worship of the covenant people throughout the biblical period. So great was the influence of Leviticus that we find its laws and commands expanded on and added to in the Second Temple period.

LEVITICUS IN THE SECOND TEMPLE PERIOD

There is little doubt that the postexilic period was heavily influenced by the Deuteronomic doctrine of centralization and worship in the rebuilt Jerusalem temple. A massively dwindled Jewish people returned from Babylon with hopes of restoring the city of

---

[17] See Daniel J. Stulac, *History and Hope: The Agrarian Wisdom of Isaiah 28–35* (University Park, PA: Eisenbrauns, 2018).

[18] See Walter Brueggemann, *The Prophetic Imagination*, 40th anniversary edition (Minneapolis, MN: Fortress Press, 2018), 63–79.

David and Yhwh's temple.[19] Sacrifices and festivals were confined to the city as Babylonian refugees sought to rediscover their identity in the practice of the Mosaic Torah.[20] Though cultic sacrifice was confined to the physical space of the temple, Judaism began to turn to other modes of worship and prayer that offered paths to holy living. The rise of the synagogue and the devotion to prayers and reading Torah in local communities did not diminish the need or desire for the temple, but it did allow those beyond Jerusalem to express their faithfulness and devotion to Yhwh in ways other than blood sacrifice.

During the period of the second temple's existence, the Levitical system remained very much intact in Jerusalem. Rotations for temple service were established for priests and the prescribed sacrifices in Leviticus continued. The Book of Chronicles accounts for the elaborate organization and activity of the priests and the rise of the temple as the religious and financial center of Jerusalem.[21]

The centralization of worship also caused a rise in pilgrimage festivals. With a decreased farming population and a large diaspora, certain festivals established in the Levitical calendar moved away from the home to the central sanctuary. The Passover became the most significant festival and even overshadowed the feast of Booths.[22] The priority on temple worship for certain festivals did not, however, hinder Jews outside of Jerusalem from ongoing local worship and devotion. In fact, an expertise in Torah began to move

---

[19] Though alternative temples were built by the Samaritans at Mt. Gerizim, and in upper Egypt by the diaspora community at Elephantine, both were held by minority groups and did not last.

[20] Saul M. Olyan, "Purity Ideology in Ezra-Nehemiah as a Tool to Reconstitute the Community," *JSJ* 35 (2004): 1–16.

[21] See Sara Japhet, *The Ideology of the Book of Chronicles and its Place in Biblical Thought* (Winona Lake, IN: Eisenbrauns, 2009).

[22] *Antiq.* 17:213–18; cf. 15:50–52.

beyond priestly circles since it was possible for any literate Jew to study and comprehend the Law.[23] This became critical in later Judaism, which was dominated by learned rabbis rather than priests after the Roman destruction of the temple in 70 CE.

The Second Temple period was also marked by great turbulence in Jerusalem. The books of 1-2 Maccabees detail Judea's struggle for liberation from the Seleucid kings and especially the persecution under Antiochus IV Epiphanes. The narratives deal with issues of Jewish apostasy and foreign rule in Jerusalem, which culminate in the desecration of the temple in December of 167 BCE. The Maccabean revolt and the recapturing of the temple led to an aggressive expansion in Palestine and parts of Syria, which gave rise to the priestly rule of the Hasmoneans. This was not, however, without conflict between different sects of Judaism who vied for power in both the religious and political spheres.

Two main groups of interpretation arose during this period. The first is broadly the rabbinic tradition that produced the Mishnah, or the oral commentary on the Mosaic law. The rabbis offered their own interpretations of Leviticus that further expanded under the Pharisees who were a group of Jewish religious leaders that arose after the Hasmonean period. The Pharisees have been called a "sect" of Judaism, but it is likely that they were a reformist group with social power that competed with other groups like the Sadducees who held different theological views.[24] The second group were also likely rabbis and priests that

---

[23] Martha Himmelfarb, "'A Kingdom of Priests': The Democratization of the Priesthood in the Literature of Second Temple Judaism," *Journal of Jewish Thought and Philosophy* 6 (1997): 89-104 (101-4).

[24] See further Amy-Jill Levine and Joseph Sievers, *The Pharisees* (Grand Rapids, MI: Eerdmans, 2021).

formed their own Jewish sect in the caves of Qumran possibly in response to the rise of the Hasmoneans. Unlike the Pharisees, the Jews of Qumran rejected the validity of the Jerusalem temple and, instead, formed their own community that utilized and developed many of the Levitical laws with an emphasis on purity.

The scrolls found in Qumran offer various glimpses into a strict sectarian approach to purity laws that may have been used to dispel any ambiguity of being God's holy people. Harrington points to several examples such as the case of the leper in Lev 14:10–20 who is required to bring cereal and drink offerings in addition to the ḥaṭṭā't. The Qumran sectarians reasoned that all are sinners and so all should bring the additional offerings (11QT 25:12–15), but the rabbis disagreed and considered the leper's offering a special case (m. Menaḥ 9:6).[25] In terms of dietary purity, the sectarians argued that even a gnat, or its larvae, must be strained out of juices to adhere to the restrictions of Leviticus 11 (CD 12:11–13), but the rabbis deemed this unnecessary (m. Ter. 7:11). In cases of sexual purity, the sectarians also preferred a strict interpretation of Lev 18:13, which prohibited a man from having sexual relations with his aunt. They inferred that a man's niece was a similar type of relationship and was thus banned (CD 5:7–11; 11QT 66:14–15). The rabbis, however, disagreed and found no direct command in the law that restricted a man from marrying his niece.[26]

---

[25] Hannah K. Harrington, "Interpreting Leviticus in the Second Temple Period: Struggling with Ambiguity," in *Reading Leviticus: A Conversation with Mary Douglas*, ed. John F. A. Sawyer, JSOTSS 227 (Sheffield: Sheffield Academic Press, 1996), 214–29 (220–21).

[26] Harrington, "Interpreting Leviticus," 223–24. Cf. Martha Himmelfarb, *Between Temple and Torah: Essays on Priests, Scribes, and Visionaries in the Second Temple Period and Beyond* (Tübingen: Mohr Siebeck, 2013), 111–90.

For the Jews living at Qumran, Leviticus was a key interpretive text as they sought to maintain the strictest levels of purity to ensure exact obedience to God's command. They saw themselves as holy, set apart, without blemish (*tāmîm*), and banned all persons with any defects from residing in the temple city (11QTemple 45:12–14). In the text of Leviticus, they found justification for their doctrines of exclusion based mainly on their religious passion for purity.[27] Other groups such as the Pharisees and Sadducees also used the laws of Leviticus to ensure that purity was maintained by the faithful of Israel. Rather than rejecting the Jerusalem temple built by Herod the Great, however, they allowed for political and social situations to exist under Roman rule while utilizing their power to maintain the sanctity of temple.

The Second Temple period was a time of upheaval and significant change. The growth of Jewish apocalyptic writings and the interest in the heavenly tabernacle and a messianic figure looked forward to a time when God would once again redeem and purify his people and his temple.[28] Theologies differed among various Jewish groups, but writings from the Apocrypha, the Pseudepigrapha, and the Dead Sea Scrolls demonstrate the

---

[27] See Moshe J. Bernstein, *Reading and Re-reading Scripture at Qumran* (Leiden: Brill, 2013). Other teachings from Qumran include ethical laws (e.g. Lev 19:18, 34) such as, "Each one must love his brother as himself, and support the poor, needy, and alien (*gēr*)" (CD 6:20–21). In this instance, however, the *gēr* is likely a reference to a proselyte who had joined the community and not to a foreigner. See also M. J. H. M. Poorthuis and J. Schwartz, eds., *Purity and Holiness: The Heritage of Leviticus* (Leiden: Brill, 2000).

[28] See Daniel Stökl Ben Ezra, *The Impact of Yom Kippur on Early Christianity: The Day of Atonement from Second Temple Judaism to the Fifth Century* (Tübingen: Mohr Siebeck, 2003).

influence Leviticus had concerning the rituals of daily life in purity and worship as well as shaping an eschatological vision for God's salvation.

LEVITICUS IN THE NEW TESTAMENT AND BEYOND

Leviticus is rarely quoted in the New Testament but its teachings on ritual, sacrifice, atonement, and ethical purity are intrinsically bound to the worldview of its authors. We have discussed how sin and defilement in Leviticus is a threat that has the potential to lead the world back into chaos and how holiness counteracts, and even destroys, these forces of death. For the New Testament authors, the power of God's holiness becomes fully manifest in the incarnation of Jesus Christ. Attested to be the Son of God, Jesus is portrayed throughout the Gospels as the physical embodiment of Yhwh's holiness (John 1:14). He is the only divine and human figure who has the authority to cast out demons, heal disease, and ultimately conquer death through his crucifixion, resurrection, and ascension.

The advent of the proclaimed Jewish Messiah in the New Testament follows the typological pattern found in Exodus and Leviticus of God's divine descent to earth. At the end of Exodus, God's glory fills the tabernacle, which is described in Leviticus as Yhwh's consecration of the altar. The descent of fire on the altar inaugurates the cult and assures his ongoing presence. In the New Testament, we find a similar pattern but this time the descent of God to his people comes in the form of a human being. The typology of the New Testament reveals that God's holiness, made manifest in Christ, is no longer confined to tabernacle/temple space but has broken into the profane world (cf. John 1:1-4, 14).

We recall that in some cases, holiness can act as a contagion (Exod 29:37; 30:26-29) and that with certain offerings in Leviticus we are told that "anything that touches them shall become holy" (Lev 6:11, 20).[29] The New Testament envisages this power of holiness to be present in the life and work of Christ and later through his death and resurrection when the curtain to the Holy of Holies was torn in two symbolizing the opening for all to approach God's holiness (Matt 27:51; Mark 15.38; Luke 23:45). The outpouring of the Holy Spirit at Pentecost (Acts 2) is another sign of holiness as a contagious force for imparting purity and wholeness outside of the temple.

Christian tradition and scholarship have long struggled with the Jewishness of Jesus and how his inauguration of the new covenant relates to the Mosaic covenant at Sinai. Christian stereotypes have often depicted first-century Judaism as a sterile religion concerned only with legal observance and ritual obedience, but lacking compassion. On the other side is Jesus, the one who shows God's mercy and casts off the stringent demands of the Law so that he can demonstrate love and bring healing. These caricatures have sadly contributed to movements of anti-Semitism over the centuries, but since the groundbreaking work of E. P. Sanders' *Jesus and Judaism*, New Testament scholarship has shifted in the last decades toward understanding Jesus within a Jewish context.[30]

In an effort to see the life and works of Jesus through his Jewish background, Matthew Thiessen examines the Gospels with a particular focus on Levitical laws of ritual purity. He argues that

---

[29] Milgrom, *Leviticus 1–16*, 443–56.
[30] Literature on the quest for the historical Jesus is vast but see e.g. the works of Richard Bauckham, Adele Yarbro Collins, Richard B. Hays, Amy Jill Levine, Geza Vermes, N. T. Wright, et al. For various essays on the topic, see Craig A. Evans, *Routledge Encyclopedia of the Historical Jesus* (London: Routledge, 2010).

Jesus' actions are consistent with Torah and need to be understood within Jewish thinking on the sources of impurity and, following Milgrom, the forces of death that lie behind them.[31]

We recall that impurity in Leviticus was never meant to be a permanent state. Contamination will inevitably come by sin or by natural means, but the goal of the purity laws in Leviticus are restoration, unity, and wholeness. God does not instruct Israel to condemn those who become defiled but to help them be reinstated into the blessings of the covenant community. It is this sentiment that is expressed through the power of holiness depicted in Jesus' encounters with those who were unclean. Rather than becoming defiled, the Gospel authors portray Jesus as the one who heals, restores, and destroys the forces of death while still abiding by the commands of Leviticus.[32]

There is not space to examine each of Jesus' encounters, but we can look to one example when he heals a man with a skin disease (*lepra*) as recalled in Mark 1:40–45.[33] We have noted extensive regulations in Leviticus on skin diseases and other outward signs of decay that are symbols of death.[34] In the immediate context of Mark's Gospel, it is important that the encounter is preceded by an earlier event in the synagogue where a man with an unclean spirit declares Jesus to be "the Holy One of God" (*ho hagios tou*

---

[31] Matthew Thiessen, *Jesus and the Forces of Death: The Gospel's Portrayal of Ritual Impurity in First-Century Judaism* (Grand Rapids, MI: Baker Academic, 2020), 14–20.

[32] Cecilia Wassén, "The Jewishness of Jesus and Ritual Purity," *Scripta Instituti Donneriani Aboensis* 27 (2016): 11–36.

[33] See Brent A. Strawn, "On Priesting," in *The Incomparable God: Readings in Biblical Theology*, ed. Collin Cornell and M. Justin Walker (Grand Rapids, MI: Eerdmans, 2023), 374–82.

[34] Jacob Milgrom, *Leviticus: A Book of Ritual and Ethics*, Continental Commentaries (Minneapolis, MN: Fortress Press, 2004), 128.

theou) (Mark 1:24). Jesus, the rabbi who teaches with power, heals, and has authority over demons, is identified as the one who bears Yhwh's holiness.

The man's plea is marked by humility. "If you choose, you can make me clean" (Mark 1:40). The Gospel author tells us that Jesus was "moved with pity" and then reaches out to touch him and heal him (Mark 1:41).[35] The "Holy One of God" also reveals the compassion and desire of Yhwh to cleanse impurity for the sake of reconciliation and wholeness. Jesus upholds the Levitical laws and tells him to go to the priest and make the offerings required so that he might be welcomed back into the covenant community (Lev 14:1–18). We recall the rite of purification where blood is placed on the right earlobe, the right thumb, and the right big toe of the healed person (Lev 14:14). The unclean man moves from exclusion to the embrace of the community and the ability to approach the temple space to worship once again.

In this passage, we find Jesus both upholding the commands of Leviticus by telling the healed man to be examined by the priests, yet not being obedient to the purity laws himself.[36] His actions can be understood in two ways. On a practical level, the unclean man must perform the appropriate ritual if he is ever to be allowed back into the community of faith to live with his family and friends and offer sacrifices at the temple, so Jesus commands him to follow the Levitical prescriptions. On another level, we find that Jesus is depicted as surpassing the purity laws because he is unable to become contaminated since he bears the fullness of

---

[35] Thiessen, *Jesus and the Forces of Death*, 55, prefers the minority textual reading that Jesus was "angered" (*orgistheis*), but the majority of texts read "having compassion" (*splanchnistheis*).

[36] Paula Fredriksen, *Sin: The Early History of an Idea* (Princeton: Princeton University Press, 2012), 20–21.

God's holiness. Unlike the Jewish priests who were called to diagnose types of skin disease without touching them and becoming impure, Jesus demonstrates that he has the power to destroy the forces of death, by touching and healing others from disease while remaining in a state of purity and holiness himself.[37]

Following the death, resurrection, and ascension of Christ, one theological issue that Jewish followers of Jesus had to reconcile with Leviticus was the fact that Jesus was from the tribe of Judah and not from a priestly line even though his sacrifice was perceived as an eschatological and cosmic work of atonement (Col 1:15–19). During the late Second Temple period, there was an apocalyptic conception of a high priest as redeemer who would liberate people on an eschatological Day of Atonement (11QMelchizedek; 1 Enoch 10).[38] Yet this messiah was from a priestly line and Jesus was not. This, however, did not prevent Christian exegesis from forming a theology consistent with Leviticus whereby Jesus is understood as the great high priest (in the order of Melchizedek), which is articulated most fully in the epistle to the Hebrews.

The author of the epistle offers an extended discussion of Christ's priestly lineage (Hebrews 1–8) and describes the earthly tabernacle as a type preparing the way for the one true high priest.

---

[37] See Joel Marcus, *Mark 1–8: A New Translation with Introduction and Commentary*, AB 27 (New York: Doubleday, 2000), 208. For further discussion on healing and purity in the Gospels, see Lidija Novakovic, *Messiah, the Healer of the Sick: A Study of Jesus as the Son of David in the Gospel of Matthew*, WUNT 170 (Tübingen: Mohr Siebeck, 2003); Thomas Kazen, *Jesus and Purity Halakhah: Was Jesus Indifferent to Impurity?*, ConBNT 38 (Stockholm: Almqvist & Wiksell, 2002).

[38] See Thomas Hieke and Tobias Nicklas, eds., *The Day of Atonement: Its Interpretations in Early Jewish and Christian Traditions*, Themes in Biblical Narrative 15 (Leiden: Brill, 2012).

"But when Christ came as a high priest of the good things that have come, then through the greater and perfect tent (not made with hands, that is, not of this creation), he entered once for all into the Holy Place, not with the blood of goats and calves, but with his own blood, thus obtaining eternal redemption" (Heb 9:11–12). The author goes on to offer a typological interpretation of the cultic system and the tabernacle to demonstrate that Christ's sacrifice is the eschatological *Yom Kippur*, which has cleansed the heavenly tabernacle by his atoning blood.[39] The cultic system established through Moses and Aaron in Leviticus became a critical interpretive tool for the author of Hebrews in identifying Christ as the self-sacrificial high priest who made, once-for-all, a cosmic atoning sacrifice that allowed for the inclusion of the gentiles into the new covenant community.[40]

Following the Roman destruction of the temple in 70 CE, both Jews and Christians reflected on the nature and purpose of the cultic commands in Leviticus. In rabbinic tradition, two conflicting opinions date back possibly to debates between Rabbi Akiva and Rabbi Ishmael concerning whether God actually *needs* sacrifices or not.[41] The midrash of Leviticus foresees a time when all sacrifices will be abolished except for the thanksgiving offering.[42] Some rabbis disagreed on account of the sacrifices mentioned in Ezekiel's vision of the new temple. The argument persisted into the medieval period between two of the great Jewish philosophers,

---

[39] Stökl Ben Ezra, *The Impact of Yom Kippur on Early Christianity*, 180–96.
[40] See David M. Moffitt, *Atonement and the Logic of Resurrection in the Epistle to the Hebrews*, SNT 141 (Leiden: Brill, 2013).
[41] Abraham Joshua Heschel, *Heavenly Torah as Refracted through the Generations*, trans. and ed. Gordon Tucker (New York: Bloomsbury, 2007), 71–92.
[42] *Lev Rab* 9:7; 27:12.

Moses Maimonides (1138–1204) and Moses Nachmanides (1194–1270).

Maimonides argued that the sacrificial system was not a part of God's original plan for Israel but that he needed to modify Israel's primitive style of worship that consisted of blood offerings.[43] In order to lead them away from idolatrous practices, God gave them specific commands concerning blood and sacrifice not because he needed offerings but so that Israel would not worship "goat demons" or be tempted to follow the ways of the Canaanites. Therefore, the tabernacle (and the cult) for Maimonides was a cultural concession that was for the benefit of primitive Israel and to designate for them a single place of sacrifice.[44]

For Nachmanides, however, the cult and the tabernacle/temple play a critical role in the life of God's people. In his commentary on Lev 1:9, he writes, "By way of truth, there is a hidden secret contained in the offerings."[45] Nachmanides argued that God desires to live in the world in the midst of his people and that the cultic system was critical to the spiritual life of Israel. The tabernacle was not a secondary intention, as argued by Maimonides, but it was necessary to satisfy the needs of God to dwell with his people. In this way, Nachmanides, and those who follow him, argue for a more mystical and sacramental understanding of God's necessary immanence on earth.

---

[43] *The Guide of the Perplexed*, 3:32. See Roy Pinchot, "The Deeper Conflict between Maimonides and Ramban over the Sacrifices," *Tradition* 33 (1999): 24–33.
[44] *The Guide of the Perplexed*, 3:47.
[45] Moses ben Nachman, *Commentary on Leviticus*, trans. Charles B. Chavel (New York: Shilo, 1974), 21. Cf. Oded Yisraeli, "The Kabbalistic Remez and Its Status in Naḥmanides' Commentary on the Torah," *Journal of Jewish Thought & Philosophy* 24 (2016): 1–30.

Beyond the practice of cultic sacrifice, the ethical and moral teachings of Leviticus remained critical for Jews whose worship moved away from the Jerusalem temple to the local synagogue. Without animal sacrifices, there arose an emphasis on the study of Scripture and prayer. The openness of Torah study (for men) in the synagogue ultimately led to a democratization of religious leadership. The institution of priests and the expertise that had been confined to the hereditary priesthood in Judaism faded as any Jew who was willing to learn could read and study the finest details of Torah. It is the rabbis who emerge as the religious leaders of Judaism as they promoted the love of Torah study and the growth of an intellectual and learned laity no matter one's background or lineage.[46]

Whereas historic Judaism leaned toward the study of Torah, prayer, the sanctification of time through the sabbath, and the liturgical calendar, the Christian church took on other ritual and sacramental aspects of Leviticus. The drama of ritual and the immanence of the divine in the material world were celebrated by Christians through the new sacraments of baptism and the Eucharist. These two sacraments stood at the forefront of Christian doctrine and practice in the early church.

Christians also relied on Leviticus for their understanding of sacred space. Within centuries of the Christian movement, we discover the growth of church architecture as it begins to reflect divisions for holy spaces and areas where only priests may be present. We previously argued that the theology of Leviticus promotes cultic worship and sacrifice at authorized locations through authorized priests rather than at a single sanctuary. In a

---

[46] See Abraham Joshua Heschel, *The Earth is the Lord's* (New York: Farrar, Straus, Giroux, 1950), 46–47.

similar manner, the early church, as described in the Acts of the Apostles, gathered in physical spaces that were authorized by the presence of the Holy Spirit under apostolic authority (Acts 2:42; 10:1–48). These spaces could exist anywhere, and were often located in peoples' homes, yet every distinct community was integral in creating the new temple of Christ (Eph 2:21; 1 Pet 2:4–5).

Initially, there were no architectural designs that reflected the temple as Christian homes in the early church served as sanctified space under the authority of its leaders. These small gatherings of believers became a new type of religious temple. This was not the tabernacle revealed to Moses in the wilderness but, rather, it was an interconnected network of small worshiping communities throughout the Roman empire. These early Christians, however, would find their ritual, liturgical, and architectural roots in the typological patterns established in Leviticus, which soon influenced the doctrine of the priesthood and the architecture of the church.

Though there was no formal priesthood based on lineage in Christianity, divisions between priests and laypeople began to take place over time, which can be seen through early church architecture. Kilde argues that the movement from home to *domus ecclesiae* occurred around the third century and can be seen at one of the earliest identified house churches found in Dura-Europos, Syria.[47] The ordinary home had been converted into a worship space sometime during the mid-second century CE and contained a baptistry, a large room for the Eucharist, and other spaces possibly for catechumens. What is notable is the inclusion of a *bema* in the largest room of the house (the triclinium) where

---

[47] Kilde, *Sacred Power, Sacred Space*, 23–24.

services were held. The *bema*, or a small platform, was reserved for the bishop or priest who led the service and acted as an architectural divide between lay and ordained.[48] The priest was slightly elevated above the congregation where he would celebrate the Eucharist, a ritual act that recalls the death and resurrection of Christ.

Through the eucharistic liturgy, the priest would consecrate the elements of bread and wine with prayers so that they became the real presence, or the flesh and blood, of Christ. Like the Jewish priests who were set apart to make daily offerings and sacrifices within the tabernacle/temple, so too did Christian priests offer the Eucharist at the altar of the church, which later became the daily Mass. In the medieval Roman Catholic Church, the divisions between priests and laypeople became more pronounced as the Mass was celebrated only for priests to consume. A typical layperson would partake of the bread and wine once a year on Easter Sunday. Historian Eamon Duffy comments, "The prestige of the Sacrament as the centre and source of the whole symbolic system of late medieval Catholicism implied an enormously high doctrine of priesthood. The priest had access to mysteries forbidden to others."[49] The priest at the altar became like Aaron in Leviticus, sacrificing in the holy of holies beyond the view of the people.

Many medieval European churches contained a rood screen that was usually an ornate partition separating the nave (where the laypeople gathered) from the chancel (where the altar resided). This blocked the laity from seeing the priest at the altar celebrating the Eucharist. Without being able to see the priest

---

[48] Kilde, *Sacred Power, Sacred Space*, 24–25.
[49] Eamon Duffy, *The Stripping of the Altars: Traditional Religion in England 1400–1580* (New Haven, CT: Yale University Press, 2005), 110.

performing the prayers of institution, the people were reliant on a bell ringing to signify when the elements of bread and wine had been consecrated. These physical and visual barriers within church architecture marked the boundaries of sacred space following the pattern of the tabernacle. The medieval Roman Catholic Church embraced the typology of Leviticus both in its understanding of sacred space and its elevation of the priesthood. In some instances, however, it moved beyond Leviticus by shrouding the priesthood in mystery and detaching it from the average layperson.

The Christian church also looked to the pattern of Leviticus 23 in its adaption of the Jewish liturgical year. Sacred time and festivals were transformed to reflect the events of the life, death, resurrection, and ascension of Christ. The basis for worship remained the weekly sabbath or what became known as "the Lord's Day" (Rev 1:10) in the church, which was celebrated on Sunday to mark the day of resurrection.[50] The establishment of yearly liturgies in the church was further developed through the monastic tradition around what is known as the Divine Office. The daily liturgy of prayer was influenced by the sacrifices of Leviticus and the daily *tāmîd* offered in the morning and evening. The heavenly pattern of marking out seven specific times followed the Psalmists confession, "seven times a day I have praised you" (Ps 118:164). Lauds, Prime, Terce, Sext, None, Vespers, and Compline were set aside for prayer, reading scripture, and meditation as an act of structuring one's day around worship.

---

[50] See Scarlata, *Sabbath Rest*, 1–35; Samuele Bacchiocchi, *From Sabbath to Sunday: A Historical Investigation of the Rise of Sunday Observance in Early Christianity* (Rome: The Pontifical Gregorian University Press, 1977).

St. Benedict established this pattern in his monasteries through a simple rule to help the brothers order their lives around worship and prayer.[51] The liturgical calendar of the Christian church embraced the Levitical understanding of the sanctification of time, festivals, and weekly patterns of rest and worship.

The Christian church has taken up and adapted many of the doctrines and practices found in Leviticus concerning sacred time and space, purity/impurity, atonement, and holiness. Gersternberger, however, argues that Christians have been "horribly ungrateful sons and daughters of our ancestors in faith" because of their refusal to recognize the church's dependency on the Mosaic laws in Leviticus.[52] His criticism is not unmerited considering the history of the church and its behavior toward the Jews. His comment is also appropriate considering the lack of knowledge in today's Christian church on the Old Testament and, in particular, the rituals, symbols, and commands of Leviticus that were so critical for the New Testament authors in being able to discern and comprehend the atoning work of Christ, the ascended great high priest.[53]

As we survey the influence of Leviticus on the Christian church, we might look at one more historic event in the Protestant Reformation that draws parallels to some of the themes that have been discussed. We argued that Leviticus was not written as an esoteric manual for a mysterious group of priests hiding behind temple walls but, rather, that its commands link the holiness of God's home with the homes of every Israelite. The text of Leviticus encourages the democratization of knowledge by laying

---

[51] Rowan Williams, *The Way of St. Benedict* (London: Bloomsbury Continuum, 2020), 47–53.
[52] Gerstenberger, *Leviticus*, 16.
[53] See Brent A. Strawn, *The Old Testament Is Dying: A Diagnosis and Recommended Treatment* (Grand Rapids, MI: Baker Academic, 2017).

bare the inner workings of sacrifice within the tabernacle and encouraging lay participation in both cultic sacrifice and ethical obedience. Leviticus is a work that decentralizes power so that all Israel is aware of their responsibility and obligation to fulfilling Torah. The theology of Leviticus gives preference to authorized priests, authorized space, and to the whole congregation as one body, called to holiness within the structures God has prescribed. In a similar manner, the Reformation sought to demystify the priesthood of the medieval Roman Catholic Church and increase lay participation in worship through the study of Scripture.

One of the most significant transformations that occurred during the Reformation was the rise of the printing press and the mass production of the Bible. In the medieval Catholic Church the scriptures had mainly been the property of priests and believers were subject to their authorized interpretation. During the Reformation, however, the proliferation of translations and publication of the Bible meant that the Word of God was placed into the hands of ordinary Christians to read and interpret. Just as Leviticus is a text that reveals the mysteries of the cult and makes known God's commands to the whole congregation, so too did the Reformation put the Word of God physically into the hands of laypeople. As Benson Bobrick argues, "Once the people were free to interpret the Word of God according to the light of their own understanding, they began to question the authority of their inherited institutions, both religious and secular, which led to reformation within the Church, and to the rise of constitutional government in England and the end of the divine right of kings."[54] Empowering the laity with the ability to read the Bible brought

---

[54] Benson Bobrick, *Wide as the Waters: The Story of the English Bible and the Revolution It Inspired* (New York: Simon & Schuster, 2001), 12.

dramatic religious and political change to the Roman Catholic West. In some ways, the theology of Leviticus anticipated such a change through its understanding of the cult, the priesthood, and how the scriptures democratized holiness in Israel.

CONCLUSION

Leviticus is a book that reveals the mystery of the divine presence to the whole congregation of Israel so that Yhwh's home and the homes of the Israelites might be holy. Direct knowledge of the cult is made available to both priest and layperson as captured in Lev 21:24: "Thus Moses spoke to Aaron and to his sons and to all the people of Israel." Of this verse Milgrom writes that the performance and behavior of the priest is *"ultimately the responsibility of the entire community."*[55] The priestly laws were meant to be part of the public domain. They were not focused on a single site of worship but were concerned with the sanctity of the people and places authorized by Yhwh. Holiness in Leviticus does not merely reflect a hierarchy of power, but it offers a division of roles, responsibilities, and service for the blessing of the whole community. The sanctification of the tabernacle, the land, and time itself was the responsibility of all the people because holiness was a communal calling and an act performed by the whole people of God.

It may be fitting to end with three fresco images from Dura Europos that broadly capture how different aspects of the theology of Leviticus have been received by both Jews and Christians over the centuries. The first is taken from a Mythrean temple where a priest stands upright with a sacred scroll in his hand. The scroll is rolled tightly and protectively covered by his arm. The

---

[55] Milgrom, *Leviticus 17–22*, 1832–34.

image conveys the priestly elite guarding the cultic and sacred mysteries reserved for the chosen few. At times throughout history, both Jewish and Christian interpretations of Leviticus have resulted in a priesthood that is removed from the people. The sacred world becomes the property of a select, elite class who are entrusted with the mysteries of engaging with the divine. This construal of Leviticus, however, is inconsistent with the commands of the text itself and represents a fundamental misinterpretation of its theology.

The second image is found in a nearby Jewish synagogue. There is an elaborate fresco of a man holding a scroll opened wide as if he is about to read. There is some debate as to whether the figure is Moses or Ezra or simply a layperson reading Torah.[56] The importance of the mosaic, however, is that it represents the Word of God being read to all Israel, which implies that God's people are accountable to even the most minute laws whether in the home, in worship, or in daily life. The public reading and study of the scriptures became central to Judaism and the Protestant Reformation, which emphasized the responsibility that all faithful believers have in their knowledge and understanding of God's word.

The final image is that taken from the Dura Europos Christian church, which had also embraced a sacramental and ritual theology from Leviticus. Along with architectural features of the *bema* and its relation to the Eucharist discussed above, there is a crude picture painted on the wall of Jesus as the Good Shepherd. It is a simple illustration of a man carrying a sheep over his shoulders. What is significant is that the image sits directly above the baptismal font, the site of one of the great sacraments of initiation into the church. The ritual washing of baptism, along with the Eucharist, celebrated

---

[56] Elias J. Bickermann, "The Septuagint as a Translation," *PAAJR* 28 (1959): 1–39 (38–39).

the triune presence of the Father, the Son, and the Holy Spirit in the believer that joined together the community of faith, the Body of Christ. Christians embraced sacramental rituals that found their symbolic roots in Leviticus. They devised sacred space and architecture that reflected the tabernacle and understood the divine presence of Christ (and his holiness) made known through baptism and his presence in the Eucharist.

The heritage of Leviticus lives on today in both Jewish and Christian circles. The lasting impact of what seems such an alien text to modern readers is a testimony to the ancient authors' understanding of humanity, worship, ritual, sacraments, and the holiness of God. The ritual practice and theology that emerges from Leviticus offers a vision of what it means to live as a holy people and as a society marked by justice, mercy, and purity expressed toward one another and toward the land. In a desacralized and secular society, Leviticus' call to holiness provides an alternative narrative to a life that recaptures the sacred and redefines our relationship with God, humanity, and creation.

The theology of Leviticus is critical for a world today that is driven by scientific rationalism and reductionism that often devalues human life and treats the environment as a material commodity rather than a sacred gift from God. The disenchantment of the secular age has lost the idea of the immanent presence of the divine in creation.[57] Leviticus, however, opens a window into an ancient world of ritual, holiness, and the reality of God's divine presence inhabiting the cosmos. It imagines a world where God will bring about the consecration of all things, where the chasm between the sacred and the profane will be dissolved and all peoples will draw near to worship him in holiness.

---

[57] See Wirzba, *This Sacred Life*, 125–54.

Further Reading

COMMENTARIES ON LEVITICUS

Although there are some recent commentaries on Leviticus that focus on theological interpretation, the majority of Jewish and Christian approaches tend to concentrate on historical and critical issues in the text. None have surpassed the depth and breadth of Jacob Milgrom's three-volume Anchor Bible Commentary, which remains the benchmark for most critical scholarship on Leviticus.

Balentine, Samuel E. *Leviticus,* Interpretation Bible Commentary. Louisville, KY: Westminster John Knox, 2002. Accessible Christian theological commentary with sophisticated insights.

Gerstenberger, Erhard S. *Leviticus: A Commentary.* Old Testament Library. Louisville, KY: Westminster John Knox Press, 1996. Constructive Christian commentary with fresh critical analysis.

Hartley, John E. *Leviticus.* Word Biblical Commentary. Dallas, TX: Word Books, 1992. Thorough critical analysis of the text with helpful theological comments.

Hieke, Thomas. *Levitikus.* Herders Theologischer Kommentar zum Alten Testament 6. Freiburg: Herder, 2014. Fresh critical analyses of the text.

Kamionkowski, S. Tamar. *Leviticus*. Wisdom Commentary Series. Collegeville, MN: Liturgical Press, 2002. A feminist approach to Leviticus.

Kiuchi, Nobuyoshi. *Leviticus*. Apollos Old Testament Commentary 3. Downers Grove IL: Apollos; InterVarsity Press, 2007. Critically conservative with in-depth analysis.

Levine, Baruch A. *Leviticus*, JPS Torah Commentary. New York: Jewish Publication Society, 1989. Accessible Jewish commentary with theological insights.

Milgrom, Jacob, *Leviticus 1–16: A New Translation with Introduction and Commentary*. Anchor Bible. New York: Doubleday, 1991.

Leviticus 17–22: A New Translation with Introduction and Commentary. Anchor Bible. New York: Doubleday, 2000.

Leviticus 23–27: A New Translation with Introduction and Commentary. Anchor Bible. New York: Doubleday, 2001.

These three volumes remain the standard for any study in Leviticus with vast historical and theological exposition though they can be challenging to navigate.

Leviticus: A Book of Ritual and Ethics. Continental Commentaries. Minneapolis, MN: Fortress Press, 2004. A more manageable version of Milgrom's full Anchor Bible commentary.

Noth, Martin. *Leviticus: A Commentary*. Old Testament Library. Philadelphia, PA: Westminster Press, 1965. Sophisticated and insightful.

Radner, Ephraim. *Leviticus*. Brazos Theological Commentary on the Bible; Grand Rapids, MI: Brazos Press, 2008. A Christian approach to Leviticus that at times resembles Jewish midrash.

Strawn, Brent A. "Leviticus." In *Wesley One Volume Commentary*, ed. Kenneth J. Collins and Robert W. Wall, 66–89. Nashville, TN: Abingdon Press, 2020. Brief but excellent commentary with parallels to John Wesley's holiness movement.

Watts, James W. *Leviticus 1–10*. Historical Commentary on the Old Testament. Leuven: Peeters, 2013.

Leviticus 11–20. Leuven: Peeters, 2023. Critical with some theological exposition.

Wenham, Gordon J. *The Book of Leviticus*. New International Commentary on the Old Testament. Grand Rapids, MI: Eerdmans, 1979. Excellent Christian commentary with critical and theological insights.

ANTHROPOLOGICAL, THEOLOGICAL, AND OTHER WORKS ON LEVITICUS

Anderson, Gary A. *Sacrifices and Offerings in Ancient Israel: Studies on their Social and Political Importance*. Harvard Semitic Monographs 41. Atlanta: Scholars Press, 1987. A comprehensive work on sacrifice that contributes to the study of Leviticus.

That I May Dwell among Them: Incarnation and Atonement in the Tabernacle Narrative. Grand Rapids, MI: Eerdmans, 2023. A theological study focused on the tabernacle, sacrifice, and other Levitical themes.

Babcock, Bryan C. *Sacred Ritual: A Study of the West Semitic Ritual Calendars in Leviticus 23 and the Akkadian Text Emar 446*. Winona Lake, IN: Eisenbrauns 2014. A thorough study on calendars and ritual time in Leviticus and the ancient world.

Balentine, Samuel E., ed. *The Oxford Handbook of Ritual and Worship in the Hebrew Bible*. Oxford: Oxford University Press, 2020. An excellent collection of essays on ritual in Israel and the ancient world.

Bell, Catherine. *Ritual Theory, Ritual Practice*. Oxford: Oxford University Press, 1992. A classic work on ritual and anthropology.

Bibb, Brian D. *Ritual Words and Narrative Worlds in the Book of Leviticus*. The Library of Hebrew Bible/Old Testament Studies 480. London: T&T Clark, 2009. A sensitive and thorough analysis with theological insights.

Douglas, Mary. *Leviticus as Literature*. Oxford: Oxford University Press, 1999. A compelling literary and anthropological approach to Leviticus.

Purity and Danger: An Analysis of the Concept of Pollution and Taboo. Reprint London: Routledge, 2002. Excellent anthropology on purity and impurity.

Eliade, Mircea. *The Sacred and the Profane: The Nature of Religion*. Translated by Willard R. Trask. London: Harcourt, Brace, 1959. Classic anthropological study on the nature of religion.

Feldman, Liane M. *The Story of Sacrifice: Ritual and Narrative in the Priestly Source*. Forschungen Zum Alten Testament 141. Tübingen: Mohr Siebeck, 2020. A literary approach to reading Leviticus with fresh insights.

Gammie, John G. *Holiness in Israel*. Overtures to Biblical Theology. Minneapolis, MN: Fortress Press, 1989. A helpful biblical theology of holiness in the Old Testament.

Gese, Hartmut. *Essays on Biblical Theology*. Minneapolis, MN: Augsburg, 1981. An excellent collection of essays exploring Old and New Testament themes.

Gorman, Frank H., Jr. *The Ideology of Ritual: Space, Time and Status in the Priestly Theology.* Journal for the Study of the Old Testament Supplement Series 91. Sheffield: Sheffield Academic Press, 1990. Excellent study on time, temple, and space in Leviticus.

Janowski, Bernd. *Sühne als Heilsgeschehen: Traditions- und religionsgeschichtliche Studien zur Sühnetheologie der Priesterschrift.* Neukirchen-Vluyn: Neukirchener Verlag, 2000. An important study on the theology of atonement in the priestly literature.

Jenson, Philip P. *Graded Holiness: A Key to the Priestly Conception of the World.* Journal for the Study of the Old Testament Supplement 106. Sheffield: Sheffield Academic Press, 1992. An important monograph on space and theology in the tabernacle.

Johnson, Dru. *Knowledge by Ritual: A Biblical Prolegomenon to Sacramental Theology.* Journal of Theological Interpretation Supplements, 13. Winona Lake, IN: Eisenbrauns, 2016. An articulate argument for epistemology and its connection to ritual.

Klawans, Jonathan, *Purity, Sacrifice and the Temple: Symbolism and Supersessionism in the Study of Ancient Judaism* (Oxford: Oxford University Press, 2006). An important study on purity and the nature of sacrifice in Leviticus.

Klingbeil, Gerald A. *Bridging the Gap: Ritual and Ritual Texts in the Bible.* Bulletin for Biblical Research Supplement 1. Winona Lake, IN: Eisenbraus, 2007. A significant work in biblical ritual studies.

Knohl, Israel. *The Sanctuary of Silence: The Priestly Torah and the Holiness School.* Minneapolis, MN: Fortress Press, 1995. Focused on the composition of Leviticus.

MacDonald, Nathan. *Priestly Rule: Polemic and Biblical Interpretation in Ezekiel 44*. Berlin: Walter de Gruyter, 2015. A helpful monograph drawing on the interpretation of Leviticus in Ezekiel.

Morales, Michael L. *Who Shall Ascend the Mountain of the Lord? A Biblical Theology of the Book of Leviticus*. New Studies in Biblical Theology. Downers Grove, IL: Apollos, InterVarsity Press, 2015. Scripturally conservative approach that attempts to connect the theology of Leviticus to the whole Bible.

Nihan, Christophe. *From Priestly Torah to Pentateuch: A Study in the Composition of the Book of Leviticus*. Forschungen zum Alten Testament 252. Tübigen: Mohr Siebeck, 2007. Thorough critical scholarship on textual and theological issues.

Poorthuis, M. J. H. M., and J. Schwartz, eds. *Purity and Holiness: The Heritage of Leviticus*. Leiden: Brill, 2000. Helpful scholarly collection of essays on purity.

Rhyder, Julia. *Centralizing the Cult: The Holiness Legislation in Leviticus 17–26*. Tübingen: Mohr Siebeck, 2019. A clear and thorough monograph on centralization in the Holiness Code.

Sawyer, John F. A. *Reading Leviticus: A Conversation with Mary Douglas*. Journal for the Study of the Old Testament Supplement Series 227. Sheffield: Sheffield Academic Press, 1996. An important collection of essays engaging with Douglas' work on Leviticus.

Stökl, Daniel Ben Ezra. *The Impact of Yom Kippur on Early Christianity: The Day of Atonement from Second Temple Judaism to the Fifth Century*. Tübingen: Mohr Siebeck, 2003. An excellent study on the interpretation of Leviticus in the Second Temple Period.

Thiessen, Matthew. *Jesus and the Forces of Death: The Gospel's Portrayal of Ritual Impurity in First-Century Judaism.* Grand Rapids, MI: Baker Academic, 2020. Detailed analysis of Jesus in the Gospels with an emphasis on the influence of Leviticus.

Warning, Wilfried. *Literary Artistry in Leviticus.* Biblical Interpretation Series 35. Leiden: Brill, 1999. Strong literary analysis of the text.

Watts, James W. *Ritual and Rhetoric in Leviticus: From Sacrifice to Scripture.* Cambridge: Cambridge University Press, 2007. A compelling argument for the rhetoric of Leviticus.

Index

agricultural, 146, 152, 195, 204–6, 217, 219, 221, 223, 241
Ambrose, 107–8
Anderson, Gary, 4, 34, 36–7, 39, 43, 58, 126, 135, 235
anointing, 60, 124, 127, 131
Anselm, 75–8
ark of the covenant, 71
atonement, 7, 12, 35, 37–8, 44–5, 53, 58, 65, 68–70, 74–5, 82, 103, 107, 127, 130, 156, 167, 169, 225, 247
   Anselm, 75–6
   in Christ, 251, 258
   Christian interpretation, 76
   definition, 44
   drama of sacrifice, 49–50, 52
   life of blood, 56–7
   purification offering, 66
   substitutionary, 76, 78
   subtitutionary, 80
   theology of, 61, 63, 65, 69–70, 74, 81
   well-being offering, 168
atonement, theology of, 81
Augustine, 77, 107–8
Azazel, 59, 68, 73–4, 164

Baal, 64, 219–20
Balentine, Samuel, 12, 50–1, 55, 67, 104–5, 130, 134, 140, 155, 159
barley, 205, 217, 219, 221, 223
Berry, Wendell, 100–1, 147, 192
blessing, 4, 14, 30, 39, 46, 48–9, 54, 85, 88, 94, 110, 129, 131, 143, 148, 155, 178–9, 203, 220–2, 228, 239, 260

blood, 35, 38, 55–7, 59, 61
   apotropaic, 56
   as contaminant, 60
   ordination rite, 60
   sprinkling, 5, 50, 52, 66
   theology of, 58
bodily discharge, 60, 86
Brueggemann, Walter, iv, 4, 6–7, 31, 141, 143–4, 214, 221, 242
burnt offering, 5, 38, 44–6, 71, 128, 167, 199, 222

Chapman, Stephen, xvi, 64, 131
childbirth, 61, 102–4, 106–7
churching of women after childbirth, 108
contagion, xvi, 102, 111–12, 247
contamination, xvi, 9, 60, 84, 102–3, 112, 126, 130, 147, 173
cosmic temple, 3, 14, 51
creation, xvi, 3, 37, 84, 231, 234, 262
   dietary laws, 91, 93–4, 97
   Priestly narrative, 50, 63
creational order, 12

daily offering, 49, 125
Davis, Ellen, 84, 99, 101, 192, 194
Day of Atonement, 38, 41, 53, 57, 62, 68, 70, 73–4, 81, 124, 162, 211, 225, 246, 251
death, 63–4, 72, 125, 135
death penalty, 59, 138–9
Decalogue, 154, 180–2, 214–15
Deuteronomy, 16, 21–2, 29, 86, 146, 153, 165–6, 185, 187–8, 212, 218, 232, 236–8

270

INDEX

dietary laws, 89–92, 97, 101–2, 159
divine drama, 51, 75, 228
Douglas, Mary, 8, 11, 13, 17–18, 25, 36–8, 50, 60, 86–92, 95–6, 120, 139–40, 158–61, 165–6, 176, 245

Eden, 3, 13, 55, 93, 99, 101, 116, 126, 129, 141, 228
Eliade, Mircea, 115, 117, 231
equinox, 71, 204, 219
ethical holiness, 19, 158, 169
exile, 144, 146, 148, 154–6, 173, 207, 215, 225, 230, 238, 241
expiation, 39, 57–8, 62, 66, 70, 72–4, 76, 78–80, 167–8

Feast of Weeks, 210, 221
Festival of Booths, 226
festivals, 204
  Babylonian, 204
first fruits, 193, 204, 210, 219–21
forces of death, 93, 103, 112, 198, 247, 249, 251

George, Mark, 9, 114, 174
Gerstenberger, Erhard, 24, 56, 58, 145, 155, 190–1, 200–1, 258
Gese, Hartmut, 68, 72, 81
Gezer, calendar, 205
Gorman, Frank, 10, 50–1, 123, 130, 210, 231, 235
grain offering, 43, 47, 103, 219–20

hand placing ritual, 49, 53–4, 68–9, 78, 110, 122, 129, 144, 225, 260
Hasmoneans, 244–5
ḥaṭṭā't, 48, 57, 66–70, 81, 127, 167, 222, 245
heave-offering, 49
Heschel, Abraham, 202, 215–16, 241, 252, 254
high priest, 41, 53, 56, 64, 67, 70, 124–5, 127, 131, 134, 136–7, 162, 196–7, 204, 251, 258
Hillel, 188
holiness code, 157
holiness school, 158
holy land, 111, 141, 148, 229, 262
Holy of Holies, 56, 70, 74, 118, 121, 127, 140, 162, 197, 248
holy time, 147, 182, 212, 216

incense, 70

Janowski, Bernd, 38, 58–9, 72–3
Jesus and Leviticus, 67, 100, 188, 230, 247–51, 261
Jubilee, 23, 143, 148–9, 152–4, 156, 211–12, 222

Klawans, Jonathan, 39, 61, 79, 104, 106

leper, 129, 198, 245
The Letter of Aristeas, 89
Levites, 2, 6, 39, 68, 122, 127

Maimonides, 1, 253
Mari, 109, 144
marriage, 171–2, 177, 196
materia peccans, 38, 62, 69, 72, 76
menstruation, 60, 62, 102, 171
minḥâ - grain offering, 43, 47
Molech, 170, 174–5, 178
moral impurity, 62
Moses, 1–3, 5, 11, 15, 30, 40, 68, 80, 89, 103, 114, 121–2, 125–6, 129–32, 135–6, 138, 144, 149, 163, 180, 218–19, 229, 237, 242, 252–3, 255, 260–1
Mount Zaphon, 220

Nachmanides, 253
Nadab and Abihu, 41, 63, 103, 134, 137–9
Noah, 5, 55, 66

oil, 39, 47, 98, 127, 129, 219
ōlâ - burnt offering, 5
ordination, 4, 40, 52, 60, 68, 121–9
Origen, 1, 107

Passover, 56, 66, 210, 212, 218, 243
paterfamilias, 15, 170–1, 176, 181
Pentecost, 211, 221–2, 224, 248
Physician, priestly role, 112
priesthood, 6, 28, 47, 132, 261
  Asronide, 124
  Aaronide, 127, 138, 159
  authority, 130, 137
  Christianity, 255–7, 259
  standardization, 26, 124
profane, 9–10, 36, 60, 62, 83, 85, 117, 126, 128, 140, 164, 199, 227, 233, 247, 262
slaughter, 44, 164, 166, 236–7

propitiation, 67, 78, 107
purity laws, 1, 22, 59, 84–5, 102, 112, 155, 162, 166, 234, 245, 249–50

Qumran, 213, 245–6

reparation offering, 48
ritual calendars, 203
ritual impurity, 62, 76, 111

Sabbath 143, 146–8
sabbath rest, 15, 143, 145–6, 148, 173, 181
sacred space, social, 118
sacred time, 156, 211–12, 215, 233, 258
scapegoat, 53, 58, 71–4
sexual purity, 15, 107, 169, 174, 178, 245
šəlāmîm (well-being offering), 5, 45–6
shofar, 223–4
Sinai, 2–3, 5, 7, 25, 33, 81, 122, 124, 132, 228, 235, 237, 242, 248
skin disease, 109–10, 198, 249, 251
Strawn, Brent, xvi, 12, 80, 92, 144, 249, 258

tabernacle, viii, xv–xvi, 2, 4, 6, 9, 11, 13–15, 17, 25, 28, 38, 48, 59, 61, 63, 70, 83, 88, 114–17, 120, 123
tenants, 143, 148, 151, 193, 222
tent of meeting, 2, 51, 62, 117, 122, 126, 163–4
trumpets, 211, 223

Unleavened Bread, 210, 217–19

vestments, 129

Watts, James, 5, 28, 127, 137–8, 159
wave-offering, 49
well-being offering, 5, 45–6, 163, 223
Wenham, Gordon, 17, 88, 93, 111, 128, 161, 163, 191, 223
wheat, 221, 223
wilderness, 3, 13, 25, 33, 41, 53, 71–3, 124, 184, 219, 227–9, 239, 255
wine, 27, 39, 50, 82, 98, 137, 219, 256–7
Wirzba, Norman, 33, 100–1, 229, 262

Yom Kippur, 41

For EU product safety concerns, contact us at Calle de José Abascal, 56–1°,
28003 Madrid, Spain or eugpsr@cambridge.org.